1850

TOWER BIBLIOGRAPHICAL SERIES

NUMBER FIFTEEN

The Hartley Coleridge Letters

A CALENDAR AND INDEX

by

FRAN CARLOCK STEPHENS

Humanities Research Center

THE UNIVERSITY OF TEXAS AT AUSTIN

© 1978 by Fran Carlock Stephens

L. C. Card Number: 76–620064

ISBN 0–87959–078–5

Frontispiece: watercolor of William Wordsworth and Hartley Cole-
ridge at Rydal, after a sketch from the life made in 1844 by John
Peter Mulcaster. Reproduced by permission of the Trustees of Dove
Cottage, Grasmere, England.

To Willis W. Pratt,

With love and respect.

CONTENTS

An Abbreviated Coleridge Family Tree

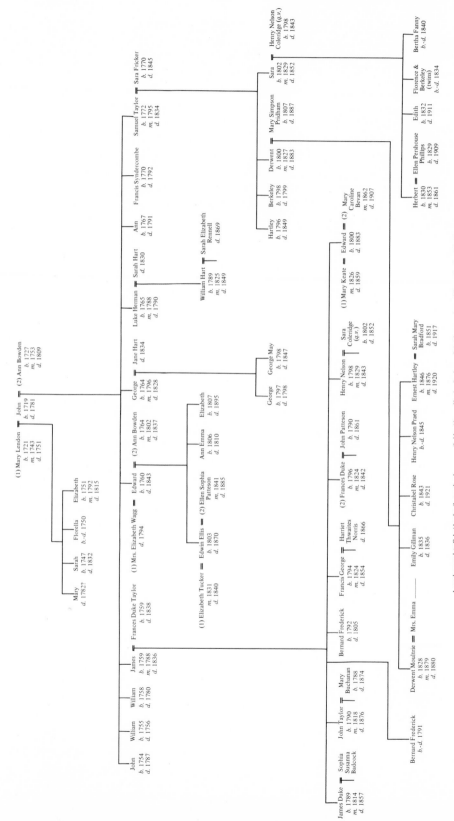

A nearly complete Coleridge family tree has been compiled by Alwyne Hartley Buchanan Coleridge, grandson of Ernest Hartley Coleridge.

PREFACE

This book is based on a doctoral dissertation which was the second in a series of calendars of part of the extensive Coleridge collection in the Humanities Research Center of The University of Texas at Austin. As the second, the *Hartley Coleridge Letters* owes much of its plan to the pioneer dissertation, Carl L. Grantz's unpublished *Letters of Sara Coleridge*. Such departures as there are from Grantz's methods of calendaring were made in the interests of simplicity and consistency.

The overall plan was derived with three objects in view—first, usefulness as a reference work for those who wish to do further work in the Humanities Research Center collection; second, usefulness to the Center in its enormous task of cataloguing the letters; and third, simplicity affording concision and clarity enough to make the reading of this preface a matter of choice.

The letters are divided into two large groups. The A group consists of letters from Hartley Coleridge to various correspondents, and the B group consists of letters from various correspondents to Hartley Coleridge. In each group the letters are arranged alphabetically by correspondent and chronologically within each correspondent series. The one exception to this scheme occurs in the Appendix at the end of the two groups. When his Leeds publisher, Francis Edward Bingley, went into bankruptcy, Hartley Coleridge enlisted the aid of his good friend James Brancker to free him from all obligations to Bingley. Since the letters, which flew thick and fast among the three men, are much easier to follow when presented chronologically, this arrangement has been used in the Appendix.

Each entry consists of three parts—bibliographical data, abstract, and publication record. The citation of data begins with a series item number, and references in the Index are to these numbers. The basic order of data is as follows:

> Bibliographical abbreviations, address of sender, date of writing or of mailing, address of recipient, number of pages of text. Miscellaneous information.

Addresses and dates are given precisely as they appear on the autograph copy with no attempt made to correct misspellings, punctuation errors and the like. In the data section, as throughout each entry, brackets have been used to enclose information not given in the original

9

document. Reliance on postmarks for dates has been so noted. Miscellaneous information usually falls into one or more of three categories: the name of the person who carried the letter; endorsement by someone other than the writer; and notation of wrappers. While hardly vital, the name of the carrier is sometimes useful in identifying a letter and might prove to be of interest to someone concerned with the movements of a carrier like William Wordsworth or Henry Crabb Robinson. Endorsements are often interesting comments by family members on the contents of the letters. Because endorsements were made over a period of many years by Mrs. Samuel Taylor Coleridge, Sara Coleridge, Derwent Coleridge, and others, it is often difficult to determine just who wrote what. Positive identifications are based either on internal evidence or on Ernest Hartley Coleridge's identifications in his transcriptions. Accompanying transcriptions, whether typed or handwritten, are not noted unless they are of particular interest. A few of Hartley's letters are in wrappers of folded note paper with outside endorsement of the contents by Ernest Hartley Coleridge. Such wrappers have been noted as part of the description of these items.

The second part of each entry is the abstract. Some effort has been made to make the tone of the abstract reflect that of the original. Hartley's letters are unique, and the reflection is, at best, a very poor one; and if the tone of some of the letters addressed to Hartley is unpleasant, the original is probably even more so. All persons, works, and significant places mentioned by the writer have been noted (usually in the form in which the writer mentions them) and so far as possible, identified. Copies of letters have been used only when the originals are no longer extant. Direct quotations from Hartley's letters have been used, sparingly, to throw light on Hartley's character, to reflect the tone of the letter, or simply out of general interest. Such material is reproduced exactly as it appears in the original, with no attempt to correct Hartley's erratic punctuation and frequent misspellings. A few letters of particular interest have been quoted in full. No attempt has been made to "strip" any letter of information valuable to scholars; it is up to the scholar to mine it for himself.

The primary source of this work is the Humanities Research Center collection of letters to and from Hartley Coleridge. It would be pointlessly pedantic to give a bibliography of secondary sources. The two books containing the largest number of Hartley Coleridge's letters are *Letters of Hartley Coleridge*, edited by Grace Evelyn Griggs and Earl Leslie Griggs (London, 1936), and the "Memoir" in Derwent Coleridge's edition of Hartley Coleridge's *Poems* (2 vols., London, 1851). *Letters of Hartley Coleridge* contains 12 letters not in the Humanities Research Center, and the Humanities Research Center has 160 Hartley Coleridge letters, 72 of which are not given in the Griggs work. Hartley's hand is extremely difficult to read. Any passages which have been mistaken in previously published versions are quoted in this work in full and without any special notation. Bibliographical information given for works mentioned by correspondents refers to the specific edition intended by the writer, to an edition which Hartley could have used, or to a first edition.

I should like to thank The University of Texas Committee on the Use of Literary and Historical Materials for making the manuscripts available; Professors Willis W. Pratt, William B. Todd, Thomas M. Cranfill, and Edwin T. Bowden for reading the manuscript and making valuable suggestions; June Moll, Sally Leach, and the entire Humanities Research Center Library staff for their unfailingly kind and cheerful assistance; Mr. A. H. B. Coleridge for his many kindnesses; and my family for making this work possible at all.

INTRODUCTION

When The University of Texas at Austin purchased the Coleridge family papers from A. H. B. Coleridge in 1964, it acquired records of more than a hundred years of English literary, social, legal, and religious history as seen through the eyes of various members of one of England's most extraordinary families. Since the prolific Coleridges (sixty-five Coleridges in three generations) were prolific writers, the Texas collection is immense. The Hartley Coleridge materials alone fill more than twelve large boxes and remain only half published. It is the purpose of this book to make available to scholars some of the valuable information in the Hartley Coleridge letters and to give a glimpse of the personality that made Hartley the most captivating of the younger Coleridges.

Hartley Coleridge (1796–1849), Samuel Taylor Coleridge's first-born, was referred to by his sister, Sara, as "our Trouble in the North," and was considered by both family and the world at large a failure. Yet this "failure" was poet, critic, essayist, biographer, editor, and a letter writer of no mean talent. Generally speaking, his criticism is competent in the longer works, shrewd in the marginalia, and often hilarious in informal letters. His essays are strongly influenced by Charles Lamb, whom he greatly admired, and his informal essays are often delightful in their Lambian lightness and whimsey. Hartley Coleridge the poet is very much like the little girl of the nursery rhyme: when he is good, he is very, very good, but when he is bad, he is horrid. Hartley lived an occasional sort of life, and much of his poetry is occasional verse, with all the lack of quality that loaded word implies. He is very, very good only in some of his sonnets, many of which are highly personal, *e.g.,* the poignant and lovely "Long time a child." By its very nature, the sonnet form imposed a discipline the poet himself lacked, while its brevity allowed for his short span of concentration. His most serious long poem, begun while he was in Oxford, at the urging of Samuel Taylor Coleridge, was a translation of the Aeschylus "Prometheus Bound," which he never finished.

> And yet if you should praise myself
> I'll tell you, I had rather
> You'd give your love to me, poor elf,
> Your praise to my great father.

13

Hartley never came close to his "great father" as a poet, yet it is impossible to read his often elfin letters without, in some measure, giving your love to him. Contemporary accounts of men who knew both father and son credit Hartley with conversational abilities quite equal to those of Samuel Taylor Coleridge. Unfortunately we have no *Table-Talk of Hartley Coleridge*. Only the letters can reflect something of the spontaneity, sprightliness, and imagination which marked his conversation.

Two factors make the collection of letters particularly valuable to literary scholars and social historians—Hartley's associates and Hartley's character. He grew up in the combined Coleridge-Southey households at Greta Hall, and the earliest letter in the collection, dated 4 March 1807, is addressed to Robert Southey. Hartley saw his father at ever less frequent intervals, but the elder Coleridge's intent for Hartley's education was followed:

> But *thou*, my babe! shalt wander like a breeze
> By lakes and sandy shores, beneath the crags
> Of ancient mountain, and beneath the clouds,
> Which image in their bulk both lakes and shores
> And mountain crags; so shalt thou see and hear
> The lovely shapes and sounds intelligible
> Of that eternal language, which thy God
> Utters, who from eternity doth teach
> Himself, in all, and all things in himself.[1]

Hartley's imagination and precocity were encouraged, and few restraints of any kind were placed upon him. From his mother he learned to read and write, and from his father he learned Greek. In 1801 Hartley and his brother, Derwent, were sent to the Ambleside school of Mr. John Dawes, who was so impressed by Hartley's agile mind that he refused any remuneration for teaching the boy. Neither in Mr. Dawes's unusual school nor in the home of his hostess, Mrs. Longmire, did Hartley meet any curtailment of his imaginative or physical freedom. In 1814 Hartley left Mr. Dawes's school and spent a year in independent study, mainly under the direction of his uncle, Robert Southey.

Schooled at home and in a village school, and allowed as much freedom as he pleased, Hartley was ill prepared for life at Oxford. His letters of this period are, for the most part, progress reports to his father and various benefactors, including George Coleridge. Despite his back-

[1]Samuel Taylor Coleridge, "Frost at Midnight," in *Selected Poetry and Prose,* ed. Elisabeth Schneider (New York, 1951), pp. 93–95.

ground, however, Hartley did well enough at Merton College. His conversational abilities and genial, if odd, temperament made him fairly popular; and his teachers, though cognizant of his scholarly shortcomings, were impressed enough by his natural abilities to give him a second class *in literis humaniorbus* in 1818. During this time Hartley's personality began to acquire a stamp which, appearing at first only in odd scraps in notebooks, later appeared in his letters and became more pronounced as he grew older. Just over five feet tall and physically unskilled, Hartley was in appearance as well as in character "different." This difference had already brought him into conflict with his school fellows, intolerant as children usually are, and during his college years, when the opinions of young women began to matter to him, it brought him further unhappiness. Increasingly Hartley turned for affection and acceptance to little children, especially babies and little girls, whose gentleness relieved his fears. William Wordsworth had predicted

> Nature will either end thee quite;
> Or, lengthening out thy season of delight,
> Preserve for thee, by individual right,
> A young lamb's heart among the full-grown flocks.[2]

And so it proved to be. To the end of his life, Hartley's best friends were among the children or the child-like dalesmen of the North.

After his graduation from Merton College, Hartley applied for a fellowship at Oriel College and in 1819 was elected a probationary fellow. And thereby hangs a tale. The Fellows of Oriel, a distinguished group including John Keble, Richard Whately, and Thomas Arnold, were noted for their strictness, sobriety, and decorum—precisely the qualities in shortest supply in Hartley Coleridge's independent nature. Hartley had found at Merton College a congenial atmosphere where he could talk freely (and with as much exaggeration as he felt necessary to make his point), take an extra glass of wine when he wished, and be the master of his own time. Recognizing his natural gifts, Oriel College accepted him, one suspects from a letter of Keble's, much as a young woman marries a man to reform him, and with about the same result. Hartley was clearly warned that he was expected to bear himself as befitted his new station, giving up his old friends, conforming to his new associates in dress, manner, habits, and (as he complained) opinions, and paying particular attention to discipline and such points as regular attendance at morning chapel. But Hartley would not conform. In May

[2]William Wordsworth, "To H. C., Six Years Old," in *The Complete Poetical Works of Wordsworth*, ed. A. J. George (Boston, 1932), p. 290.

of 1820 the Provost, Dr. Edward Copleston, warned Hartley that his conduct had been "not only irregular, but grossly immoral" and that his position as a fellow was endangered. The sensitive and idealistic Hartley, remembering "two passing wine parties," promptly confessed to the charges and threw himself upon the mercy of the college. Inquiries were instituted among college servants and others, and on 30 May 1820 the Provost and Fellows decided that in their formal meeting in October they would not confirm Hartley as a fellow of Oriel College, a decision unprecedented in the history of the college. The Dean, James Endell Tyler, suggested to Hartley that he should spare himself the disgrace of formal dismissal by resigning before the October meeting. The charges against Hartley were intemperance, keeping low company, and failure to attend properly to "certain duties." As far as the truth can be ascertained, the "intemperance" referred to Hartley's returning to his lodgings tipsy on two or three occasions; the "low company" referred to Hartley's old Merton College friends, whom he refused to drop; and the "failure to attend to certain duties" referred to Hartley's absences from chapel. Hartley argued his case before the Dean, the Provost, and the Fellows. Finding them adamant, he finally fled Oxford altogether.

In June Samuel Taylor Coleridge learned of his son's trouble from his nephew John Taylor Coleridge, who had been given Keble's account of the affair. Derwent Coleridge was dispatched to Oxford, and reported. Letters of this period fall into two groups: Hartley's account of the affair to his friends and relatives; and letters concerning Samuel Taylor Coleridge's fight to have his son confirmed. The forces were aligned, the battle fought, and the fellowship lost. Samuel Taylor Coleridge called this loss one of the greatest disappointments in his life; Hartley emerged with a sense of guilt and failure which remained with him to his death. This group of letters, though of questionable literary value, sheds a great deal of light on the characters of the men involved and on the temper of the times. The letters of the Oriel party are unrelentingly correct, pious, and sententious; those of the Samuel Taylor Coleridge party full of love for and understanding of Hartley. The elder Coleridge wrote Dr. Copleston at great length. On 15 October Coleridge and Copleston met in Oxford and on 19 October in London. At his father's urging, Hartley, now returned from his weeks of wandering and lodged with Basil Montagu in London, sent the Provost and Fellows a formal defense (A143). All efforts on Hartley's behalf proved vain, and later in October he was formally deprived of his fellowship. The Oriel authorities, obviously feeling themselves exceptionally severe in the dismissal, offered Hartley a gift of £300. Samuel Taylor Coleridge, with Hartley's full concurrence, indignantly refused the money.

16

John Taylor Coleridge, however, kept in touch with Keble, and the sum was finally given, by 15 January 1823, to Hartley's mother.

Hartley's failure to be confirmed at Oriel in large measure determined the circle of his friends and the set of his character for the rest of his life. After a brief fling at the London literary world (during which he wrote an unpublished, charmingly irreverent metrical letter to his brother, Derwent, A21), Hartley was shipped back to the North, where temptations were fewer and the Wordsworths could keep an eye on him. There he remained, for the most part, until his death in 1849.

His friends and his reading now became the centers of interest in Hartley's frequent letters to his immediate family in London. He kept the Coleridges fully informed about the activities of their northern relatives and friends, particularly the Wordsworths. He met and wrote of a host of lesser figures who either had homes in the north, as did the John Wilsons of Elleray and the Thomas Arnolds of Fox How, or came on visits as did Henry Crabb Robinson and Branwell Brontë. These letters are, of course, especially valuable to scholars who wish information about the activities of various literary figures of the period.

Hartley's closest friends (aside from the Westmorland and Cumberland farmers) were the Fells, the Claudes, the Branckers, and the Foxes. Mrs. Louise Claude, with whom Hartley had studied German when she had lived in Ambleside, was the widow of a Liverpool merchant and mother of three girls and a boy. Her letters are filled with housewifely concerns—the health of her children, the education of her son, the routine activities involved in running a household. Perhaps Hartley was hungry for precisely this ordinariness and regularity of family life, for the Claudes became his most frequent correspondents. William Fell, a doctor in Ambleside, married Mrs. Claude's sister-in-law and became one of Hartley's closest friends. Although the collection contains only one letter from Hartley to Fell (A126), a number of Hartley's letters were written from the Fell home, where he was a frequent guest. Here, too, Hartley found the rather ordinary family life which he seemed to seek, and he once wrote Mrs. Claude that he envied Fell "the Family party letters he receives" (A8).

James Brancker, a mutual friend of Hartley's and Mrs. Louise Claude's, was a businessman and a politician in Liverpool and had a summer home in Ambleside. Most of the surviving Hartley-Brancker letters deal with Hartley's Leeds business affairs (see Appendix), but the closeness between the two men is indicated by the fact that Hartley was one of the very few people Brancker would see just after the death of his first wife, Jane Moss Brancker.

Of Sarah Fox, Hartley wrote his mother, "She is as kind, as lively,

and as lovely as ever. We never quarrel about religion, or politics"
(A114). Indeed, Hartley and Mrs. Fox seldom, if ever, quarrelled about
anything. That delightful lady had such singular sweetness of character
and lightness of touch that she could watch over Hartley without
smothering him and reprove him in such a way that he was delighted
with reproof. During her stay at Dale End, Mrs. Fox was able to help
look after Hartley, and after her removal to Perryn, Cornwall, they ex-
changed charming letters.

The balance of personal humility, humor, and shrewd critical acumen
in Hartley's nature makes his frequent comments on the characters of
such people as Sara Hutchinson, the Wordsworths, and Robert Southey
worth careful perusal. He was, for example, perfectly able to keep
Southey the constant example, Southey the man, and Southey the laureate harmoniously balanced. Hartley wrote his mother that the quickest
way to make a boy hate a man is to hold that man up as a perfect
ideal, as she constantly held up Southey to him. He expressed great
sympathy and compassion to various correspondents about the contro-
versial second marriage of Southey to Caroline Bowles. He wrote to
Derwent of Southey's just published "Vision of Judgement,"

> O Tempora, O Mores – And is it come to this? And our dear
> good mother gave me such a hint to praise in her last letter!!! . . .
> Seriously speaking, our late lamented Monarch did not deserve
> such an insult to his memory. And who, but a converted Revolu-
> tionist, would ever have dream'd of spurring the wind-gall'd,
> glander'd, stagger'd, bott-begrown, spavin'd (Oh – for the Com-
> plete Farrier) broken-down gelding, that has turn'd blind with
> facing year after year the same round of Court Compliments –
> who, I say, but Southey himself would have forced the poor old
> beast into the Hexameter long trot; and so mounted as on another
> Rosinante, set off in search of adventures, in the world of spirits?
> (A26)

Although the letters pointed out here cover a wide range in time,
they reflect no change of feeling but a clarity and balance of vision
which make the whole collection valuable. Indeed, Hartley Coleridge's
letters may be looked upon not merely as sources of information but as
literary products in themselves. The habitual procrastinator is hereby
advised to brave Hartley's atrocious hand and note carefully the grace-
ful and ingenious excuses with which the poet's letters usually begin.
The letters are marked by a spontaneous style now serious, now whim-

sical, which makes them as delightful for reading as they are useful for research.

The 268 letters to Hartley Coleridge from some 90 different correspondents do not, with a few notable exceptions, match Hartley's in charm. Sara and Henry Nelson Coleridge wrote Hartley in detail of their preparation of editions of Samuel Taylor Coleridge's works, publication dates, and sales records, and Hartley responded with comments on both his father's works and that of the editors. Derwent Coleridge wrote often of family and church concerns and sprinkled his letters with sermonettes intended to improve Hartley's moral character:

> Oh my dear Brother, need I remind you what this cruel enchantment has cost you? that it has cut you off from those who yearn to have you with them. . . . My circumstances have ever been such that the possibility of your losing your self-respect has put it out of my power to see you. . . . Not to say that my health would immediately give way under the misery which it w^d occasion me. (B88)

Another great "improver" of Hartley's character was his mother, whose letters seldom stray far from lectures on pubs, the state of Hartley's clothes, and her own penury and ill health. Typically, the first letter of her series, B111, contains a half-page folio, closely written, on how to pack a trunk, and the last of the series, B125, contains a plea for Mrs. Wordsworth's sympathy because she (Mrs. STC) is so tried by Sara Coleridge's sufferings. Letters from the London Coleridges are, in fact, packed with news of the illnesses of Derwent and Sara, both of whom outlived Hartley.

Among letters of interest from correspondents outside the Coleridge family are those from Joseph Henry Green, M. C. Minto, Barry Cornwall, and Charlotte Brontë. The first letter from Joseph Henry Green is dated 21 August 1834, and gives a detailed account of the last days and the death of Samuel Taylor Coleridge. The second letter from Green, dated 27 November 1848, reviews the discovery and publication of the manuscript of Samuel Taylor Coleridge's *Hints Toward the Formation of a More Comprehensive Theory of Life*. Green comments on the purity of the text and discusses Coleridge's philosophy at length. M. C. Minto's letter is a patchwork quilt of over-sweet compliments, requests for charades, vague generalizations, and, unexpectedly, astute criticism of Robert Browning and of two new volumes, Medwin's *Life of Shelley* and Charlotte Brontë's *Jane Eyre*. Barry Cornwall's letter, while of little or no scholarly importance, is full of the warmth and personality of the man, and is a neat example of how to compliment an author gracefully.

The Brontë correspondence really forms a little sub-group of its own.[3] In this group are two letters to Hartley from Charlotte Brontë (one unsigned and the other signed "Currer Bell") and an unfinished reply from Hartley to Branwell Brontë. The unsigned letter from Charlotte Brontë has been the subject of some scholarly debate and heretofore was thought to exist in rough draft only and to have been directed to William Wordsworth. Hartley's letter to Branwell Brontë is a reply to Branwell's second batch of poetry sent to Hartley for criticism. The letter opens with a critique of Branwell's translation of Horace's first ode and is accompanied by a heavily annotated transcript of some poetry, possibly Branwell's.

Many of the letters to Hartley Coleridge are letters of little importance from people of little importance. There are the inevitable requests for autographs and original poems, often "for a friend." The invitations and letters of introduction from and in behalf of people who simply wanted to meet one of the local "literary lions" vary in little but degree of frankness. These letters have been included and duly abstracted not merely because they form a part of the collection, but because Hartley's responses to them reveal his kindness and patience. He sent autograph after autograph, often Southey's or Wordsworth's or his father's as well as his own. He wrote poem after poem for dead relatives and new babies. While these poems certainly do his literary reputation no good, they *are* indicative of his kindness as a human being.

If a man can be remembered for what he was as well as for what he did, so it should be with Hartley Coleridge. His letters reveal what he was, and the picture is perhaps the more lovable because it is a flawed and very human one. Painfully sensitive and introspective, Hartley could always see into himself, and his own vision is, perhaps, the clearest one:

> Long time a child, and still a child, when years
> Had painted manhood on my cheek, was I, —
> For yet I lived like one not born to die;
> A thriftless prodigal of smiles and tears,
> No hope I needed, and I knew no fears.
> But sleep, though sweet, is only sleep, and waking,
> I waked to sleep no more, at once o'ertaking
> The vanguard of my age, with all arrears
> Of duty on my back. Nor child, nor man,
> Nor youth, nor sage, I find my head is grey,

[3]For a full account, see my "Hartley Coleridge and the Brontës," *TLS*, 14 May 1970.

For I have lost the race I never ran:
A rathe December blights my lagging May;
And still I am a child, tho' I be old,
Time is my debtor for my years untold.

ABBREVIATIONS

A.	autograph
DC	Derwent Coleridge
EHC	Ernest Hartley Coleridge
Grantz	Carl L. Grantz, *Letters of Sara Coleridge: A Calendar and Index to Her Manuscript Correspondence in The University of Texas Library*, unpublished doctoral dissertation
HC	Hartley Coleridge
HNC	Henry Nelson Coleridge
i.	initialed
(inc.)	incomplete
L.	letter
LHC	Grace Evelyn Griggs and Earl Leslie Griggs, *Letters of Hartley Coleridge*, London, 1936
Memoir	Derwent Coleridge, "Memoir," in Hartley Coleridge, *Poems*, 2 vols., London, 1851
N.	note (one page or less of standard-size note paper)
n.d.	no date
n.p.	no place
s.	signed
SC	Sara Coleridge
STC	Samuel Taylor Coleridge
Mrs. STC	Mrs. Samuel Taylor Coleridge

The Hartley Coleridge Letters

Letters from
Hartley Coleridge

EDWARD BAINES, JR.

A1 A.L.s./copy in unidentified hand, Ambleside, 1841. To: Leeds. 3 pp. A penciled note identifies the hand as that of Sara Coleridge. A reply to B6.

> Is sorry to have been so slow to reply to Baines's request for a copy of the poem [to Eleanor Dawson] Mrs. Baines burned by mistake. Kept no copy but will enclose "a small piece" ["To a Snowdrop," DC ed., HC, *Poems*, London, 1851] rather than doing "as Ben Johnson on a similar occasion" and composing "Execrations to Vulcan." Mentions Mr. [John] Crossfield and Baines's father [Edward Baines, M.P. for Leeds].

LADY [MARGARET WILLES] BEAUMONT

A2 A.L. (inc.) [25 Bedford Square, London], [n.d., December 1820]. To: [Coleorton Hall or Grosvenor Square, London?]. 4 pp. See introduction for an account of the Oriel affair.

> An account of the Oriel affair to his benefactress. Explains the system of a probationary year for Oriel fellows. "I have heard my fellow-probationers, whose conduct has past without reproach, complain of it, tho' they were acquainted with the severity of it, before they offer'd themselves as Candidates, which I was not." Not only is strict conduct required at Oriel, "but a devotion to its wishes, a preference of it to all other company, a partaking of its spirit, and, with regard to certain matters . . . an adopion of its opinions." Alludes to the difficulty in dropping one's own friends in favor of a new, and possibly incompatible, set. Speaks of the espionage and misrepresentation to which a fellow is subject. "In fact he has the rank of a Fellow and more than the restrictions of an Undergraduate." Encloses a copy of the Protest delivered through the Provost to the assembled fellows. Admits "on one or two instances"

25

drinking too much, being seen with undergraduates, neglecting the rules of the college, and staying out late. Denies charges of habitual intemperance. "It might be, that when men, not distinguish'd for Academic regularity applied to me for assistance, either literary or other, I only thought of them and their need; and neither of their character nor my own." The fellows of Oriel "invented no slander—they heard some disagreeable facts, and being prepossessed by them, and my general eccentricity against me, believed all that was said by I know not whom." Has convinced STC "of my comparative innocence." STC has been to Oxford, had an interview with Dr. [Edward] Copleston, and presented the Protest [see A143]. Tells of the £300 offered by Oriel and of his father's reply. Has written the Warden of Merton a full account. STC has acted on the advice of Mr. [Samuel] Mence, minister of Highgate and formerly Tutor of Trinity, Oxford. Both men advise HC to return to Oxford and take private pupils. Derwent [DC] is at Cambridge. Is staying with [Basil] Montagu in Bedford Square. No conclusion.
Quoted in full in *LHC*, pp. 51–55.

THOMAS BLACKBURNE

A3   A.L.s./copy in unidentified hand, [n.p.], [n.d., 1847]. To: [n.p.].
6 pp.

Blackburne has reproved his long silence, but he was unsure whether or not his letter would reach Blackburne. Is sorry Blackburne intends to leave his present situation because his pupil could learn a great many things from him, even if Latin was not one of them. Admires both of Blackburne's poems. "The Rich Man and the Poor" is beautiful, and [William] Fell has copied it. Quotes a stanza of the poem and comments on it. Remarks that the winter has been long, mentioning Dr. [Samuel] Johnson's *Life of Savage* [*An Account of the Life of Mr. Richard Savage, Son of the Earl Rivers*, 1744], [Matthew] Prior's *Robber*, and the Vicar of Wakefield [Oliver Goldsmith, *The Vicar of Wakefield, A Tale*, 2 vols. 1766]. The primroses in Rydal Wood were a month behind. Now it iss pring, "but if any thing could reconcile me to the running of cold iron through the bowels of this beautiful country it would not be the aesthetic advancement of the Manchester Operatives – but – Cheap Coals." Has Blackburne seen Wordsworth's railroad sonnets ["On the Projected Kendal and Windermere Railway" and "Proud were ye, Mountains, when, in times of old"]? If Petrarch could not win Laura with sonnets, "how could the Bard imagine or fancy that 14 lines, though each line were instinct with living fire like an Electric Telegraph, would mollify the Philantropic no-heart of a Railway Company?" But should not speak so of Wordsworth at this time, for his daughter is dying [Dora Wordsworth Quillinan died 9 July 1847]. "If you had seen her as I have seen her and seen how a beautiful Soul can make a face not beautiful most beautiful, if you had seen how by the mere strength of

26

affection she entered into the recesses of her Father's Mind and drew him out to gambol with her in the childishness that always hung upon her womanhood, you would feel, as we do, what earth is about to lose and Heaven to gain.

Quoted in full in *LHC*, pp. 291–293.

A4   A.L.s./copy in unidentified hand, [n.p.], [n.d.]. To: [n.p.]. 7 pp.

Would have answered Blackburne's letter of 26 July earlier, "but besides my usual *irresponsiveness* (the word in its epistolary sense is from the mint of the Revd. Derwent Coleridge) I was puzzled what medicine to prescribe in your disease albeit it was essentially the same from which I suffered myself at intervals from earliest youth to commencing eld from which I escapped only when youth – I had well nigh said when Hope had left even." Never could discover the whereabouts of Gilead, though "Balms of Gilead have been advertised by more Quacks than Dr. Soloman." Found some relief in versificatioon and the study of languages. Found the fit "accelerated and exacerbated" by unsympathetic consolation like that of Bildad the Shuhite, Eliphaz the Temanite, and Zophar the Naamathite to Job. Would have had fewer and less severe relapses had he used his lucid inervals better. Enjoyed Blackburne's description of his home near the ocean. "P——— certainly sounds better than Reverend Mrs. ———. Though I certainly hope that the Rev Mrs. William Fell will one day be Right Revd. Mama." Mentions Mr. Fosberry and a series of typical books of religious verse. Would Blackburne object to his showing "your lines of Dr [Thomas] Arnold to the family?" Is glad Blackburne was pleased by the sonnet. Will try what he can do for the Lines [?] Of Synesius. Comments on Blackburne's theory of the Church. Cannot read Blackburne's German. Had a narrow escape during a thunderstorm of Helvellyn; the party was weatherbound at Nag's Head. Mentions Witheburn, "Benjamin the Waggoner," Sir Charles Wetherall, Stockport, Cobden, and Manchester. Was recently thrown out of a gig. "The world also might have lost the chance for perpetual motion for the unfortunate Phaeton (what can people expect who call their Vehicles by such ill omened names?) contained a very gallant and aged mechanician who thinks he is near solving that long disputed problem." [William] Fell intends to add a few lines.

JAMES BRANCKER

A5   A.L.s./two copies in two unidentified hands, Grasmere, June 25th, 1834. To: Doe Park, near Liverpool. 5, 6 pp. A note at the top reads "autograph given to Lord Wolseley. E.H.C."

Brancker's advertisement [for the sale of Croft Lodge, his Ambleside home] fell on them like a thunderbolt. Will now hate the Westmoreland *Gazette*. Many cannot believe Brancker is selling Croft Lodge, and HC hopes he will find no purchaser. "In sober earnest (for I am always apt to be nonsensical when I am really sorry) it is a general topic of regret that you should find it necessary to leave us, just when we had begun to recon you ours, and when your long architectural labours were drawing to a close." Mentions the regret of Mr. Warden and "the fair widow." Speaks of Louis [Claude] and the Miss Claudes [Annie, Jane, Louisa, Mary] who are taking dancing lessons "heedless of the denunciations of the godly." Mentions William Penn and "the Hector of Librality" [identified in a MS note on the first TS copy as Henry Richard V——— Fox]. The Ambleside singers are being trained by Mr. Shepherd. Joseph Harden has lost the cure of Hawkshead, which "has been bestowed on a thirteenth or fourteenth cousin of Sir Ro^t Peel's." Mentions the present Chancellor of the Duchy of Lancaster, [Thomas] Spring Rice, and "that best and handsomest of men, the quandam mentor of the Limerick Telemachus." Sends news of Grasmere, Mrs. Ashworth, Mrs. Dawson, Mr. Parry, and "the man at Wyke." Respects to Mrs. [Jane Moss] Brancker, Brancker's father and father-in-law, and "Raw Material."

DR. W. BRIGGS

A6 A.L.s./copy in unidentified hand, Sedberg, Decr 18, 1838. To: [n.p.]. 4 pp.

Is gratified that [Thomas] Clarkson was pleased by the sonnet ["Long hast thou laboured, long, and very hard," Griggs, *New Poems*, p. 75] and rightly appreciates Clarkson's "delicacy in declining to be concerned in the publication of a Sonnet denouncing woe on the sons of his departed friend" [Robert Isaac and Samuel Wilberforce, who published the *Life* of their father, William Wilberforce, 5 vols., 1838]. Has no copy of the sonnet and cannot "tell whether the rest would have any force or meaning if the *damnatory* clauses were omitted but I have no wish to send forth anything which might give pain or offense to many pious persons without benefit to any important cause or principle." Discusses at some length Clarkson's role in the early abolition movement and the hardships he endured. Wilberforce had "the easier task of bringing the evidence into the Court," and perhaps his highest service was "that he engaged the religious feeling of all religious bodies in the right side." Digresses on the effects of the "connection of the Religious Establishment with the Monarchic and Aristocratic part of the State." On the whole, had rather the sonnet not be published "because I contemplate a longer poem on Perseverance in the good cause in Old Age wherein I shall endeavour to do justice to both Clarkson, Wilberforce and all other grey headed Reformers." Kindest respects to Mrs. [Anna Maria] Briggs and "your amiable daughters" [Anna Maria, Margaret, Mary Jane, and Sara].

PATRICK BRANWELL BRONTË

A7 A.L. (inc.), [Nab Cottage, Rydal], Nov. 30th or December 1st [1840]. To: [n.p.]. 2 pp. Accompanied by 3 pp. of poetry in an unknown hand heavily annotated by HC.

"I fear you have thought me unkind or forgetful in neglecting so long to notice your letter and the enclosed translations. [Branwell wrote HC 27 June 1840 and sent translations of Horace and a portion of a Henry Hastings story.] Believe me, I would not be the one and could not be the other, but I am a sad Procrastinator. I run in debt to Time, and debts of that nature bear compound interest. The longer unpaid, the more difficult to pay. I have however been wiping out a few old scores – this evening – and though I know not whether it be today – or tomorrow – whether Nov. 30th or December 1st, I will make an installment to you forthwith. You are by no means the first or the only person who has applied to me for judgement upon their writings. I smile to think that so small an asteroid as myself should have satellites. But you have heard the distich –

> Fleas that bite little dogs have lesser fleas
>   that bite em,
> The lesser fleas, have fleas still less, so on,
>   ad infinitum.

Howbeit, you are, with one exception, the only young Poet in whom I could find merit enough to comment without flattery, or stuff enough to be worth finding fault with. I think, I told you how much I was struck with the power and energy of the lines you sent before I had the pleasure of seeing you. Your translation of Horace is a work of much greater promise, and though I do not counsel a publication of the whole – I think many odes might appear with very little alteration. Your versification is often masterly – and you have shown skill in great variety of measures – there is a racy english in your language which is rarely to be found ever in the original – that is to say – untranslated and certainly untranslatable effusions of many of our juveniles, which considering how thorough Latin Horace is in his turns of phrase, and collocation of words – is proof of sound scholarship – and command of both languages. But we will, if you please examine a few odes – rather critically – and analytically.
    The first is not one of Horace's best, and I must say that it is your worst. Whatever merit it has in the original, is in the precise word, and juncture, for which our language cannot ever compensate. That Mecaenas, astavis edite regibus – Had Horace set about of malice prepense to cast the infirmities of our old mother lingo in her teeth, I could not have done it more provokingly. For what is the English of Atavus? Great-great-great grandfather! There is no language which I know the least of – that is so miserably off for terms of lineage as ours. Pater, Avus, Proavus, Abavus, Atavus, Tritavus, is a line of Plautus which it would be impossible to render into any modern language. I do not know whether Horace meant to compliment Mecaenas with that precise degree of descent from the Etruscan Monarchy [Cilnii] but yours – Sprung of

29

kingly line – is far too weak and vague. The feeling is much the same as if you were to address a welsh squire, as a descendant of Caractacus [king of the Silures, ca. 48–51] or Howel Dda [king of Wales, d. 950] –

> Oh, Davy Dear, sprung from the blood
> That was True Welsh before the Flood,
> And royally from sire to son
> Descended ere the world begun –

I once essayed to imitate the ode, in an irregular metre – somewhat in this fashion –

> Mecaenas, sprung of kings renownd in story,
> At once my sure defense, and pleasant glory,
> There we that have a might gust
> For trophies of olympic dust,
> When the glowing wheels have nicely turnd
> The goal, and the palm is nobly earnd,
> Nobly earnd and justly given
> It lifts the Lords of Earth to Heaven.

But your four lines –

> Whom dust clouds drifting oer the throng"

[The letter breaks off at this point. Cf. Patrick Branwell Brontë, tr., *The Odes of Quintus Horatius Flaccus Book I*. London, 1923.]

Quoted in full in "Hartley Coleridge and the Brontës" by Fran Carlock Stephens. *TLS*, 14 May 1970.

MRS. LOUISE CLAUDE

A8 A.L.s., Grasmere, Sept., 1838. To: [No. 36 Faulkner Street, Liverpool]. 10 pp., including a 2 pp. postscript sent under separate cover.

Feels she understands him and does not make the mistake of taking seriously things he says in fun. "Yet I have known the same defect [mistaking a humorous statement for a serious one] in persons of acute minds and fine sensibility, by no means destitute of humour, but from a certain earnest simplicity of nature, a sturdy matter of fact imagination and a habit of putting the heart into every thing, if they do not positively take jokes for grave propositions, and confound fiction with falsehood speak, feel, and judge, as if they did. The elder Miss [Dorothy] Wordsworth was an instance of this." Few people can understand grave irony, "which disguises deep meanings and powerful emotions under a garb of sportiveness." Is envious of [William] Fell for the "Family party letters he receives" [Mrs. Claude and Mrs. Fell are related]. Describes a ball at Green Bank where, "jammed in a corner with others of the superannuated list, [he] meditated on the evils arrising from a superabundant population." Saw two special favorites, Jessy Harden and Mary Dickinson. Played cards with Alderman Partridge, with Captain Lutwidge and Mr. Maltby as opponents. Gives an elaborate and humorous description of Alderman Partridge as Master of the Pack. Says to tell Louis [Claude] that Mr. Woodard started the hunt in a new scarlet coat. Fears the girls miss their Ambleside home. Sends to Mary "a sonnet [see A17] addressed to her favorite Mr. [Frederick] Faber," who has stirred up a great deal of religious controversy in Ambleside. "The terms Popistic and Calvinistic have been banded about by Persons who know not in what either Popery or Calvinism consist, unless perhaps they have taken the trouble to look for those articles in [John] Evan's sketches of all religions [*A Sketch of the Denominations of the Christian World*, London, 15th ed., 1827], or the Pocket Encyclopaedia, or some other equally profound, orthodox, and portable compendium of Xtian knowledge." Feels controversy has no place in the pulpit and is really a form of breaking the Sabbath. Faber's success is due, in no little part, "to his elegant manner, the impressive cast of his features, his ascetic paleness, his fine tones, and his almost aristocratic gentility of bearing." There is also something in names, "and I doubt whether Timothy Snook or Able Shufflebottom would produce such an agreeable impression in the pulpit as Frederick Faber." Heard "the Revd T[homas] Brancker" [nephew of James Brancker] and dined with the Branckers at Croft Lodge. Mentions [Owen] Lloyd; Mr. Harris [a new curate at Grasmere]; Monsieur Galippe; Louisa, Jane, and Mary [Claude]; Mr. Withington; and Mrs. Green "the elder" [of Grasmere, the Rev. Isaac Green's mother]. Adds his thanks for the letters and books. Visited at Croft Lodge [James Brancker's Ambleside home] with Mr. [John] Dawes, M. Galippe, [William] Fell, and Mrs. [Jane Moss] Brancker. Louis [Claude]'s old friend Dory came "with his master Isaac [Green]" to Mrs. Green's funeral. Mentions Janetta and Adolph [Claude], Mr. Pritchard, Lily Greenwood, and Mrs. Greenwood. Closes

> And so good night
> If night it be,
> For I verily think
> It is going for three.

A9 A.L.s., [Grasmere], [n.d., between January and June 1839]. To: No. 36 Faulkner Street, Liverpool. 3 pp. Carried by Mr. James Brancker.

Says he has a formidable job to complete before the first of June [*The Dramatic Works of Massinger and Ford*, see A49]. Thanks Louisa [Claude] for her copy of one of his sonnets. "Could all my works be so fairly transcribed, it would save the printers, and myself too, no small trouble. . . . I think I shall not publish it. The strain of self-accusation in which it is written though if I know myself at all – perfect sincere and unaffected – is too [much] a public confession, and I have no mind to invoke the eyes of the world upon my personality."

Describes his work on Massinger and Ford, of whom Mrs. Claude may never have heard. "You may perhaps remember that poor Ander [EHC, "Archer." Claude?] told you, Shakespeare was very like [August Friedrich Ferdinand von] Kotzebue only *not so moral.* . . . Now the Truth is that Shakespeare of all writers of his age the least resembled Kotzebue. None of them, indeed, resemble him in the mode of treating their subject, which is far more elevated and poetical. The sentimentality of Kotzebue would not have served for a clap-trap even to the sturdy spectators of Elizabeth's day, (for in the theaters of that age, the galleries were appropriated to the aristocratic portion of the audience, the masses standing in the pit)." Speaks of the fondness of the old dramatists for violent situations "pushed to an extent quite outrageous" though not without parallel in modern literature. Mentions the incest theme in Massinger and Ford. Says he works for "Mr. Wordsworth's publisher [Edward] Moxon, who pays most liberally. He is to publish my essays and Poems in the autumn" [Moxon, perhaps because of HC's tardiness on the Massinger and Ford, declined to do so].

A10   A.L.s., [Grasmere], [n.d., probably late March 1839]. To: [No. 36 Faulkner Street], Liverpool. 5 pp.

Intended to write from Keswick, where he has just attended the marriage of Bertha Southey [to Herbert Hill, 12 March 1839]. Sends condolences on the death of Mrs. Claude's daughter [Annie]. Mary Anse has also died. The weather has been bad, but Bertha's wedding day was fair. "In Bertha's case, I believe the Parson, who is used to such things, and myself, who cannot weep, however deeply I may be affected, were the only dry vessels." Mentions Herbert Hill's pupil, son of the Archbishop of Dublin [Richard Whately] and discusses the character of Aunt [Edith Fricker Southey], whom Kate [Southey] much resembles. "Bertha is very tall, lady-like, almost rather aristocratic in her appearance. Kate is of a small scale but with features exquisitely formed." Says Herbert Hill has no preferment but will live at Rydal and take pupils. Mr. [Robert] Southey intends to marry Miss Caroline Bowles [on 4 June 1839], "An authoress of much genius – if she be as good in herself as she appears in her books, she will not confirm the vulgar prejudice against step-mothers" [Southey's marriage caused a bitter family quarrel.] Southey is visiting Miss Bowles, and Mr. Wordsworth is going to Bath. Sends news of Mrs. STC, Mrs. [Jane Moss] Brancker, and Mr. [John] Dawes. Plans to do the lives of Massinger and Ford for [Edward] Moxon [*The Dramatic Works of Massinger and Ford*, London, 1840] "at five and twenty guineas a sheet, more than double of what I ever received before." Also plans an essay on STC for a new edition of *Biographia Literaria* [fragments published in *PMLA*, December, 1931]. "This I despair of doing to my own satisfaction, but it is earnestly desired by several friends, and if I do it not, somebody else may do it worse." Plans a second volume of poems and a volume of essays [not published during HC's lifetime]. Mentions Mr. J[ames] Spedding, Louis [Claude], Jones [Greenwood] at Sedbergh, Mr. [James] Brancker, and Mr. Shepherd.

A11   A.L.s., Ambleside, Fell's, July 13, postmarked 1840. To: No. 36 Faulkner Street, Liverpool. 4 pp.

Elaborately excuses the tardiness of his letter. "I was most agreeably surprised to see Louisa [Claude]. She is herself magnified. At least I see in her the same little darling as in times of yore." Louis [Claude] "has a good deal of the man about him" and still resembles Herbert White. The name "Captain C. H. White" appeared on the list of those slain at Guznee, but HC cannot believe that it is Herbert. Loves to hear Janetta [Claude] speak German with Fell. Discusses the sounds of different languages. "Before I heard you speak it I used to think [German] the cruelest torture which the presumption of the builders of Babel had inflicted on the ears of man." Mentions the Withingtons, Agnes and Fanny [Withington daughters], and Dulwich. Asks if she has seen the College [Dulwich College] founded by Edward Alleyn [1566–1626] and tells a story of Alleyn's seeing the devil. "I am the worst possible newsmonger and Fell the best." Dr. Briggs has just turned seventy and HC has "written a few lines on the occasion" ["To Dr. Briggs, on his 70th birthday," Earl Leslie Griggs, ed., HC, *New Poems*, London, 1942]. Sara [Briggs] is convalescent. Has been asked to be godfather to SC's expected child [Bertha Fanny Coleridge, b. 13 July 1840, d. 24 July 1840]. Has shifted from Grasmere to Nab Cottage. Misses [James] Brancker and Mrs. Claude. Love to Mary and Jane [Claude]. Mr. [Frederick] Faber preached yesterday at Rydal.

A12   A.L.s., Surgery, Ambleside, March 21, 1841. The product of *six* pipes – Small – False – I only smok'd one pipe and a precious black one. To: [No. 36 Faulkner Street, Liverpool]. 4 pp.

Says [William] Fell says he is a sinner for not having written her. Has not acknowledged Mrs. R[ichard (Hannah Mary Reynolds)] Rathbone's book [*Childhood*, 1841, to which HC's contributions were "The Sabbath Day's Child," "The First Birthday," "Primitiae," and "To K. H. J."]. Two of the poems came from Jane and Louisa [Claude]'s albums. Wishes he had appended a note, ["To K. H. J."] to explain that Katey Jones is the darling of a blind grandfather. [The poem is so subtitled in the *Poems*, 1851, but the *J* is changed to *I*.] Could have supplied poems on children in classical and older English literature. "It is remarkable, how abundant the authors, male and female, of the last half century, have been in baby poetry." Mentions poetry to children by [Matthew] Prior and Ambrose Philips. "I know not that any English poet before [Isaac] Watts ever wrote serious poetry for children, and some of his hymns, where the Calvinist did not predominate over the poet and Christian, are really beautiful." Mentions [Frederick William] Faber's book [*Cherwell Water Lily and Other Poems*, London, 1840], which has been sent to Mary [Claude] by Thomas Troughton [Ambleside bookseller]. Understands Faber is on his way to Jerusalem with his pupil [Matthew Harrison]. Wishes Mr. [James] Brancker a good purchaser [for Croft Lodge, his Ambleside home]. Is glad to hear H[erbert] White, who had been reported "fall'n at Guznee," is alive. Louis [Claude]'s friend Jones Greenwood is at home. The Adolph's [Claudes] have arrived at Valparaiso. Enjoyed their journal as translated by

33

Mrs. [William] Fell. Speculates on the effects "of a foreign clime" on little Janetta [Claude]. Wishes Mary [Claude], "who is as great a noddy about Babies as myself," could see Katey Hill [daughter of Herbert and Bertha Southey Hill], upon whom he has written a poem ["To Dear Little Katy Hill," DC, ed., HC, *Poems*, London, 1851]. "I also made some to the Queen in her character as wife and mother ["A wanton bard in heathen time," DC, ed., HC, *Poems*, London 1851], which Miss Spring Rice (now Mrs. J. G. Marshall) presented to her Majesty." Love to Jane and Louisa [Claude].

Quoted in full in *LHC*, pp. 247–250.

A13   A.L. (inc.), [Nab Cottage, Rydal], [n.d., April–May, 1841]. To: [1 Brighton Road, Waterloo, near Liverpool?]. 2 pp.

Apparently an unfinished reply to B53. Reports on James Brancker, as she requested. Brancker's health appears good. "I can see that *it* [Jane Moss Brancker's death] is at his heart, but he has put away the great burden from the region of its worst pressure and bears it stoutly up. I made no allusion to the loss, of course, and avoided everything that look's that way." Is sorry to hear Louisa [Claude] is depressed. Says he never saw the sea "without a sense of glory." Sends nineteen lines on the sea, "It comes, it goes — it ebbs, it flows" [Earl Leslie Griggs, ed., HC, *New Poems*, London, 1942]. Speaks of the coast of the Isle of Wight.

A14   A.L.i., Ambleside Octr. 11th, 1841, without a pipe in his mouth. To: No. 36 Faulkner Street, Liverpool. 4 pp. The letter is on paper illustrated by an engraving of Blea Tarn cut by William Banks.

Begins with the poem " 'Into the heart of mountain Solitudes' / Where one low dwelling, with its neighbor trees" [*LHC*, p. 251]. Speaks of the dismal weather, mentioning Mrs. [William] Fell. "I never myself took any fancy to these closets in the hills, as places of permanent residence, since I was fifteen." Even Robinson Crusoe was on a green, sunny island with much animal life. "Though sulky and misanthropic enough at times," has not yet come to that state which "seeks solitude as something less intolerable than . . . society." Sometimes finds Nab Cottage "rather too retired." Mentions Mr. [James] Brancker and Louis and Louisa [Claude]. "My muse, however, has been productive of late, but I cannot produce either prose or verse to please myself completely, and some times when I read the trash that is so liberally set forth, I am tormented with the suspicion that my own is no better." The worst writer always has friends who will praise him. Mentions [Frederick] Faber and his "Pupil"; Mr. Combe's synagogue; Sir Wilfred Lawson of Braymore Hall; Janetta [Claude?]; Herbert Southey Hill; and Mary, Jane, and Louisa [Claude].

Quoted in full in *LHC*, pp. 251–253.

A15 A.N.s., [n.p.], [n.d.]. To: [n.p.]. 1 p. The back of the note is filled with historical notes in HC's hand.

His clumsiness has caused an ink stain on the margin of Ferdinand and Isabella [W. H. Prescott, *The History of Ferdinand and Isabella of Spain*, London, 1837?] "it is of no use to say with Lady Macbeth 'out, out damn'd spot,' for I fear it will remain. . . . But let the blame fall on the offender. Let me arouse, as just penance, the wrath of the awful secretary, and whatever more substantial penalty the sable sin may have incurred."

LOUISE CLAUDE W.*

A16 A.L.s., [Nab Cottage, Rydal], [n.d., early March 1842]. To: [36 Faulkner Street, Liverpool]. 4 pp.

Excuses the tardiness of his letter, explaining that he has had "a stupifying head-achey cold, which sticks to me like a poor and homeless relation, in spite of the broadest hints to depart." Speaks of the murder of Julius Caesar and the current rumors that London will be swallowed up by an earthquake. "London's rich and famous town / Hungry earth shall swallow down." "I wonder you could hesitate at all to ask about the drift of my emblematic verses, but then, I sometimes wonder how any one can call my hand-writing illegible, though the purblind printers not only protest that it is so, but prove their assertion by making all sorts of imaginable and unimaginable blunders." Says she is right in supposing that there is a language of gems as of flowers, animals, etc. [See B56]. Understanding of these "languages" is necessary to understand the "old Poets, Divines, and Philosophers." Mentions Sir Hildebrand and Mr. [James] Greenwood. Quotes nine lines on gems from [Thomas] Carew [1595?–1645?]. Speaks of some of the alleged powers of gems. Has been to a party at Captain Lutwidge's with [William] Fell. Mentions Louis [Claude], Louis's friend Jones Greenwood, and the verses he has written on Owen [Lloyd] ["A Schoolfellow's Tribute to the Memory of the Rev. Owen Lloyd" and "Epitaph on Owen Lloyd," DC, ed., HC *Poems*, London, 1851]. Thanks Mr. [James] Brancker for the *Athenaeums* he sent by Mr. [James] Greenwood. "Mr. Wordsworth is bringing forth a volume [*Poems, Chiefly of Early and Late Years; Including The Borderers, A Tragedy*, London, 1842]. It will doubtless create a sensation." Calls Wordsworth "the last of the Poets," now that [Samuel] Rogers and [Robert] Southey write poetry no more. "Wordsworth and [Thomas] Campbell are the sole survivors of the Poets of my youth. They are not likely to have any successors. We have now plenty of clever men, but no great Man, and no promise of greatness." Congratulates Louisa that [Herbert] White is safe in England [he had been reported killed in the siege of Guznee]. Love to Mrs. [Louise] Claude. Adds a postscript on the flowers.

*On 14 January Louise Claude married John W., whose last name is given nowhere in the correspondence. "W." has been included here and elsewhere to distinguish daughter from mother, for while HC addresses the daughter as "Louisa," her mother and sisters refer to her as "Louise," and she signs herself so.

A17 A.L.s., [Grasmere], [n.d., September 1838]. To: [No. 36 Faulkner Street, Liverpool]. 2 pp.

Encloses sonnet [see A8] "To the Reverend Frederick Faber" [*LHC*, p. 225]. "Knowing your partiality for the person to whom it is addressed (in his clerical capacity I mean) I thought you would not be displeased to see that Heretic as I must needs appear in his eyes – I hold him in high honour." Has never had the courage to call on Mr. Faber. "He has made some converts, I believe, to the High Church . . . But I am afraid he has prevail'd upon nobody to fast upon Fridays." Advises Mary not to listen to controversy.

Quoted in full in *LHC*, pp. 225–226.

A18 A.L.s., [Nab Cottage, Rydal?], [n.d., 1840]. To: [No. 36 Faulkner Street, Liverpool]. 2 pp.

Has dined at the Claudes' old house with John Crossfield, his brother, their wives, and the Rev. Anderson, who is officiating for Mr. Boutflower. Mary's flowers are flourishing. "I was delighted, my dear Mary, with your mother's telling me of the impression the Nightingale's song made on you, but still more, should I have been delighted, had my father been alive, in as much as he was the first modern Poet, to explode and defy the fancy, of the Nightingale's *Melancholy* song, and to call her (or, gallantry apart, it should be – him – for I believe only Male *Birds* sing)" [quotes ll.43–48 of "The Nightingale," Elisabeth Schneider, ed., STC, *Selected Poetry and Prose*, New York, 1951]. Sends poem "The Nightingale" [written 27 September 1840; DC, ed., HC, *Poems*, London, 1851].

Quoted in full in *LHC*, pp. 243–245.

A19 A.L.s., Knabbe [Cottage, Rydal], Nov. 18, 1840. To: [No. 36 Faulkner Street, Liverpool]. 4 pp.

Has just returned from [William] Fell's, where he won £3.6. Mrs. [W. (Anna Maria)] Briggs's note informs him that Mr. and Mrs. [John] Crossfield are going to Liverpool. By them he will send this letter and a copy of [Frederick William] Faber's poems [*Cherwell Water Lily and Other Poems*, London, 1840, see A12]. Gives local news mentioning "your Mr. Jones," Mr. Warden, Tommy [Troughton] and Mrs. Nicholson [Ambleside booksellers], Mr. [William] Richardson, and Mr. Reckam [a relative of William Fell's] and his wife. Suppose Mrs. [Hannah Mary Reynolds] Rathbone's work is now ready for publication [*Childhood*, 1841]. Sends along a ditty "Lollypops" [Earl Leslie Griggs, ed., HC, *New Poems*, London, 1942] which Mrs. Rathbone may use as she wishes. "But you must not let the mercantile or dissenting public conceive, that it is ascribed to the Bard of Rydal Mount" [Wordsworth]. Speaking of Faber's poems, HC says "Seriously, I do think, that they shew more genius, than I find in any of the young Poets, Alfred Tennyson excepted, but genius as yet undisciplined and not very well supplied with material to work on." Says man cannot create "But combine, transpose, and modify." Regards to the Misses Withington. Mentions Mr. [James] Brancker, Croft Lodge, Mrs. [Jane Moss] Brancker, "the popish Mayor of Kendal," Katey Hill, the needle in Jane [Claude]'s foot, and Louisa [Claude]'s bad teeth. Love to Mrs. [Louise] Claude. "I cannot refrain from visiting London much longer, for my poor Mother is aged, and I fear sinking. I have never seen my niece or nephew [Edith and Herbert Coleridge], and my brother [DC] has become a minister and a husband and a father since we met." Asks her to send a copy of the sonnet about the Nightingale ["The Nightingale," DC, ed., HC, *Poems*, London, 1851].

One sentence quoted in *LHC*, p. 248.

A20 A.L.s., [Fell's, Ambleside], [n.d.]. To: [No. 36 Faulkner Street, Liverpool]. 1 p. Written on part of a letter from William Fell to Mary Claude.

HC's letter consists mostly of twenty-four lines of verse beginning "When thoughts too mighty crowd upon the brain" [*LHC*, p. 277]. Speaks in a general way of birth and death. Alludes to the death of "the long, in pain, expecting sufferer," and life after death. Adds a prose note "Very bad – but they hint at my meaning." Promises to write more.

Fell writes at length of "Poor Jane Briggs," who has never recovered properly from her last confinement. Her husband, Robert, does not behave well toward her. Miss Milligan, a neighbor, is the local authority on the Briggs' affairs. "Hausechen" [Mrs. William Fell] sends love and promises an account of the baby [Jeanette Fell]. Coleridge is here and says to leave him room to write.

Quoted in full in *LHC*, p. 277.

DERWENT COLERIDGE

A21 A.L.s., [25 Bedford Square, London, and Highgate, London], postmarked Dec. 11, 1820. To: St. John's College, Cambridge. 4 pp. Endorsed on address face by DC "1820 Metrical letter."

A 196-line verse letter. Congratulates Derve [DC] on some recent success. DC has not written either him or Mrs. [James] Gillman.

And permit an old culprit in friendship to mention
That she thinks a great deal of a slight inattention.

Won't go to Highgate because he has a cold and a "Rheumatical" shoulder.

Tis a Paradox, perhaps you may think, that I say,
But I'm ten years more aged in March than in May:
In November I'm fifty, fourscore in December,
In a snow storm a snuff, in an East wind an ember;
But when the May moon has replenished her cresent,
I feel my old bones getting quite juvenescent.
....
Twere a mighty great bore to grow old as Tithonus,
Unless growing young were thrown in as a Bonus.

Proposes a plan to import fine days from Italy or Turkey. Gives, in a delightful
imaginative passage, his version of how England got its bad weather. Discusses
current political affairs. Hopes DC sticks to the Queen [Caroline] and is glad
"the Bill" [of Pains and Penalties against the Queen] was thrown out [dropped
after it had passed its third reading in the House of Lords by a majority of
only seven]. Though STC has been slandered,

I wish that we both were a conscience as easy
At fifty may bost of his moto, ΕΣΤΗΣΕ
["He stood;" in nineteenth-century pronoun-
ciation a pun on STC.]

Mentions Robespierre, Lord Castlereagh, Paley, Hume, Sidmouth, Lord Yar-
mouth, Clarence [later William IV], Wilberforce, Lord Donoughmore, John
Scot, Baron Eldon, Lord Keeper, "Colombia's countess," Canning, Copley, Cun-
ningham, Whately, Judge Best, The Queen's Son-in-Law [Prince Leopold], and
John Tarus [Bull]. Says he wants to tell DC about the Oxford affair, but not in
verse. The Rydal family is visiting their brother at Trinity [Christopher Wordsworth, master of Trinity College, Cambridge]. Intends to complete a volume of
poems for Christmas and invites DC to join him in the volume. Saw DC's Miss
Hall and was not impressed. Goes to Highgate, after all. Wishes DC better luck
at Cambridge than he has had at Oxford.

And if e'er her odd whims your disposed to take
    tartley,
Pray remember the fate of your poor brother
    Hartley.

A22 A.L., postmarked Oxford, [date of postmark almost illegible]
Jan [1820]. To: Keswick, Cumberland. 4 pp.

Put DC's last letter aside to read when he had more time, "(for in very truth,
my dear Brother, your hand out-villains villainy)" and lost it. Has been work-

ing hard with his student St. Aubyn, but St. Aubyn failed his exams. Speaks of St. Aubyn's character, concluding "His faults are the result of his situation – his virtues are his own." Will advise St. Aubyn's father and brother, who is now at Cambridge, that the young man should not make a third attempt. Has been to Ottery St. Mary and was agreeably surprised by his reception there. "*Entre nous*, however, Fanny [Frances Duke Coleridge Patteson], Aunt Luke [Sara Hart Coleridge], and Frank [Francis George Coleridge] were the only people who came up to my notions of perfection." Comments on Aunt [Anne Bowden] and Uncle Edward [Coleridge], Aunt George [Jenny Hart] and George [Coleridge], Mrs. Colonel [Frances Taylor] and the Colonel [James Coleridge]. "Then for the juniors" mentions Edwin [Ellis Coleridge] and his sister "little deaf Bessy" [Elizabeth Coleridge]. Moves from Bessy's defect to the divine bounty of the universe. "This . . . is a strange transition, but I hope my scrawls will never be published. . . . You see that some of my earlier feelings are alter'd, that my religion . . . is become cheerful." Hopes more correspondence with DC will be beneficial to them both. Gives a charming description of Fanny [Frances Duke Coleridge Patteson]. Says DC's account of "your beauty" [Miss Hall?] was charming, "tho' any thing like love in you or I, is the height of fatuity. I can't either condemn it or get rid of it in myself, so I'll not be intolerant towards you." Cautions DC to be careful; some girls, even the nicest ones, are incapable of love. "M. [Mary Harris?] is as lovely and beloved as ever, tho' I am better reconciled to hopelessness than I was formerly. I know, at least I think, she does not care for me. I almost believe that she has no conceptions that I more than like her, and perhaps it is as well it should be so." [*LHC* notes that John Taylor Coleridge wrote James Gillman in June 1820 "I am informed . . . that he has contracted an attachment for a young person, the daughter I think of an architect; I hear her well spoken of individually, but any such engagement at his time of life and under the circumstances is to be deplored."] Presently has no pupils but Cousin Ned [Edward Coleridge]. Plans some theological studies and extensive work on the "Prometheus." Mentions Mrs. STC, SC, Wilsey [Mrs. Wilson, Greta Hall housekeeper], "our good old King" [George III], STC, Cousin Harry [HNC], [Henry Peter] Brougham and [William] Lowther [Lord Lonsdale].

Quoted in full in *LHC*, pp. 26–30.

A23 A.L., Highgate, [London], February 19, 1821. To: St. John's Coll., Cambridge. 3 pp. Endorsed on address face by DC "1821 – Feb. My bills | Blank verse." Seal face has been used for math and Latin notes in pencil.

Uses DC's nickname "Snifterbreeches." "Doctissimus" [James] Gillman bids HC tell DC the latter's bills are paid. Gillman has drawn £80 from George Frere "being the amount due to you by Mr. J[ohn] H[ookham] Frere" [who set aside £300 understood to be for DC's college expenses]. Gillman has put the money "into the counter-drawer" of Mr. [Thomas] Coutts [Coutts & Co., Strand, bankers of George III]. Mentions Mr. [Thomas] Calvert, fellow and tutor at

St. John's College, Cambridge; Mrs. [Ann] Gillman; and Remorse [STC, *Remorse*, London, 1813]. Sends eight lines of verse "Come, listen to a woeful story" [*LHC*, p. 58]. Has improved his blank verse, but "I certainly succeed better in intricate and difficult, than in plainer and simpler textures. The Sonnet is my favourite." Had a letter from "Snouderumpater," [Mrs. STC] enclosing Wilsy [Mrs. Wilson, Greta Hall housekeeper]'s legacy of £200. Refers to "old George Rose's" [1744–1818] fortune "drawn out of the pockets of the people" [George Rose and members of his immediate family held a large number of salaried government offices]. Mrs. STC's letter mentions DC and SC. "Not a word about [Robert] Southey." Charles Owen [HC's pupil] has not paid him. Mentions "Prometheus" [not completed; DC, ed., HC, *Poems*, London, 1851], Mrs. [Ann] Gillman, and STC. Closes with six lines of doggerel, "Write when you can" [*LHC*, p. 59].

Quoted in full in *LHC*, pp. 56–59.

A24 A.L.i., [25 Bedford Square, London?], postmarked May 2, 1821. To: St. John's Coll, Cambridge. 4 pp.

Has set aside another letter to DC to write on a more serious topic. Has seen DC's letter to STC. [DC asks to be changed from St. John's College to Trinity College.] "Your objections to St. John's seem to fall under two heads: your small chance of success there, and your dislike to the society." Advises DC to consider "the advantages of an early competence, and a fixt home – goods, which I have learned to value. . . . But I am decidedly of the opinion that you could not contend on equal grounds with some of your tough-headed competitors without the risque of your life, or at least, of all that can make life valuable." Therefore advises DC to pursue the Fellowship as a possibility rather than as a necessity. "Do not expect it, and do not throw it away. So doing, you will satisfy yourself, your truest friends, and all reasonable people, you are not dazzled by the name of Fellow, which I suspect was the case in some degree, with poor dear Mama." As to DC's second objection, his dislike of the St. John's society, HC hopes his own Oriel experience will not weigh on DC's mind. "If you do continue there, by all means keep in sight of the Superiors." Feels that DC's temperament will allow him to be more successful in society than he was. Reviews his Oxford career. At Merton he was "in a great measure . . . master of my own time." He became pessimistic about people, and his very pessimism caused him to overrate good qualities when he found them. "This was not a good preparatory discipline for Oriel. And indeed, from the first moment that I conceived the purpose of offering myself as a Candidate [for the Oriel Fellowship], I felt that I was not consulting my own happiness. But duty, vanity, and the fear of being shipped off to Brazil – determined me on the Trial." Reviews the strictness and incompatability of Oriel, where he felt subject to "a kind of espionage." "I thought most of them [his Fellows and superiors] Bigots, ignorant deciders upon the conduct of others, conceited of their own dignity, and rather disposed to tyrannize. The natural effect of all this on my mind was a tendency to resistance, and I was not bold enough to fight, or prudent enough to make peace." Begs DC to consider carefully whether Trinity might not be quite as incompatible as St. John's. "I am not now speaking of Studies, or even of Society, these are points you may ascertain. But I speak of a certain cold-heartedness – and confined feeling – which every body of fellows have more or less of. College pride is as specific a feeling as Family pride and far less connected with inward nobleness." Mentions Bob [Robert Jameson], Mr. [James] Gillman, and STC.

Quoted in full in *LHC*, pp. 59–63.
Quoted in part in *Memoir*, pp. lxxxvii–lxxxviii.

A25   A.L., Grays Inn [London] August 27, 1821. To: St. John's Coll., Cambridge. 4 pp. Endorsed on address face by DC "Funny-things."

"I am thoroughly convinced there is nothing so wholesome for mind and body, as talking Nonsense. Writing it is not half so good – it's like sending Sal volatile by the waggon with the cork out, but situated as we are, what can one do better." Nonsense should be written only to one's intimates, whose memories can supply "proper looks and tones." Pen and ink are the destruction of a funny thing. "Woeful it is to reflect that of all the wonders that you and I and the Maum [Mrs. STC] have produced in that way, not one can be of the slightest benefit to Posterity." Can only laugh at what is "exquisitely bad" and purely accidental. "Indeed, a praemeditated funny thing is worse than a praemeditated piece of sensibility. . . . I never laugh now at Hogarth, or Fielding, or Cervantes. . . . But at our old Funny things I can laugh by myself for an hour together – nay, they furnish me with a reservoir of laughter for all needful occasions." Alludes to a family joke concerning DC. Writes on domestic matters, mentioning Monday and Slatter [tradesmen], Mrs. STC, [Robert] Southey, Netherhall, and STC. Finds himself lonely. Robert [Jameson] and his friends are all busy, "and, what is worse than all, I know neither girls nor children. You must not be surprised if I Hang myself, tho' I have no determined thoughts that way at present." Discusses the Milnes [neighbors of the Gillmans] and the [James] Gillmans. "When you are closely united, by interest or gratitude, with a family, never be too intimate with their intimate neighbors." Quarrels are bound to arise, and then one is put into a most difficult position. Mentions Bob [Robert Jameson].

Quoted in full in *LHC*, pp. 68–71.
Quoted in part in *Memoir*, pp. xc–xcii.

A26   A.L.i., [25 Bedford Square, London?], [n.d., 1821]. To: St. John's College, Cambridge. 4 pp. Seal face bears math equations.

Thanks DC for his last letter, "(in which only one sentence was absolutely illegible)." Has been ill at Highgate and Mrs. Milne's [neighbors of the Gillmans]. Writes at length to assure DC he [DC] has not lost his poetic powers. DC's love "spread a sort of color'd mist about your feelings. . . . Thus passion, gaining the permanence of thought, and thought the warmth and vitality of passion, you had but to add a tone . . . and the simple record of the goings on of your heart and mind came forth as sweet poems." Believes that DC's loss [of his love, Miss Hall?] will prove a gain, forcing him "to look abroad, to call on your imagination, to observe more, and invent more." Mentions his "Prometheus" [DC, ed., HC, *Poems*, London, 1851], Miss Maria Battley, his "friend and pupil" C[harles] Owen, Fred Gunning, and Charlotte Owen. "Have you seen [Robert] Southey's Vision of Judgement [London, 1821] ! ! ! ! ! O Tempora, O Mores – And is it come to this? And our dear mother gave me such a hint to praise in her last letter!!! I came off, I think, pretty well, saying that I did not think it the *best* of S.'s poems. Seriously speaking, our late lamented Monarch did not deserve such an insult to his memory. And who, but a converted Revolutionist, would ever have dreamed of spurring the . . . broken-down gelding . . . into the Hexameter long trot." Launches into a long discussion of the advantages and disadvantages of hexameter verse, mentioning [John? Thomas?] Wilkes, Milton, Sir Philip Sidney, Pope, and Dryden. Sends local news of Bob [Robert Jameson], James and Henry [Gillman], STC, Mrs. [James] Gillman. Gives a very amusing description of Mrs. Gillman's sister, Miss Jane Harding. Love from Mr. and Mrs. G[illman], Robert [Jameson], and Mr. [Basil] Montagu. "I hear nothing of the *when* between Miss Skepper and Barry Cornwall [Barry Cornwall married Anne Skepper, Basil Montagu's step-daughter, in 1824], but I should doubt whether that gentleman were in a state either of health or purse, to make marriage advisable." Mentions Worship [?], Henry [HNC], [Richard] Townsend, SC, and Mrs. STC.

Quoted in full in *LHC*, pp. 63–68.

A27   A.L.i., Ambleside, May 2, [1823]. To: St. John's Coll., Cambridge. 4 pp. Endorsed on address face by DC *"Extract | school."*

Is in low spirits. Intends to take orders in two years. "I have found more kindness both here and elsewhere than I have earn'd." Is in no immediate distress. Receives cheerful letters from SC, STC, and Mrs. STC. All these things "do make me thankful and they ought to make me cheerful." Asks DC about his progress. Feels a curacy would suit DC better than a Fellowship. "Remember, that it is to you that Sara [SC] will look. I must and will do my utmost – but all that I can ever do will be less than she deserves and requires." Mentions Mrs. STC, STC, his Uncles, [William] Green the artist, and Jane [Green]. Sends local news of Mr. and Mrs. Wordsworth, who are now at Lee Priory in Kent; Miss [Dorothy] Wordsworth; Dorothy [Wordsworth Quillinan?]; the [Robert] Southeys; Aunt [Mary Fricker] Lovell; Mrs. Bobson; Mr. Longmire; the Dicksons [Dixons], who are leaving Old Brathay [for Field Head]; Eliza Dixon; Mr. [John] Dawes; John Marshal; and J[ohn] Wordsworth [son].

Quoted in full in *LHC*, pp. 78–80.
Quoted in part in *Memoir*, pp. xcv–xcvi.

A28   A.L., [Ambleside], postmarked June 24, 1823. To: J[ohn] Moultrie Esqre, for D. Coleridge Esqre, Eton Bucks, Berkshire. 5 pp. Page five is crosswritten on page one.

Having just dismissed his pupils for the midsummer holidays, "I will bestow some pages of my tediousness upon thee, little as thou has provoked such a return at my hands." Has burned DC's letter, as requested, but "had they been posted on the church door . . . no one would have been the wiser. Thou dost write the most incomprehensible cypher that ever baffled mortal curiosity." Refers to [Richard] Bentley's edition of *Paradise Lost* [London, 1732], Lord Portsmouth, and George IV. Warns DC to beware of jealousy: "you are framed to make women false." At any rate, were he [HC] "disposed to act the part of Don Juan, I would choose a younger and less affected Julia than Mrs. P. [?]." Is sorry DC has been ill and depressed and tries to comfort him. Reviews his owns trials. "I am now not happy, but I am at ease, I am content, and I am cheerful. I have no hopes, and not many wishes, which lie at the mercy of chance, and I have strength within me which is the more secure because I have learn'd not to confide in it." Discusses DC's resignation of "the pursuit of Academic honours." Advises DC to be "very cautious in your conduct" to STC and to the [James] Gillmans. Mentions SC and Mrs. STC, who is "not much more Jobish." Promises an article for DC's magazine [*Knight's Quarterly Magazine*] and advises DC not to do much for it until he has taken his degree. [DC contributed a number of articles usually signed Davenant Cecil.] Sends news of the Rydal Mount group. "W[ordsworth] has been in Holland. John [Wordsworth, son] is laborious as an Ass. Dora [Wordsworth Quillinan] is a sweet, good humor'd girl. Little Will [Wordsworth] is a bore." Mentions Fanny White; Mr. Moy; the Dixons, who have moved from Old Brathay to Field Head; Eliza [Dixon]; Miss Marshall, "George Crump's inamorato"; Elizabeth Crump; Mr. [John] Dawes; and Edwin [Ellis Coleridge].

Quoted in full in *LHC*, pp. 81–84.
Quoted in part in *Memoir*, pp. xcvi–xcvii.

A29 A.L., [Ambleside], [n.d., 1827]. To: Helston, Cornwall. 5 pp. Favoured by Mrs. [Charles (Sarah Hustler)] Fox. Endorsed on address face by DC "On my going into orders."

Addresses DC by his nickname "Snifterbreeches." Playfully speaks of Mrs. [Sarah Hustler] Fox and of Daniel Lambert [1770–1809; the fattest man on record, weighing at his death 52¾ stone, or 738½ lbs.]. Rejoices to see DC in his new position, which "I know you have not taken upon you lightly . . . but with due sense of all its aweful responsibilities." Speaks at length on the character and duties of clergymen. Has nearly finished a long article [(The Old Batchelor), "De Omnibus Rebus et Quibusdam Aliis," *Blackwood's Magazine*, July 1827] for Ebony [William Blackwood], who "owes me nearly 10 Guineas, which I wish he would pay." Comments on the *Quarterly Review*, the *British Critic*, Joseph Hume, *Knight's Quarterly Magazine*, and *Blackwood's Magazine*. Discusses DC's "A Lecture on Wordsworth" [(Derwent Coleridge), *Metropolitan Quarterly Magazine*, Vol. 1, No. 2, 1826], mentioning Thomson, Cowper, and Milton. "Wordsworth's prose has done more to retard his fame, than the *simplest* of his poems. Why do you say nothing of the 'White Doe' [William Wordsworth, *The White Doe of Rylstone; or The Fate of the Nortons, A Poem*, London, 1815] – so sweet, so beautiful? What a mighty genius is the Poet Wordsworth! What a dull poser is W. W. Esqre. of Rydal Mount, Distributor of stamps and brother to the Rev'd. the Master of Trinity [Christopher Wordsworth]. I hope we shall have the remainder of the *Recluse* ere long, and that W. will have the courage to let his poetical or philosophical creed stand on its own bottom, and not pursue the worse than useless attempt to disguise Spinoza in the ragged Surplice of a Westmorland Curacy." Mentions Greta Hall, Mrs. STC, STC, and SC. Wishes SC had formed another attachment. "Worldly considerations apart, I do not think the author [HNC] of the *Six Months' Residence* [*Six Months in the West Indies*, London, 1826] the likeliest person in the world to accord with the exquisite tenderness and susceptibility of her moral and physical constitution. . . . Sariola will require delicacy in a husband." Mentions the [James] Gillmans. Comments on the *Six Months*, which "is very clever, and tolerably sensible, but there is a flippancy, a vulgarity about it, which I cannot esteem." Mentions [Thomas Babington] Macaulay, DC's engagement [to Mary Pridham], and Mrs. STC's opinion of that engagement. Sends local news of Mr. [John] Dawes, Mr. Harden, Owen Lloyd, Jonson Jackson, Billy Scambler, Herbert White, and Fanny and Sophy White.

Quoted in full in *LHC*, pp. 90–94.

A30   A.L., [Grasmere], Begun August–Finished August 30 [1830]. To: Helston, Cornwall. 20 pp.

A long, fanciful letter conveyed by "the hand of a Quaker" [probably Mrs. Sarah Fox]. Has been unable to collect money due him for tutoring [unsuccessfully, for Oriel College, Oxford] St. Aubyn and leaves the business in DC's hands. Regrets that he is a financial burden to Mrs. STC and "the poison which such worldly dealings mingle with the pure streams of affection." Congratulates DC on his happiness in marriage and makes many general comments on the married state. Mentions Mary [Pridham Coleridge], Prior's Solomon [Matthew Prior, *Solomon de Mundi Vanitate*, Oxoniae, 1734–1736], Mrs. [Elizabeth] Fry [the prison reformer], and Dervy [Derwent Moultrie Coleridge]. Says Mary [Pridham Coleridge] would be impossible to describe, but DC should send a long description of the baby [Derwent Moultrie Coleridge]. "Yet, God bless it [any baby], the good gossips hold it up to the light (as if it were a bottle of claret) to the infinite discomfort of its small eyes, and with noticable inconsistency, in one breath pronounce it 'a little beauty' and yet the very moral of the ugliest of all its ugly Aunts, Uncles and Cousins." Speculates on Dervy's appearance, mentioning STC, Mrs. STC, and SC. Discusses SC's marriage [to HNC, 3 September 1829]. Wishes HNC were richer, but is glad SC has escaped Greta Hall, where she felt herself to be in bondage. Discusses "Henry's book on Homer" [HNC, *Introduction to the Study of the Greek Classic Poets*, London, 1834]. HNC is very near the theory of [Friedrich August] Wolf and [Christian Gottlob] Heyne, "a theory which if I did not abhor puns of all sorts, and particularly good ones, I should pronounce Wolfish and Heinous." [Both STC and HNC advocated the theory that the *Iliad* was composed by several

44

authors.] Mentions the possibility that he will review the book for *Blackwood's* [*Magazine*] or the *Quarterly* [*Review*]. [No such review exists.] Thanks DC for the razors and clothes. Sends Westmorland news, mentioning Wordsworth; C[hauncey] H[are] Townshend; John Wordsworth; Lord Lonsdale [William Lowther]; Miss [Isabella] Curwen; Henry Curwen [Isabella's brother?]; Dora [Wordsworth Quillinan]; the *Recluse*; Uncle [Robert Southey]; Edith May [Southey Warter]; Bertha [Southey Hill]; Kate and Cuthbert [Southey]; Mr. [John] Dawes; Owen Lloyd; Miss Jane Moss [Brancker]; [James] Brancker; Croft Lodge; Mrs. Brancker [Sr.]; Mrs. Robinson; the [John] Hardens and children Jane, Alan, Jobby, and John William; Elleray [John Wilson's home]; Mrs. Machel; Christopher North [John Wilson]; Professor [John] Wilson; Ebony [William Blackwood]; Mrs. [John] Wilson and children Maggy, Mary, James, and Jane; and Chucky Doro [Dorothy Wordsworth Harrison (Mrs. Benson Harrison)]. Hopes to produce two volumes of prose and verse [none published at this time]. Adds a description of Grasmere. Mentions Mr. and Mrs. [Charles] Fox, St. Bob [Robert Peel], Mrs. STC, SC, T[homas] Poole, and Sir Thomas Lethbridge. Encloses sonnet "Can Man rejoice in joys he may not know" [*LHC*, p. 119]. Adds notes on Mrs. [Sarah] Fox and her two girls; Mr. Longmire; Mrs. Robinson; Mrs. [Charles (Sophia)] Lloyd and her children Grosvenor and Owen; Mr. [Charles] Lloyd; and "my Nephew" [Derwent Moultrie Coleridge]. Encloses poem "To My Unknown Sister-in-law" [somewhat different from published versions; HC, *Poems*, Leeds, 1833]. Mentions [John Gibson] Lockhart, [William] Gifford, John [Taylor Coleridge], and Mrs. [Felicia Dorothea Browne] Hemens.

Quoted in full in *LHC*, pp. 105–124.

A31 A.L., Grasmere, August 1st, 1834. To: Helston, Cornwall. 4 pp. Endorsed on address face by DC "Father's Death."

"We are both alike – both fatherless children. I never felt before – how much we are brothers." Longs to see DC. "I never felt, never acknowledged, the value of a father, and of such a father, till I knew that I had no Father." Speaks of the grief DC must feel and of how much of a comfort DC must have been to STC. "For me, I can only hope that no painful thought of me adulterated the final out gushing of his spirit." Feels his own sorrow is scarcely adequate to the occasion. Speaks of STC as "a powerful preacher of Jesus. For myself I can speak, that he, he only made me a Christian." Often forgot himself, but never forgot STC, "and wherever the final bolt of judgement may drive me, it will not be into the frozen region of sons that loved not their fathers." Will always regret that he was not with STC at the end. Alludes to DC's troubles and mentions Dervy [Derwent Moultrie Coleridge]. Intends to publish a second volume of poetry [not published during his lifetime]. "God help us – it is a sad piece of vanity, when a great spirit is departed from the earth, to think of one's own silly verses; and yet, I shall finish Prometheus half as well as if he, who praised the commencement so far beyond its deserts, had been alive to judge it. Heaven grant I may never write what he would not have approved on earth, or may not approve in Heaven." Speaks of their duty to Mrs. STC. Mentions

Mary [Pridham Coleridge], Derwent Moultrie Coleridge, HNC, and [Winthrop Mackworth] Praed.

Quoted in full in *LHC*, pp. 162–164.
Quoted in part in *Memoir*, pp. cxi–cxii.

A32   A.L.i., [Grasmere], [n.d., 6 October 1835]. To: Helston, Cornwall. 4 pp., including a letter from S[arah] H[ustler] Fox, dated Oct. 6, 1835. Endorsed on address face by DC "Sonnet of Hartley." The first half of pp. 1–2 has been cut off.

"I felt . . . that you were destined to be a happy husband, and I to be an insignificant old Batchelor." Is thankful that DC has found a good wife [Mary Pridham Coleridge]. Praises, mentioning [Francis] Hopwood, DC as a preacher. Would like to see Derwent Moultrie Coleridge. "I would never call you Filthsoul or Rotten guts in his presence and not often Snifterbreeches, though I certainly do think the latter appellation the happiest effort of my fancy." Commends DC for calling his daughter Emily [Frances Gillman Coleridge, b. 1835, d. 1836], "But what in the name of Belzebub, . . . Moloch, . . . and all the rest of 'em could possess you to call her Gillman?" Goes on at length about DC's choice of "Gillman." Encloses sonnet "Oh, why my Brother are we thus apart" [Earl Leslie Griggs, ed., HC, *New Poems*, London, 1942]. Hopes DC will see Hal [HNC] and Sara [SC]. Mentions the family joke about Derwent's blowing his nose in his nightcap.

Mrs. Fox's letter says of HC "I hope he has written legibly, but this is not often the case with his productions now." Comments on HC's warm heart and love for his family. Reports that HC has been sober and industrious and for six months has returned to his lodgings every night. Speaks in the most complimentary terms of HC's intellect and "his greatly increased capacity for *continued & systematic* exertion of the mind." Says the Wordsworths are grieving over the death of Miss [Sara] Hutchinson [23 June 1835] and that the shock "*annihilated her* [Dorothy Wordsworth's] *mind*. She is now like a child." Mentions Mrs. W[ordsworth], Dora [Wordsworth Quillinan], Emily [Frances Gillman Coleridge], Miss E[mily] Trevenen, Charles [Fox] and Derwent [Moultrie Coleridge].

A33   A.L.s., [n.p.], [n.d., Christmas season, possibly 1840]. To: [n.p.]. 4 pp. The letter is partially burned and badly blotted.

Regrets the long silence between the two and says Derwent is often the companion of his dreams. Used to call Derwent names, "and yet loved all the while." "My best apologist you always were, because you were the only man who ever knew me, the only man to whom I dared tell the whole truth about myself . . . in fact the only man that ever knew enough of my faults to forgive them." Met a man who knew Derwent and Mary [Pridham Coleridge] and entertained him for three days. "You are probably not ignorant of the facts which would make the wishing a merry Xmas to Kate [Southey] sound like a hollow mockery." Says of Aunt [Mary Fricker] Lovell "I cant invent anything which would comfort her." [The series of family quarrels resulting from Robert Southey's marriage to Caroline Bowles eventually resulted in Kate Southey and Mary Fricker Lovell's being turned out of Greta Hall.] "Dear Derwent, think not unkindly of me that I have never acknowledged your book" [DC, *A Christian Minister's Account with Time: A Farewell Sermon Preached at Helleston, in Cornwall on Sunday, 10th January, 1841*, London, 1841?]. Encloses a sonnet to Mrs. STC, "Now is the time, as old Tradition tells" ["Christmas Day, 1840," Earl Leslie Griggs, ed., HC, *New Poems*, London, 1942]. "I will write more rationally and better when you have written to me." Love to Mrs. STC and everybody.

A34   A.L., [Nab Cottage, Rydal], postmarked August 22, 1842. To: Herbert White, Stanley Grove, Chelsea, near London. 7 pp. The signature has been cut away. Endorsed on address face by DC "Self-reproval | Views on the church | my poetic hymns."

Thanks DC for his pamphlet [? DC wrote many pamphlets and reports for his superiors], praising his clearness of statement, plain English, and matter of fact style. Feels unworthy to address, much less to meet DC "not only because, for manifold derelictions I am unworthy to be call'd your brother; but, because, even in my best of hours, in my wishes, hopes, and prayers, I am not as you are." Speaks of [Zachary] Macaulay, societies, and the church. Describes the beautiful summer in Westmorland. Mentions Wordsworth's *The Excursion* [, *Being a Portion of The Recluse, A Poem*, London, 1814]; Herbert White and his family; and the deaths of Fanny, Sophy, and Howard White. Discusses Herbert White's character, his educating his natural son as a doctor, and his wife. Would like to have the music for DC's "Sea-song." Has written words to the tunes of "My lodging is on the Cold Ground," "Rousseau's Dream," "Poor Mary Anne," "Robin Adair," and "God Save the King." Thinks his sonnet "What sound awakened first the untried ear" [*Poems*, Leeds, 1833] is his best. Mentions Wordsworth, Massinger [HC, *The Dramatic Works of Massinger and Ford*, London, 1840], STC, [Robert] Southey, and [Sir Walter] Scott. Comments at length on Wordsworth's last volume [*Poems, Chiefly of Early and Late Years; Including The Borderers, A Tragedy*, London, 1842]. Mentions Shakespeare, *Titus Andronicus*, and *King Lear*. Continues the letter more than a week later. Mentions Dervy [Derwent Moultrie Coleridge], his master [Dr. Benjamin Hall] Kennedy, STC, [Dr. Thomas] Arnold, and Mary [Pridham Coleridge].

Quoted in full in *LHC*, pp. 255–259.

A35   A.L.s., [Nab Cottage, Rydal], postmarked June 19, 1848. To: St. Mark's College, Chelsea, London. 3 pp.

Feels for his brother in his sorrow. [Derwent Moultrie Coleridge has just been expelled from Oxford.] Says sympathy does very little practical good and sends his views of the affair. "Wreck'd as I am upon a barren rock, I have observed something, and my inward experience is much. I do not believe that your son has fallen either from excess of sensuality (for we are all by nature sensual) nor for misdirected pride, and satanical defiance, nor as I did from impotence of will, but merely from the hereditary vanity of our family, from which I never knew a Coleridge, except Sara [SC] and the Judge [John Taylor Coleridge] to be free." "Insulting and mortifying" this pride only makes it worse; hope for defeat of pride can come only through the example of Christ. Is very angry about an article in Edinburgh ["Coleridge and Southey," *Edinburgh Review*, April, 1848]. "It behoves me to remember that I am writing to a Clergyman, or I might even write _____ _____ those who have caught up the too little considered words of our parents, themselves always yes *always* provoked by the virtual falsehoods of the word-catchers to make a separation of love and esteem between the two men." DC must not be surprised if he starts to write on public affairs. "But I will be, if not exactly . . . conservative, the advocate of peace, order, loyalty on religious grounds. As for the symbolic and the chivalrous – you cannot keep them any longer." Sympathy to DC.

Fragment quoted in *Memoir*, p. clxvii.

MRS. DERWENT [MARY PRIDHAM] COLERIDGE

A36   A.L.i., postmarked Ambleside, Dec. 16, 1842. To: Stanley Grove, Chelsea, Near London. 3 pp. Endorsed on address face by DC "Poem about | *Uncle* | Henry's life."

Has been informed by Mrs. STC of Fanny [Coleridge Patteson]'s death [27 November 1842]. "I saw her but for a week or so, but that was long enough. We were Cousins at first sight, and it did not need a seven years apprenticeship to learn to love her. She had then all the richness of vernal womanhood— she felt her 'life in every limb,' and knew nothing of pain, or sorrow, or sickness, but from that keen sympathy which enabled her to feel not only for, but with, the sick and the afflicted. . . . You are not ignorant that there is a life [HNC, who dies 26 January 1843] for which I would not only lay down my own (that were not sacrifice, no self-denial) but consent to endure it under any trial which Providence might think fit to inflict on me. But this is idle talk. I have not the strength to wrestle with the Lord. If I had, all the blessing I would ask would be, th[at] he would be pleased to restore Henry [HNC] to his family, and dispose of me according to his infinite wisdom." Speaks of his little Niece [Edith Coleridge] who has been with the DCs. Can love little girls in the abstract, but finds it hard to love "the mere abstract idea, Boy." Sends a fragment of a poem to Derwent [Moultrie Coleridge], "Nephew, a term few poets dare to use" [unpublished]. Best love to Derwent [DC]. Mentions Mrs. STC. "Arent you glad W[ordsworth] has got £300 a year at last?" [In October 1842 Sir Robert Peel granted William Wordsworth a pension of £300 a year from the civil list.]

A37 A.L.s., [Nab Cottage, Rydal], postmarked Nov. 16, 1844. To: Stanleigh Grove, Chelsea, Near London. 3 pp.

Thanks Mary for making him some shirts. Has been prevented by a cold from fitting his essays for the public eye "which after all, I hope is not quite so critical as your Husbands, for he, much over-rating my ability, perceives motes in my performance, which ordinary spectacles are not magnifying enough to discover." Thanks "Madame Mere" [Mrs. STC] for the pens; he is at present writing with a goose quill. Longs to see "Christabel Rosa" [Coleridge]. "May God enable me to break through the wall which my sins and follies have builded between us." Sends poem "To Christabel Rose Coleridge," [DC, ed., HC, *Poems*, London, 1851]. "I am ill at these numbers. Derwent [DC] will cut the sonnet up, I know, But give my love to him." Mentions Mrs. STC.

THE REV. GEORGE COLERIDGE

A38 A.L.s./copy in unidentified hand, Merton College, Oxford, Nov. 4th, 1815. To: [Ottery St. Mary, Devon]. 3 pp. Bound in "Samuel Taylor Coleridge Letters I."

Is grateful for kind mentions of him in letters to Mr. [Robert] Southey and for "the advantages which you have been in great measure the means of procuring for me." [George Coleridge was probably the most active of the Ottery group in helping HC at Oxford.] With his promised help and that of Sir George Beaumont and Mr. [Thomas] Poole, his situation will be more than adequate. Is disappointed that Cousin William [Hart Coleridge] has left, but hopes he will do well; William was most kind and helpful to HC during his first months at Oxford. Looks forward to meeting Cousin George [May Coleridge] when he comes to Oxford. Has begun the study of Herodotus, Aristotle's Ethics and Poetics, Tully, Horace, mathematics, and Latin composition. Details his expenses and asks that part of the promised allowance be sent to him. Spent his vacation with STC in Wiltshire. "He was busily employed, during the whole of it, in a work which is now finished and in the press, called Autobiographia Literaria, being a history of his own literary Life and opinions, with remarks on some living writers, particularly Southey & Wordsworth [STC, *Biographia Literaria or, Biographical Sketches of My Literary Life and Opinions*, London, 1817]. Afterwards he intends to bring out a tragedy, and then he will devote his principle attention to the great philosophical work, he has been collecting materials for so long, a treatise on the Logos, human and divine, in which he proposes to confute the Socinians, and to defend the doctrines of the Trinity and of Redemption. I have received a letter from him since my return to Oxford, which took place on the 20th ult." Sends news of Mr. and Mrs. [Robert] Southey and Miss [Edith May] Southey, who have been in Flanders. Mentions Mrs. STC, Little Sara [SC], and Derwent [DC]. Respects to Mrs. [Jenny Hart] Coleridge.

A39 A.L.s., Mert[on] Col[lege, Oxford], December 6, 1818. To: Ottery St. Mary, Devon. 3 pp.

George [May Coleridge] and Edward [Coleridge, James's son] probably have informed George Coleridge that HC has passed his examination. Does not yet know his place on the list. Was "respectable" in logic, Latin composition, Aristotle, and History; "above par" in divinity and ethics; failed in Sophocles; "stumbled" in Virgil; was "not far amiss" in Pindar; has cause for shame in the "O-dyssee." Mr. [Nathaniel] Ellison [fellow of Merton College] was very kind, and Mr. [John] Keble offered his assistance. Mentions Mr. [Robert] Southey's current works [*Life of Wesley*, London, 1820; *History of Brazil*, vol. iii, London, 1819; and *History of the Peninsular War*, vol. i, London, 1822], Derwent [DC], and Sara [SC]. STC is engaged in a series of lectures [at the Crown and Anchor Tavern, 14 December 1818 – 25 March 1819]. Hopes to see STC and William [Hart Coleridge?] at Christmas. Respects to Aunt George [Jenny Hart Coleridge]. Ought to have thanked Uncles Edward [Coleridge] and the Colonel [James Coleridge] "for their kind remittance."

Quoted in full in *LHC*, pp. 18–20.

A40 A.L.s./copy in unidentified hand, Oriel Coll[ege, Oxford], March 31st 1820. To: [Ottery St. Mary, Devon.] 2 pp. Bound in "Samuel Taylor Coleridge Letters I."

Had the pleasure of introducing George [May Coleridge] to Derwent [DC], who is on his way to Cambridge to enter either St. John's or Jesus [DC entered St. John's College]. Expects DC to do well at college. Comments on George's strengths and weaknesses as a student. Has been reading Aristotle with Edward [Coleridge, James Coleridge's son]. Mentions John [Taylor Coleridge] and his wife [Mary Buchanan Coleridge], Fanny [Frances Duke Coleridge Patteson], and Sir T[homas] Ackland. Has been busy at the essay, which he hopes will please the judges. Derwent brings news from the north that Mrs. Wilson ["Wilsy," the Greta Hall housekeeper] has died and that Sara [SC] is gaining strength. Mentions Mr. Newcomb and sends remembrances to Aunts George and Luke [Jenny Hart Coleridge and Sara Hart Coleridge], the Colonel's and Uncle Edward's family [James Coleridge and Edward Coleridge], Fanny [Frances Duke Coleridge Patteson] and Bess [Elizabeth Coleridge].

A41 A.L.s./copy in unidentified hand, Oriel Coll[ege, Oxford], April 20th, 1820. To: [Ottery St. Mary, Devon.] 2 pp. Bound in "Samuel Taylor Coleridge Letters I."

Should have written before, but was in town, where he found STC well and left Derwent [DC] with him. Derwent will be entered in Cambridge shortly. Speaks of George [May Coleridge]'s scholarship and spirits. James [Duke Coleridge] and Edward [Coleridge] are at a musical party. Was sorry to hear of Mrs. Lee's death. Remembrances to Aunts George and Luke [Jenny Hart Coleridge and Sara Hart Coleridge], William [Hart Coleridge], the Colonel's family [James Coleridge's family], Fanny [Frances Duke Coleridge Patteson], Aunt and Uncle Edward [Edward and Anne Bowden Coleridge], and Bessy [Elizabeth Coleridge]. Begins a new pupil tomorrow.

GEORGE MAY COLERIDGE

A42   A.L.s., Ottery St. Mary, Jan. 3, 1820. To: Christ Church, Oxford. 3 pp.

Tells his cousin George how much the Ottery world misses him. Describes his unfortunate journey to Ottery through bad weather. Asks about George's studies. Promises to introduce Scratchey, who is "very expert at interpreting Aristotle; as in fact that Philosopher was very little more than his Amanuensis." Mentions [Robert] Burton and Sam Archer. Speaks of a gathering at Aunt Luke's [Sara Hart Coleridge's], mentioning the Newcomes [father and daughter], Ned [Edward Coleridge], Frank [Francis George Coleridge], and Fanny [Frances Coleridge Patteson]. "She [Fanny] absolutely condescended to speak to me at the ball, which raised me 15 degrees at once in female estimation." Also at the ball were Miss Smith, Mr. Lowe, Edwin [Ellis Coleridge], Miss Risk, and Mrs. Hodge. Sends love from George's parents [George and Jenny Hart Coleridge], Aunt and Uncle Edward [Edward and Anne Bowden Coleridge] and Bessy [Elizabeth Coleridge]. Mentions Miss Green and his kitten.

Quoted in full in *LHC*, pp. 24–26.

HENRY NELSON COLERIDGE

A43   A.L.i., [Grasmere?], April 15, postmarked 1832. To: No. 1 New Square, Lincoln's Inn, London. 4 pp.

Has received a letter from "Ebony" [William Blackwood, of *Blackwood's Magazine*] asking him to use his influence to get STC to write another series of letters similar to the Fletcher Letters [eight "Letters to Judge Fletcher," *The Courier*, 20 September–10 December 1814]. Says he feels STC's health is too precarious to allow him to write the series. Tells of his new job—"namely to revise a Biography of Yorkshire and Lancashire Worthies" [HC, *Biographia Borealis; or, Lives of Distinguished Northerns*, Leeds, 1833]. [Previously the series of *Lives* had been entrusted to Mr. John Dove, "A Whig and a Dissenter."] Has just returned from Keswick and sends news of Uncle [Robert Southey], Aunt [Edith Fricker Southey], Edith [May Southey Warter], Aunt [Mary Fricker] Lovell, and Aunt Eliza [Fricker]. "You must not be angry if I contradict your Lycanthropic Lesen, very flatly in print—All's fair you know— and I must Defend Old Homer" [HNC, *Introduction to the Study of the Greek Classic Poets*, London, 1830]. Is learning German to please STC: "Would to God I could do something better to sustain his declining years." Mentions Miss [Dorothy] Wordsworth, SC, Mary Pridham Coleridge ["Derwent's Sermon"], Mrs. STC.

Quoted in full in *LHC*, pp. 139–142.

A44 A.L.i., Grasmere, Sunday, Sept. 29th, 1833. To: No. 1 Downshire Place, Hampstead, London. 4 pp. Pages three and four are crosswritten on pages one and two.

Has left Leeds only because Mr. [Francis Edward] Bingley has shut up his house. Will return if Bingley wishes to publish more of the *Worthies*. Apologizes for Bingley's hot letter to HNC and calls Bingley "one of the best natured, best-hearted, and not one of the strongest headed boys . . . that I have ever met with." Counts on paying his bills with the £50 from *Poems* and the expected third of the engaged price for *Worthies*. Has received £5 from [James] Brancker, who ordered six copies of *Poems*. Mentions Mrs. STC, SC, and SC's children. Speaks of the review of *Poems* in *Quarterly Review* [vol. xlix, 1833]. "Why, in the Devil's name cannot they review my book, gentle or semple, without a fling at poor Wordsworth?" Mentions Mrs. STC, Aunt Eliza [Fricker], and Miss [Janetta] Smith.

Quoted in full, *LHC*, pp. 151–154.

A45 A.L.i., [Grasmere], Jan 11, postmarked 1836. To: No. 21 Downshire Hill, Hampstead, London. 4 pp.

Tells HNC of his difficulties with [Francis Edward] Bingley. [Bingley had invited Hartley to resume *Northern Worthies* on terms which Hartley felt were unacceptable.] [James] Brancker is trying to emancipate Hartley from Bingley. "No one, not even Bingley, would have thought have [of?] continuing the work had it not been for your panegyric" [HNC's review, *Quarterly Review*, liv, Sept. 1835]. Defends his account of [William] Roscoe. Discusses the difficulty of spelling animal sounds, the pronunciation of ancient Greek and of modern Latin, and the place of the classics in the curriculum. Mentions [William] Mitford [*The History of Greece*, 5 vols., 1784-1818; 10 vols., 1818–1820]. Greatly admires the execution of HNC's *Table Talk* [HNC, ed., *Specimens of the Table-Talk of the Late Samuel Taylor Coleridge*, 2 vols., London, 1835], but has fears lest it prove a bad example. Has not seen Allsop's book [Edward Thomas Allsop, *Letters, Conversations and Recollections of S. T. Coleridge*, 1836] but thinks "he deserves a trimming." Mentions by inference Thomas De Quincey's articles on STC [*Tait's Edinburgh Magazine*, September 1834–January 1835]. Mentions Mr. Smith, "who *does* Asia and America for the Ency. Brit." Is thinking of doing an article on Massinger. Speaks of [William] Gifford [ed., *The Plays of Philip Massinger*, London, 1805] and [F. A. M.] Retzsch's *Outlines for Shakspear, Macbeth* [1833]. Mentions Miss [Dorothy] Wordsworth, Aunt [Edith Fricker Southey], Dora [Wordsworth Quillinan], Mrs. STC, SC, and DC.

Quoted in full in *LHC*, pp. 178–182.

A46 A.L.s., Grasmere, May 8, 1836. To: [Heath's Court, Ottery St. Mary, Devon.?]. 13 pp. including A55 to SC, 3 pp., A.L.i. No address; carried by William Wordsworth.

Comments upon the fortitude of the family in the face of ill health and upon his estrangement from Miss [Sara] Hutchinson before her death [23 June 1835]. Apologizes for teasing SC. Says of STC "he would never have approved of the . . . reforms" though "he did perceive the necessity of deep and vital changes." Discusses his father's political idealism and his movement toward conservativism as he grew older, though "when I was last with him at Highgate" he spoke "very harshly of the political subserviency of W[ordsworth] and S[outhey]." Comments upon the quarrels among the three poets. Says he has pleaded with STC for Southey though "I did not and do not, admire any of his laureate poetry." Writes at length on the various duties of government; on the distribution of powers and functions; on official, clerical, and personal privilege; on oaths; and on the separation of church and state. Promises the Macbeth article [see B102] containing his translations of Schiller's substitutions [see "Schiller's Translation of Macbeth," DC, ed., HC, *Poems*, London, 1851]. Speaks of having been paid £5 for an [unknown] article on [Sir John] Sinclair. Will send HNC Charles Lloyd's transcription of STC's "Essay on Faith" [HNC, ed., *The Literary Remains of Samuel Taylor Coleridge*, 4 vols., 1836–1839]. Mentions having read [Friedrich Ludwig Georg] von Raumer's *England* [in 1835, Sarah Austin, tr., London, 1836] and [Henry] Taylor's *Philip Van Artevelde* [1834].

Quoted in full in *LHC*, 187–194.

A47 A.L.i., Sedbergh, Revd. I. Green's, March 27, 1837. To: Downshire Place, Hampstead, London.

Describes his experiences in teaching school again. "I engaged, however, under the express understanding that my functions terminated with the lessons; for I know myself both morally and physically incapable of exerting authority or enforcing discipline." Says Mrs. STC need not worry; he is not sarcastic with the dull boys. Outlines in some detail his essay on his father [fragments published in *PMLA*, December 1931]. Will try to clear STC "from the imputation of being a Metaphysical poet. Undoubtedly in some of his early poems, he did versify Metaphysics, but then he ceased to be a Poet at all." Says the only metaphysical poet is Wordsworth, not Davis [John Davies?], Lord Brooke, nor Henry More. Mentions Derwent [DC] and Mrs. STC.

Quoted in full in *LHC*, pp. 209–211.

A48   A.L.i., [n.p.], [n.d., 1837?]. To: [No. 10 Chester Place, Regent's Park, London]. 2 pp.

Encloses a sonnet not for the public eye. "Not a word in prose or verse will I ever publish that can be tortured into a reference to our domestic affairs, or even to my own circumstance." Of the enclosed sonnet he says "I protest I would not show it to Wordsworth on any account. His austere taste would be mortally bored with the confusion of Astrology, Mythology, Scripture, and Hylozoism it exhibits." Thanks HNC for his aid to STC. "You caused him to die in good will with all men—save the Reformers and the dissenters—happily unconscious what a pack of resurrection rascals were hovering around his deathbed." Mentions Mrs. STC, SC, and [John Gibson] Lockhart. Encloses sonnet "Kinsman, Yea – more than kinsman, brother, friend – " ["To H. N. Coleridge," DC, ed., HC, *Poems*, London, 1851].

Quoted in full in *LHC*, pp. 217–218.

A49   A.L.i., Grasmere, October 24, 1839. To: 10 Chester Place, Regent's Park, London. 4 pp.

Says he is in great haste to finish his job for [Edward] Moxon. [Early in 1839 Moxon requested Hartley to prepare a biographical introduction and a critique for an edition of Massinger and Ford. Hartley procrastinated, and Moxon was driven to desperation. The edition finally appeared in 1840. *The Dramatic Works of Massinger and Ford*, London, 1840.] Mentions SC, Mrs. STC, Derwent Moultrie and Edith Coleridge. Describes Mrs. [Frances] Trollope at great length. "I had pictured her . . . an excellent, genteel, comely fine-lady. . . . By the Holy Power, she is a mighty respectable, comfortable looking dowdy, weighing 13 stone at the least . . . – some thing between a house-keeper and a Land-lady." Alludes to the anger aroused in America by Mrs. Trollope's *Domestic Manners of the Americans* [London, 1832]. Describes the terms of his agreement with Moxon and the possibilities of Moxon's purchasing the remainder of *Poems* and *Worthies*. Speaks of Mr. J[ames] Gillman's death [1 June 1839] and of Derwent [DC]'s Sermons [DC, *The Scriptural Character of the English Church*, London, 1839]. Mentions Mrs. [James] Gillman, Mrs. STC, Mary [Pridham Coleridge], Bertha [Southey Hill], [Herbert] Hill, and the Wordsworths.

Quoted in full in *LHC*, pp. 233–235.

A50 A.L.s., The Nab [Cottage, Rydal], July 10, postmarked 1840. To: No. 10 Chester Place, Regent's Park, London. 5 pp.

At HNC's request HC agrees to be godfather to the child SC is expecting [Bertha Fanny Coleridge, b. 13 July 1840, d. 24 July 1840]. Encloses a sonnet [written for Caroline Green] expressing his feelings about being a godfather ["The God-child," DC, ed., HC, *Poems*, London, 1851]. Asks HNC if he has seen James Frazer's [sic] article on STC in the January *Blackwood* [James Frederick Ferrier, "The Plagiarisms of S. T. Coleridge," *Blackwood's Magazine*, March, 1840]. Says he feels, first, that the charges are exaggerated and, second, "that when writing the Biographia, my father copied not from Schlegel [Schelling] – but from his own memorandum-books – and had literally forgotten what was his own, and what was translation." Speaks of the circumstances surrounding the composition of STC's *Biographia* and of STC's poor memory. Mentions his *Massinger and Ford* and his plans to edit Spenser [he did not do so]. Is sorry [Edward] Moxon is in "hot water" about Shelley. [In 1840 Moxon issued Shelley's *Poetical Works*. He was tried for and found guilty of blasphemous libel. No sentence was passed.] Mentions Professor [John] Wilson, Mr. Wordsworth, Dora [Wordsworth Quillinan], Bertha [Southey Hill] and family, Derwent and Mary [Coleridge], Mrs. STC, SC, and Miss [Emily] Trevenen.

Quoted in full in *LHC*, pp. 239–243.

A51 A.L.s., Knabbe [Cottage, Rydal], May 21, 1841. To: No. 10 Chester Place, Regent's Park, London. 3 pp.

"The Penny post (let us get all the good we can out of it, while we have it) enables us to write successive letters—after the method of Richardson's Pamela and Clarissa, something between letters and chapters." Has received and read DC's Farewell Sermon [DC, *A Christian Minister's Account with Time: A Farewell Sermon, Preached at Helleston, in Cornwall on Sunday, 10th January*, London, 1841]. Speaks of Derwent's religious views and ill health. Chides himself for not being in a position to help Derwent. Is working on "Prometheus." "I could indeed produce a vol. longer than the last – of sonnets and shorter pieces – immediately. But I know you would prefer seeing Prometheus at the head." Speaks of literary arrangements with [Edward] Moxon. Feels deeply obligated to so many people. Says a Leeds bookseller [John Cross] has on hand 60 copies of *Poems* and 200 or 300 copies of *Biographia Borealis*. Love to Sara [SC] and children. Mentions Mr. and Mrs. [James] Brancker, [Herbert] Hill, Bertha [Southey Hill], the [Edward] Quillinans.

MRS. HENRY NELSON
[SARA] COLERIDGE

A52 A.L., [Clappersgate, near Ambleside], [n.d., late May or early

June, 1814]. To: [Greta Hall, Keswick]. 4 pp. Paper is watermarked "J. Dickenson & Co. [Ltd.] | 1810."

A charming letter entirely in "unpolished dogrel rime" [89 ll.]. Compliments SC on her French, Latin, Italian, and dancing. Says vacation will soon begin and he and Derwent [DC] will soon be home, Hartley for good. Comments on SC's garden.

> I really grieve a thoughtless clown Should tread your fairest flower down,
> Which you ta'en such pains to rear; I wonder not you shed a tear
> To see it cut off in its pride; And while its sad remains you eyed
> You thought perhaps how slight a blow, Destroys the fairest things below.
> [The following line is struck through but readable]
> Your grief excites not my surprise, But with your tears I sympathize.

The "pretty Dolly" has left Rydal. Dora [Wordsworth Quillinan] is well. Sends news of Chucky [Dorothy Wordsworth Harrison; Mrs. Benson Harrison] and her elder sister, Miss Barker, and Miss Fletcher. Is very concerned that he has not heard from or had news of STC [who is at 2 Queen's Square, Bristol, the home of Josiah Wade]. Speaks of news from Bristol telling him of the death of a man who had been very kind to him. Apologizes for writing her in verse.

> Say not I think myself a poet, And that I anxious am to show it.
> But kind affection, is no worse, I hope, for being put in verse.

Says Uncle [Robert Southey] is probably upset about the "hapless" revolution in Spain, mentioning "Master Ferdinand" and the constitution. [Ferdinand VII of Spain returned from captivity to abolish the Spanish constitution in March 1814.] Mentions Mrs. Wilson ["Wilsey," Greta Hall housekeeper], Mr. and Mrs. Charles Lloyd and the [Greta Hall] children.

Quoted in part in *Memoir*, pp. lx–lxii.

A53   A.L.s., Greta Hall, [Keswick], March 24, postmarked 1834. To: 1. Downshire Place, Downshire Hill, Hampstead, 3 pp. Endorsed on address face by DC "Hartley in K[eswick] | p. 68 [of manuscript for 'Memoir' in DC, ed., HC, *Poems*, London, 1851] | March 1834 | Greta Hall, on oldtimes." Endorsed on seal face by Mrs. STC "a good deal about *the 'Doctor.'* " and "Droll letter from Hartley is his | first letter from Keswick after | the departure of his Mother & sister | 1834."

Is glad SC has seen [at Keswick] "your old playmate and cousin bride" [Edith May Southey, who married John Wood Warter 15 January 1834]. Reminisces of past times at Greta Hall. "To walk with reverted eyes, to live in the days that are gone, is commonly accounted to be the natural propensity of old age, or the acquired indulgence of affliction. For myself, I remember not a time when it was not so with me." Longed, as a child, for the freedom of an adult, yet had a "praesentiment, that I was enjoying rather more freedom than I could ever expect again." Speaks of Ejuxria [the imaginary country he invented as a child], Robert [Lovell], and Wilsy [Mrs. Wilson, Greta Hall housekeeper]'s kitchen. Things have changed, and "the church-yard is full of our hopes and affections." Mentions Uncle [Robert Southey] and [John Gibson] Lockhart's conjecture that he [HC], assisted by STC, is the author of *The Doctor &c.* [Robert Southey, *The Doctor, &c.,* 7 vols., London, 1834–1847]. Comments on the book and says he plans to review it in *Blackwood's* and "throw out some sapient innuendoes respecting the authorship, just to lead wiseacres astray." [Griggs in *LHC* feels that the authorship of two unsigned articles, "The Doctor. First Dose" and "The Doctor. Second Dose" in *Blackwood's Magazine,* August and October 1835, may be attributed to HC on internal evidence. *The Wellesley Index* attributes these articles to John Wilson.] Intends to return to Grasmere on the next day. Love to Mrs. STC and Henry [HNC].

Quoted in full in *LHC*, pp. 158–160.
Quoted in full in *Memoir*, pp. cvi–cviii.

A54 A.L.i., Grasmere, Day before Easter Sunday, postmarked April 21, 1835. To: No. 1 Downshire Place, Hampstead, near London. 4 pp. Endorsed on address face by Mrs. STC "Hartleys metrical letter."

The letter is mostly in verse which begins in a high vein but soon degenerates into news-filled doggerel. Encloses a sonnet, a slightly different version of "Twins" [DC, ed., HC, *Poems*, London 1851]. Notes that "my poor foolish Editor [Francis Edward Bingley] has failed."

He'll blame me much: and troth, I must confess—
I am to blame for his foolhardiness.
He thought in me he had a mine of gold,
My talents known, my weakness all untold.

Asks SC what she thinks of Harriet Martineau's political novels [HC and Miss Martineau despise each other].

Were I a woman, I should blush for shame
That such a thing should bear a woman's name.

Heard of Bingley's troubles not from the publisher or his assignees but from the bookseller, [Thomas] Troughton. Will apply to James Brancker for help in settling his affairs. Will not write for *Fraser's Magazine,* and mentions [J. A.] Heraud's doing so ["Coleridgeiana," *Fraser's Magazine,* January 1835]. Mentions HNC, *Quarterly* [*Review*], and [John Gibson] Lockhart. Has three articles in hand for *Blackwood's* [*Magazine*]. [Possibly among them are "The Doctor. First Dose," and "The Doctor. Second Dose," *Blackwood's Magazine,* August and October 1835. *The Wellesley Index* attributes these articles to John Wilson.] Mentions Mrs. [Mary Harris] Bernard; Bertha [Southey Hill]; Kate

[Southey]; John Wilson, Jr. of Elleray; and HNC. Is not sure how many copies of *Poems* [HC, *Poems*, Leeds, 1833] were printed. Speaks of Aunt [Edith Fricker Southey, who became insane about this time]. "May God put a speedy end to all our troubles—for hers, I fear, there is but one."

Quoted in full in *LHC*, pp. 169–172.

A55   A.L.i., Grasmere, May 8, 1836. To: [Heath's Court, Ottery St. Mary, Devon.?]. 3 pp. This letter is an addition to a letter to HNC [see A46].

Speaks of SC's health, the weather, and SC's children. Saw Owen [Lloyd] and Mrs. B[enson, "Chucky Doro"] Harrison at a party at Mrs. [Louise] Claude's. Mrs. Claude suits him exactly, though "she is a shade too easy and happy for your ideal of a widow." Mentions Mr. and Mrs. Hernden, Mr. [John] Dawes, Mrs. Parry and Mrs. Woollam. Finds Kate Woollam a dear creature but Johnny Woollam "not quite enough of the boy." Remembering his own school days, is glad that "Uncle [Robert Southey] relinquished his intention of sending Cuthbert [Southey] to Westminster. . . . I consider a public school a very expensive way to Hell." Mentions Kate and Bertha [Southey]. Intends to read Southey's Cowper [Robert Southey, *The Works of William Cowper. With a Life of the Author*, 15 vols., 1835–37]. "For so excellent and unoffending a man Uncle [Robert Southey] certainly has the luck to make many literary enemies." Love to Mrs. STC and SC's children. Asks about Mrs. [Edith Southey] Warter.

A56   A.L.i., [Grasmere], postmarked Sept. 7, 1837. To: 10 Chester Place, Regent's Park, London. 4 pp. Endorsed on the address face "STC's Poetry."

Thanks SC for her "Fairy Tale" [SC, *Phantasmion*, London, 1837]. Is now settled [on return from Leeds, with William and Eleanor Richardson at Nab Cottage]. Is hard at work on essay on STC [fragments published in *PMLA*, December 1931]. "It were indeed, no very hard matter to review the poems, somewhat more intelligently than they have ever been reviewed before." Comments on STC's poetry at some length. Has divided STC's poetry into three phases—first, juvenile poems, the best of which is "Lover's Resolutions"; second, "attempts to embody in poetry his philosophic mind and moral aspirations, as they existed in his early manhood"; third, "Products of his pure imagination." "The 'Remorse' forms a transition between the second and third classes." Comments upon the education of Herbert and Edith [Coleridge]. "I do think it a great waste of youth, in nine instances out of ten, to devote to dead, aye, or living languages. There are more good books in any one language than life is long enough to master." Speaks of his sleeping habits, his Sedbergh bills, Mr. and Mrs. Isaac Green and Caroline [Green, his goddaughter]. Has read [John Henry Newman's] *Lyra Apostolica* [Derby, 1834] and the Professor [Adam] Sedgwick's work [*A Discourse on the Studies of the University*, 1833]. Mentions Mr. Curwen, John Wordsworth, Mrs. Wordsworth, Mrs. [Sarah] Fox, Berkeley [HC's brother who died in infancy], Derwent [DC], Derve [Derwent Moultrie Coleridge], Mrs. Parry, Mr. [James] Brancker, Aunt Eliza [Fricker], Mrs. P[rofessor John?] Wilson, Mrs. Narver, Mrs. [Louise] Claude, Aunt [Edith Fricker Southey], Uncle [Robert Southey], and "my host and hostess" [William and Eleanor Richardson].

Quoted in full in *LHC*, pp. 212–216.

A57 A.L.s., Grasmere, October 9, 1838. To: No. 10 Chester Place, Regent's Park, London. 4 pp. Endorsed on address face "1838 Bishop and Archbishop."

Discusses Mrs. [Sarah] Fox's [Quaker] religion, which is less a matter of choice or conviction than of education. "There is nothing Quakerish about her mind." Denies SC's charge that he cares little for Bishops and Archbishops and says they are "highly useful." Wishes Queen Victoria would appoint younger men than [William] Howley [Archbishop of Canterbury] and says she needs better advisers than [William Lamb, Lord] Melbourne and Johnny Russell. Encloses his version of "God Save the Queen" [DC, ed., HC, *Poems*, London, 1851]. Has not seen Mr. [James] Gillman's book [*The Life of Samuel Taylor Coleridge*, London, 1838]. Will send an essay [?] on the return of James Spedding who "has given me carte-blanche to send any thing of what ever weight under cover to him at the colonial office." Sends local news, mentioning Mr. Wordsworth; his nephew [John Wordsworth], son of R[ichard] W[ordsworth]; Willy Wordsworth; Mrs. B[enson (Dorothy Wordsworth)] Harrison; George Muckle; Miss [Anne] Bristowe; Margaret Muckle; and Uncle [Robert Southey]. Does not have vol. 5 of Doctor [Robert Southey, *The Doctor, &c.*, 7 vols., London, 1834-1847]. Discusses clothing. Says Mr. [Isaac] Green's mother has died. Two chapels to be dedicated, one at Howgill and one at Cowgill. "[I] like Prof[essor Adam] Sedgewick almost the best of any man I ever saw." Mentions Cornwall paper, *Whitehaven Gazette*. "Sent a sonnet – translated from Michel Angelo ["From Michelangelo," DC, ed., HC, *Poems*, London 1851]—to a work [*The Tribute*] published for the benefit of [Edward] Smedley's family, under the patronage of Lord Carmarthen." Sent another sonnet for a "book to be sold at a Bazaar for the benefit of a church near Bendford." "The Editor [John Walker Ord] of the Conservative Journal wants me to send something from the 'Gift' which is to [be] dedicated to her Majesty" [See B213]. Love to Henry [HNC], the Maum [Mrs. STC], Edith and Herbert [Coleridge]. Mrs. [Eleanor] Richardson is pregnant.

A58 A.L.i., Greta Hall [Keswick], Feb. 23, 1839. To: [No. 10 Chester Place, Regent's Park, London]. 4 pp.

The changes in Greta Hall are "melancholy" and would disturb Jacky [Mr. Jackson] and Wilsy [Mrs. Wilson, Greta Hall housekeeper]. The weather is "rascally," spring being much later than usual. Describes the mountains as "looking like great black giants badly white-wash'd." While "I am as impartial in my tastes for books as the old Topper in 'Gammar Gurton' [William Stevenson, *Gammar Gurton's Needle*, 1575] in regard to Ale," he finds the Greta Hall library rather overpowering. Has read his poems to Kate and Bertha [Southey] but not to Uncle [Robert Southey]. Describes at length Southey's person and spirits and comments on Caroline Bowles. "Should I judge her by her writings, she must [be] a goodly sample of womanhood." Alludes to the family quarrel about Southey's coming second marriage [to Caroline Bowles, 4 June 1839] and to Bertha [Southey]'s coming marriage [to Herbert Hill, 12 March 1839]. Describes Kate [Southey]. Mentions Lady [Frances Duke Coleridge] Patteson, James [Duke Coleridge]'s movements, John [Taylor Coleridge]'s getting Heathcourt [his father's estate], Herbert [Coleridge]'s schooling, Mrs. [John] Lonsdale, Aunt [Mary Fricker] Lovell, and Mrs. STC. Has received "Church and State" [STC, *On the Constitution of Church and State*, London, 1830; ed. HNC, London, 1839] and "Italy" [John Edmund Reade, *Italy, A Poem with Historical and Classical Notes*, London, 1838]. Has read Mr. Gillman [James Gillman, *The Life of S. T. Coleridge*, vol. 1, 1838, no more published], which he finds "a good hearted, noble minded book," although "it is not a well-written or well constructed book." Love to Mrs. STC, HNC, and "Bairns" [Herbert and Edith Coleridge].

Quoted in full in *LHC*, pp. 226–230.

A59   A.L.i., (inc.), [Nab Cottage, Rydal], postmarked Aug. 20, 1842. To: No. 10 Chester Place, Regent's Prk, London. 1 p. Endorsed on address face "after S. & H.N.C. | Antwerp trip." A reply to *Grantz* 515.

"Your letter descriptive of your travels, was beautiful and your remarks [wildly favorable] on Rubens admirable. The pictures by which Rubens is known in England are, I suspect, chiefly of his later day." Speaks of a growing need of prayer and self-examination as one grows older. "Pictures however, intended for vast Churches, have [no; not?] fair play in English galleries. The Painters calculated on the perspective of distance. Rubens was I believe – like Paulo Veronese – a scenic painter. . . . When will we have the other half of Hogarth?" Will write an essay on the topic to complete the volume for [Edward] Moxon. Love to Mrs. STC, HNC, and Darl[ings].

A60   A.L.s., Rydal, March 21, postmarked 1843. To: No. 10 Chester Place, Regent's Park, London. 4 pp. Letter and accompanying envelope have black borders and seal.

Feels too unworthy to be consulted in regard to the trusteeship [of the literary and other property of STC following the death on 26 January 1843 of HNC]. Feels "The Justice [John Taylor Coleridge] is the fittest person" but may be too busy. Mentions [Edward Thomas] Allsop, Mr. [Basil] Montagu, and Mr. [John Hookham] Frere. "I fear I am at present under such a cloud, I have shown myself so little worthy of reliance, that it is vain to make any offer of personal services in the only way in which I could be of use – that is to say, in regard to the care of the Works." Intends to finish the essay [fragments published in *PMLA*, December 1931] which he had rather appeared with the *Poems* than the *Biographia Literaria*, which is "more fragmentary and worse put together than any of them." Wishes he could be more useful. [Robert] Southey has been seized with typhus, from which there is small chance of his recovering [Southey died 21 March 1843]. Mentions Derwent [DC], Mrs. STC, and William [Wordsworth] Junior's impending marriage [in July to Mary Monkhouse. Miss Monkhouse went out of her mind in late April, and the match was ended]. Despairs of ever obtaining SC's forgiveness.

Quoted in full in *LHC*, pp. 262–263.

A61   A.L.i., [Nab Cottage, Rydal], Feb. 25, 1844. To: No. 10 Chester Place, Regent's Park, London. 4 pp. With accompanying envelope with black border and seal.

Discusses his clothing and bills. Is glad to hear such a good account of "the young ones" [Herbert and Edith Coleridge]. Nab Cottage "is not yet quite out of quarantine" and the weather is miserable – snow and rain. "I am or should be very busy – but work without hope – you know the strain. I will try however not to despair. The times it is true are very bad, and tho' prices are looking up a little, I'm afraid that wont much improve the book market." Is glad the sale of STC's works is improving, but feels he himself has no capacity for writing anything "original and great. Had I access to books I might indeed be a useful compiler, for I have the knack of dovetailing miscellaneous particulars into something like continuous compositions in a readable style." His differences from the rest of the family on "matters of temporary interest" make him mistrust himself. Thought SC had seen "the verses on Cornelia [Nicholson] in which H. N. C. is mention'd" [HC, "On the Birth of Cornelia," a broadside dated January 28, 1843]. Mr. [Edward] Quillinan has "the sonnet on Southey" ["XL. Keswick," DC, ed., HC, *Poems*, London, 1851?]. Mentions Derwent [DC], Miss Katherine Pridham [Mrs. Thomas Helmore], Kristy [Christabel Rose Coleridge], and Dora [Wordsworth Quillinan]. "Poor Betty [Kate Southey's old servant] yet lingers on."

A62   A.L.s., Nab [Cottage, Rydal], October 11, 1845. To: No. 10 Chester Place, Regent's Park, London. 8 pp. With note on inside of accompanying envelope. Endorsed on address face of envelope "1845 His Mother's death."

A letter of condolence on the death of Mrs. STC [who died suddenly on 24 September 1845. HC had not seen her since 1831]. "I cannot shed above a few unsatisfactory tears, rather at the recollections of past days and tendernesses, and funny things – memories new dressed in mourning, from a competent feeling of great bereavement." Gives his reactions to the news [in a letter from Mary Pridham Coleridge, see B96] of his mother's death. Discusses at length his faults as a son. "Yet for none of my offenses, not even for those which added shame to her sorrow, and made her almost despise while she pitied me, am I so sharply self-reproached as for this, that I have loved her too little." Miss [Isabella] Fenwick has given him Edward [Coleridge]'s letter containing details of the funeral. Mentions Derwent [DC], the Judge [John Taylor Coleridge], and Mrs. STC's burial at Highgate. Speaks of his grandmothers, [Mrs. Stephen Fricker], of whom he has "a rather repulsive imagination," and [Mrs. John Coleridge] whom "I only remember as a sufferer." Speaks of the poems, ridiculed by "the anti-jacobian brutes [of the press], on their grandmothers published by C[harles] Lamb and C[harles] Lloyd." [Charles Lloyd printed a volume of verse memorials on the death of his grandmother in 1796. But HC's reference is probably to "Poems on the Death of Priscilla Farmer" by Charles Lloyd and "The Grandame" by Charles Lamb in *Poems by S. T. Coleridge, Second Edition, To Which Are Now Added Poems by Charles Lamb and Charles Lloyd*, Bristol, 1797. SC's inventory of books from HC's library in her possession, *Grantz* 63, includes "*Poems*, single vol.," and the Humanities Research Center has the STC *Poems* 1797 with SC's signature on it.] Called at Rydal Mount with Mary [Pridham Coleridge]'s letter but found it vacant except for Miss [Dorothy] Wordsworth. "Her words are rational, sometimes beautiful, but her manner is strange and irregular." Mentions Mrs. [Elizabeth, wife of Thomas] Cookson, Mr. J[ohn?] Hutchinson, J[ohn] Wordsworth, and Dora [Wordsworth Quillinan]. Speaks of the death of Mr. [John] Dawes. Mentions D. [DC], the Judge [John Taylor Coleridge], Mrs. [James] Gillman, Mr. J[oseph] H[enry] Green, and Mary [Pridham Coleridge].

Quoted in full in *LHC*, pp. 283–286.

A63   A.L., Nab [Cottage, Rydal], [between 11 and 21 October 1845]. To: [No. 10 Chester Place, Regent's Park, London]. 4 pp.

Has received a letter from Derwent [DC] with "a most beautiful summary of our dear mother's excellences" [B87]. "Miss [Isabella] Fenwick comissions me to tell you, that she will be most happy to see you in her present abode in Ambleside, with your daughter and Nurse [Mrs. Ann Parrott] and Herbert at the holidays . . . – she thinks that it would have a healing influence on your mind, body, and soul, to be near your native mountains and to have the opportunity of conversing with the earliest surviving friends." Speaks of the comfort Miss Fenwick has been to Kate [Southey] and of Miss Fenwick's character. "She greatly admires your essay on rationality ["On Rationalism," HNC, ed., STC, *Aids to Reflection*, 2 vols., London, 1834. Volume II, Appendix C., pp. 335–556], and indeed, the perfect sympathy of your religious and political opinions would make your dwelling together especially happy," although Miss Fenwick is decidedly high-church. SC must make up her own mind about coming. Feels Derwent [DC]'s opinions not influenced by his circumstances. "I don't think either that he would care a straw for the abuse of the Record [*The Record* (Anglican), January 1818–] if he were firmly supported in high quarter." Berates "gentlemen of the press" but stops just short of saying all men are liars. "I believe Ebenezer Elliot and Mr. Aubrey De Vere to be perfectly honest."

A64 A.L., [Nab Cottage, Rydal], [October 1845?]. To: [No. 10 Chester Place, Regent's Park, London]. 2 pp.

Introduces to SC Miss Wilkins "whose acquaintance will I think be a pleasure to you" since she "inclines to your views in matters of church and state without however any stiffness or virulence. I do not mean that virulence or malice are characteristic of your side, but some of *you* – *Ladies particularly* are very apt to talk as if all the private and domestic virtues, all true piety, nay all historical faith in Christianity belong'd to the . . . Pittites." Thanks Edith [Coleridge] for her drawing. Has had his picture painted "at the special request of a young artist [see B257] who intends to put it into the exhibition" [probably the same painting, by Robert Tyson, which SC bought for £12–10–0 between 1 and 8 June 1846]. Wonders who has the drawings of SC and Edith [Southey Warter?] by [Edward] Nash [d. 1821]. Says SC or Mrs. [James] Gillman probably has SC's portrait by [William] Collins.

A65 A.L.i., [Nab Cottage, Rydal], [n.d., 1846?]. To: [No. 10 Chester Place, Regent's Park, London?]. 3 pp.

Has made few changes in the enclosed document [?]. "I thought non-mention of the Judge [John Taylor Coleridge] injurious, which I have done my best to remedy." Has dined with Miss [Isabella] Fenwick and Kate [Southey], who "gives good accounts of Aunt [Mary Fricker] Lovell, Cuthbert [Southey], and family. . . . A report has reach'd Grasmere through the Ecclesiastical Gazette that Derwent [DC] has been appointed to a Canonery of St. Paul" [DC "became a Prebendary of St. Paul's in 1846," EHC]. "I am going to send you a heap of sonnets and other poems on religious subjects. . . . I would fain devote rather more than a little of my talent, be it what it may, to the direct service of God." SC is to mark any passage "which you conceive could offend any pious person of any denomination" and he will change it. Sends "one of my latest compositions – not many days old," the sonnet "No Revelation has withdrawn the veil" [DC, ed., HC, *Poems*, London, 1851]. Feels "that our first Parents may have remained millions of years in innocence while all the geological changes were going on." Love to Edith [Coleridge].

A66 A.L., Nab [Cottage, Rydal], April 10th, 1847. To: [No. 10 Chester Place, Regent's Park, London]. 8 pp.

Has lectured "in the Museum of the Natural History Society of Kendal on the final Cause of Poetry, which went off pretty well on the whole, tho' some complained that it was too abstruse." Gave "readings of the English Poets, with observations interspersed" on the 8th and 9th and is to do the same for "Dryden, Pope, and their followers and compeers" on the 12th. Has received £4 for the lectures and been at no personal expense, transportation having been provided by Mrs. [Louise] Claude and Mrs. George Crawdson. Has dined with [Thomas Gough, a surgeon] the son of John Gough, "the famous blind naturalist." Miss M[ary] Arnold, with the Misses Whately as bridesmaids, was married "by the Rev. Mr. [John] Penrose, Mrs. [Thomas] Arnold's Brother," not, as HC had thought by the Archbishop [of Dublin, Richard Whately]. "But what right has a Malthusian like him [Whately] either to marry himself or to marry other people?" Writes news and descriptions of the Claude family – Mrs. Claude and her daughters Louisa, Mary, and Jane. Mary Claude has done some translations from the German "very sweetly, and I believe accurately, without any of that un-English construction of German prose, and particularly the cumbrous length and stiff convolution of German sentences (which remind me of petrified snakes)." Mary and Jane Claude have published *Verses for a Child of Six Years Old*. Strickland Cookson is to bring SC "My ballad printed for the relief of the distressed Irish." [HC wrote several poems which were printed and sold for the Irish Relief Fund. "Laugh No More: A Ballad in Behalf of Poor Paddy," Earl Leslie Griggs, ed., HC, *New Poems*, London, 1942]. "Miss Trevanion has sent for ten shillings' worth of them." Mentions Edith [Coleridge], Christy [Christabel Rose Coleridge], Derwent [Moultrie Coleridge], Derwent [DC] and Mary [Pridham Coleridge]. "I see that the Baby [born 8 December 1846] is called Ernest Hartley, after, I suppose, the King of Hanover and his poor Ne'er-de'well uncle—I hope he will take after neither." Mentions Dora [Wordsworth Quillinan], Nurse [Mrs. Ann Parrott], Mr. Wordsworth, and William Green.

Quoted in full in *LHC*, pp. 288–291.
Quoted in part in *Memoir*, pp. clxxv–clxxvi.

A67   A.L.i., Nab [Cottage, Rydal], May 18th, 1847. To: No. 10 Chester Place, Regent's Park, London. 3 pp.

Is very worried because SC has not acknowledged the income tax papers he has sent her [*Grantz* 533, 535]. Reports on Dora [Wordsworth Quillinan]'s health. "She has been at her own request, fully informed of her state, and is not only resign'd but happy." The Wordsworths "bear up like Christians, but are quite absorb'd by their sorrow." The doctor has advised HC that he can be of no use or comfort, so he will stay at home. William [Willy Wordsworth] came from Carlisle to take leave of Dora, and John [Wordsworth] administered the sacrament to his sister [Dora]. "I anticipate it will not be long" [Dora Wordsworth Quillinan died at Rydal Mount 9 July 1847]. Love to Edith [Coleridge]. Adds that Mrs. [Louise] Claude has returned.

Quoted in full in *LHC*, p. 294.

A68 A.L., Mrs. Claude's [Ambleside], Nov. 16—of course you know
the anno Domini, postmarked 1847. To: No. 10 Chester Place, Regent's
Park, London. 2 pp.

"Mr. Benson Harrison being absent, I applied to the Rev. F[letcher] Fleming
[Rydal vicar] . . . , who signified the fact of my existence in the flesh" [for the
settlement of Mrs. STC's estate]. Mr. [Joseph Henry] Green [co-administrator
with John Taylor Coleridge of the estate after HNC's death] says the form of
the certification was not proper and has sent printed forms and other necessary
information. Says he will get a regular certificate from Mr. [Benson] H[ar-
rison]. Love to Edith [Coleridge]. "I saw Mr. and Mrs. W[ordsworth] at Chapel
on Sunday, pretty well. Dr. Christopher Wordsworth preach'd ! ! ! ! ! ! ! ! alas
too."

Quoted in full in *LHC*, pp. 296–297.

A69 A.L.i., [Nab Cottage, Rydal], Jan. 28, [1848]. To: [No. 10 Chester Place, Regent's Park, London]. 6 pp.

Is sorry he has not answered her letter; he cannot plead it is his humor, for
"in these days of Homeopathy, Hydropathy, and Mesmerism – the humoral
pathology is out of fashion." Has much to do but hasn't done it. "Your account
of the children is delightful." Longs to see Edith, but is afraid. Had he seen her
as a young child he might, by his "fondness," have passed muster as an uncle.
"But when Misses and Masters are in their teens, an Uncle stands in a serious
relation. . . . I can be serious, but not grave, earnest but not solemn, indignant
when need is, but not calmly austere." Has learned from experience that while
he has a talent for teaching, he is "wholly incompetent to discipline." Can never
"act Uncle" unless it be such a one as "my Uncle Toby" [in *Tristram Shandy*].
"I must be content to stand in the position of an elderly Cousin. It is hard to
say, what powers might have been develop'd in me had it pleased God that I
should have been a Father. My knowledge of my own infirmities might have
made me painfully suspicious on moral points." Would have been pleased to
have studious children, both boys and girls. "I do not think that intellectual
development necessarily tends to make any man good. It does not even exempt
him from the tyranny of the lower appetites." Therefore, can not sympathize
with her regrets that Edith [Coleridge] is not studious. "I was never studious.
. . . But our revered Father . . . while he lamented my lack of zeal, was not
blind to the cause of it. He remember'd, that in his childhood and boyhood,
books were all in all to him. They were his duty, recreation, family, friends,
the only world in which he had either enjoyment or liberty. The very fulfilment
of his own aspiration 'For thou my Child, &c,' ["But *thou*, my babe!", l. 54
from "Frost at Midnight," Elisabeth Schneider, ed., *Samuel Taylor Coleridge:
Selected Poetry and Prose*, New York, 1951] made it impossible that study
could be to me what it had been to him. While I inherited that absence of
ambition that made him as I have heard him say, keep at the bottom of his
class . . . ." Hopes neither Edith nor Herbert [Coleridge] has inherited his

65

"morbid" oversensitivity "which was the guilty origin of all those wanderings and hidings, which turned my mother's love to grief." Says part of the above was written long ago, in 1847. Wishes SC and family a happier year than the last. "It's snowing – it will spoil the ice, which lies bright and beautiful before my window, often dotted with gay skaters," among whom is Dora Harrison, daughter of "Chucky Doro" [Dorothy Wordsworth Harrison (Mrs. Benson Harrison)]. Dora is engaged to "a most amiable and sensible young man named Bolland," a nephew of the judge [Sir William Bolland]. The young man "has little but his learning and his friends," but Benson Harrison is wealthy. Dorothy Wordsworth Harrison "wears better than any woman I know," is very pretty, and "looks more like 27 than 47," though she has just lost a grandchild. Matthew Harrison, 'father of the dead child, is "an English Gentleman rather of the Squire genus, without the least turn either for business or study." Describes Matthew Harrison and his four brothers. Dickey, the youngest, is under Mr. Dobson at Cheltenham. Dobson married Mr. Harrison's daughter by his first wife. "Dora has the sense of the family." Sends a sonnet "Stay where thou art. Thou cans't not better be" [DC, ed., HC, *Poems*, London, 1851] written upon Dora's failure to convert when [the Rev. Frederick] Faber followed Newman into the Roman Catholic Church. Post time is nigh, and he is to dine with "my dear old infirm, Whiggish friend Dr. Briggs" and his wife and daughter, Anna Maria. John Wordsworth has called and does not give as good an account of his father as one might wish. "Says there is no getting him to stir." Thanks SC for her remittance to Mrs. [Eleanor] Richardson. Mentions Herbert [Coleridge] and Derwent [Moultrie Coleridge]. Admires SC's contributions to the Bio. Lit. [HNC and SC, eds., STC, *Biographia Literaria*, London, 1847]. Plans to examine "the Spenser question" in *Frazer['s Magazine]* at the request of the new editor, [John William] Parker.

A70 A.L.i., [Nab Cottage, Rydal], Feb. 18, [1848?]. To: No. 10 Chester Place, Regent's Park, London. 16 pp. Endorsed on envelope by DC "Politics, Mrs. Fletcher | Derwent [Moultrie Coleridge]. | Primitive Churches." On envelope in HC's hand "Favoured by Mrs. Fletcher." Also on the envelope in unknown hand is the date 1847, but internal evidence would indicate 1848.

Introduces to SC Mrs. [Archibald] Fletcher and her daughter Mrs. John Davy, wife of the physiologist and anatomist and sister-in-law of Sir Humphry Davy. Says the only Tories he can get along with are Miss [Isabella] Fenwick and the Judge [John Taylor Coleridge]. Speaks of loyalty and of the popularity of George IV, "who was almost detested in the first years of his reign but to the bulk of the people . . . was endeared by his dauntless personal courage, his plain living, his dining at two o'clock . . . his shaking his sides at a Clown . . . in a Pantomine." Speaks at length on the character and reputation of George IV. Speaks of Derwent Moultrie Coleridge's misconduct and subsequent expulsion from Oxford. "I am glad his parents take the most favourable view that the case admits," but believes the expulsion will do him good. "All the Coleridges I ever knew were vain except the Judge [John Taylor Coleridge] and yourself and perhaps Lady [Frances Duke Coleridge] Patteson." Disagrees with

SC's opinion, "expressed in your essay on the disadvantages of beauty which I am glad you did not publish." Mentions Elizabeth Crump and says "I do not believe that beauties have less than their share either of talent or good sense. Indeed I think that Miss [Sara?] Hutchinson and Miss Barker were the only decidedly superior women of my acquaintance whom not even a lover could think pretty." Mentions John Wordsworth, [Edward] Moxon, Derwent [DC] and Mary [Pridham Coleridge], Edith and Herbert [Coleridge], George [May Coleridge], Mr. [Richard Hurrell] Froude, and HNC.

A71   A.L.i., Knabbe [Cottage, Rydal], October 29, [1848]. To: [No. 10 Chester Place, Regent's Park, London]. 6 pp.

Speaks of a bill of his from Mrs. Nicholson [Ambleside bookseller], who is "not to be blamed for being exact to the letter of the law." Borrowed the five shillings from Mr. Monroe, not Mr. Bullock, who "is a friend of Mr. Clark, but not acquainted with Derwent." Comments on how personally some people take their names. Mentions Wordsworth's *Peter Bell*[, *A Tale in Verse*, London, 1819]. Hopes she enjoys her visit to St. Mark's and sends love to Christabel [Rose] and Ernest [Hartley Coleridge]. "I like to think of him [Ernest Hartley] by his other name. I am as superstitious about names as Mr. Shandy [Walter Shandy in Sterne's *Tristram Shandy*]. I have known more than one Hartley, and none of them were all that could be wish'd either in themselves or their circumstances." Speaks of Dervy [Derwent Moultrie Coleridge]'s becoming twenty. Twenty would seem a natural age to be "the year of majority. Twenty one was probably fix'd upon as the multiple of the sacred numbers 3 and 7. . . . But for any common sense reason, I can see no . . . claim that 21 has to be considered the age of discretion." Is to dine with Dr. Hollenforth, a physician of Hungarian descent. Describes Miss [Mary] Minto, "a great friend (as I believe I told you of Miss Barrett) now Mrs. Browning." Mentions Miss Stolterforth, who has a copy of his poems, and Dr. Stolterforth, whom he likes very much. "Indeed I am not sure, that . . . I do not like the medical faculty the best of the professions. Were my course to run again, I would not be a Physician myself. But rather than be without a settled occupation," HC would submit to the tyranny of a desk job, like Charles Lamb. Speaks of DC's fitness for his job. Asks if it is [John] Sterling's song "that Mr. [Henry?] Taylor repeats so well. Few songs are worth repeating. I except however many of Barry Cornwall's." Asks for James Spedding's address. Must write DC. Has read SC's "Tennison" ["Tennyson's *Princess: A Medley,*" *Quarterly Review*, March 1848] and will look out for the B. and F. [SC, "Dyce's edition of Beaumont and Fletcher," *Quarterly Review*, September 1848]. Remarks on the friendship of Beaumont and Fletcher. Mentions Mrs. [Louise] Claude; Mr. [John] Crossfield; Mrs. Claude's daughter in India [Louise Claude W.], who has a little girl; and Mary Claude's new book *Twilight Thoughts* [London, 1848], which he recommends.

A72   A.L. (inc.), [Nab Cottage, Rydal], [n.d., 1848?]. To: [No. 10 Chester Place, Regent's Park, London]. 2 pp.

Says he has written to thank Mr. [John Wood] Warter for the book [probably the one vol. ed., J. W. Warter, ed., Robert Southey, *The Doctor, &c.*, London, 1848. See B259] which SC has promised to send. "Unquestionably it [*The Doctor, &c.*] is a delightful book to take up and put down—a wonderful Museum of odd fancies, strange facts – [John?] Taylor's Gehenna of shreds and remnants – old things and new, cloth of gold, and scarlet, and beggars' velvet . . . – Material for a hundred workers in mosaic – but I cannot [see] that it is a skillful piece of Mosaic itself." *Tristram Shandy* is unified by the assumption "that Tristram is always the speaker." Will not put Southey on the level of Sterne, who is a dishonest plagiarist, although "the very humor and originality of Walter Shandy is to talk out of books." "But S[outhey]'s nonsense is never worse than nonsense, which cannot be truly said of Sterne's." *The Doctor, &c.* suffers from periodic "dogmata" and from Southey's lack of skill in delineating character. "Every poetic personage . . . should testify to its own truth, without reference to an original which few can ever have seen, none can longer see. This it is, that divides true imitative Art from mechanical Imitation." But the truest characters and landscapes are drawn from real life. Wordsworth "glories" that every character, etc., in his work is drawn from life and proposes to give Miss [Isabella] Fenwick an account of the facts from which his imagination has worked – "a precious commentary it will be" ["the Fenwick notes" first appear in William Wordsworth, *The Poetical Works*, 6 vols., 1857]. Fielding, Sterne, Smollett, Addison and Sir Walter [Scott] all sketched characters from real life. "Dickens should never draw without a model. It is the same with Painters," Hogarth, Raffaelle, Michel[angelo], and Titian.

Quoted in full in *LHC*, pp. 294–296.

SIR JOHN TAYLOR COLERIDGE

A73   A.L.s., Ambleside, Jan. 15, postmarked 1823. To: No. 2 Pump Court, Temple, London. 2 pp.

Asks his cousin JTC to send STC £15 "on my account." Wishes to give the remainder of his £300 Oriel gift to Mrs. STC. Speaks of Sara [Coleridge]'s visit to Ottery—"Fanny [Coleridge Patteson] and she will be a lovely pair." Sends regards to Mrs. J[ohn] C[oleridge], Henry [HNC], and Willam Hart [Coleridge]. Speaks of an article on Aeschylus promised to Mr. Lisle [this article is unknown].

Quoted in full in *LHC*, p. 76.

A74   A.L.i., Ambleside, Feb. 12th, 1825. To: No. 65 Torrington Square or Pump Court, Middle Temple, London. 3 pp.

Explains that his strained thumb has delayed this letter. Congratulates JTC on his editorship [of the *Quarterly Review*] and on the birth of his daughter [Mary Frances Keble Coleridge]. "I am as fond of Babies as if I had twenty– perhaps fonder. It is, I believe, a family failing with all the Coleridges." Discusses a possible book review and the limitations of his isolation. "My Uncle S[outhey] is indeed very kind in lending whatever I wish for, but I am not able to avail myself of his Library on the spot, far less of the stores of his memory." "When you see Mr. [Edward] Smedley [editor of *Encyclopaedia Metropolitana*], you will oblige me by asking him when the article on Poetry will be call'd for." Speaks of Henry [HNC]'s joining William Hart Coleridge in the West Indies. Mentions Mrs. [Frances Duke Coleridge] Patteson, Frank [Francis George Coleridge], Derwent [DC], and Sara [SC]. Finds teaching "is not an absolute sinecure. Great boys are the least agreeable animals in creation." Asks to be remembered to Ottery friends.

Quoted in full in *LHC*, pp. 87–89.

A75 A.L.s., [Grasmere], [n.d., October, 1836]. To: [Fox How, Grasmere]. 1 p. Endorsed in unknown hand "1836 | Oct. | Hartley Coleridge | Grasmere." [Following Dr. Thomas Arnold's return to Rugby, John Taylor Coleridge occupied Fox How, the Arnolds' Grasmere residence.]

Promises to see John Taylor Coleridge at four. Has been thinking about the essay on STC [fragments published in *PMLA*, December 1931]. "I should not shrink from the task, were [it only] my father's character as a poet, A Critic, and in general a literateur (will it not offend his manes to be characterised by a French word?), but I am hardly capable of arguing his philosophy at present. Indeed my opinion is that no view of it should be attempted, till his remarks are all before the public."

Quoted in full in *LHC*, p. 198.

A76 A.L.s., [Grasmere], postmarked Fe. 20, 1839. To: London. 4 pp.

Tells of witnessing the consecration of a chapel at Sedberg, where the Rev. I[saac] Green is incumbent. Distinguishes between the terms "rite" and "ceremony." Speaks approvingly of the demeanor of Dr. Longley [Charles Thomas Longley, Bishop of Ripon]. When in company of the Bishop, could not speak and "fell into a reverie or speculation as to what the conversation would have been had STC been present." Says he has read the first volume of Gillman's life of STC [James Gillman, *The Life of Samuel Taylor Coleridge*, London, 1838], and supposes the second volume is out [no more published; Gillman collected material for a second volume but destroyed it before his death]. Because of Gillman's friendship "and yet heavier obligations . . . any thing like censure [would be] ungracious and ungrateful. Besides, I have to thank him for much that he has not said." Mentions that Gillman "has not omitted above three or four lines of Christabel." "G[illman] evidently dislikes Southey -- for speaking of the story of Doctor Daniel Dove, he describes it as an old tradition which 'some literary man has used for pegs to hang a story and the contents of his scrap book upon.' Now G[illman] knows well enough that S[outhey] is the author. *Entre nous* – I do not think that great and excellent man has acted wisely in publishing the Doctor [Robert Southey, *The Doctor, &c.,* London, 7 vols., 1834–1847]." "He had better reserved his *facetiae* for his own after supper fire side." Comments on *The Doctor, &c.* "Sterne was a miserable sentimentalist and at best a second-hand humourist, but he was an admirable dramatist. In fact, should I select an instance of Genius, eclipsed but not totally eclipsed, diseased, yet not poison'd by moral debility, my instance should be Sterne." Speaks of intention to publish a small volume of "sonnets &c. on scriptural subjects" [never published separately]. Some of the sonnets would not accord with STC's ideas on some subjects. Recommends a friend, William Sandford, for a church appointment to Australia: "I myself will testify to his orthodoxy, for he has been very angry with me when he thought me heterodox."

A77   A.L.s., Ambleside, May 12, 1840. To: London. 3 pp.

Recommends Robert Temple of York, Barrister, for the vacancy in the list of commissioners of bankruptcy. Doubts his influence with "the *graced* members of the flock." Is not sorry that Derwent [DC] has not gotten a position in the City of London School as "he is not the man . . . to succumb to . . . purse-proud vulgarity, far less to submit to ignorant dictation." Asks if JTC has seen the January [March] issue of *Blackwood's* charging STC with "gross and unacknowledged plagiary." "I would spend the last hour of my life to do [confute] it – if it were possible." Sends respects to Lady [Mary Buchanan] Coleridge and love to children, "more particularly to her of the beauteous locks, that did not put forth an angry hand against the kiss of a grey headed man and a cousin. You cannot conceive how grateful I am for these things—even from a child."

Quoted in full in *LHC*, pp. 237–238.

A78   A.L.s., Rydal, January 9, 1846. To: [Heath's Court, Ottery St. Mary?]. 3 pp. Endorsed on back of letter "Mr Justice Coleridge | 1847 | Consent to arrangement." Page one of letter has black borders.

Agrees to settlement of Mrs. STC's estate [Mrs. STC died 24 September 1845] proposed by John Taylor Coleridge and Joseph Henry Green, who administered the estate. Must make arrangements "to render care of my concerns less burdensome" to SC and Mrs. Wordsworth than it had been to Mrs. STC and Mrs. Wordsworth. Has not been idle. Wishes he could spare SC the toil of preparing the *Biographia* [HNC and SC, eds., STC, *Biographia Litearia*, London, 1847]. Promises the essay on STC [fragments published in *PMLA*, December

1931], but does not feel competent to speak on STC "as Politician, Philosopher, or Theologian." Mr. and Mrs. Wordsworth are grieved by the death of their grandchild [Edward Wordsworth], son of the Revd. John [and Isabella Curwen] Wordsworth, in Italy. Remembrances to Lady [Mary Buchanan] Coleridge.

Quoted in full in *LHC*, pp. 287–288.

SAMUEL TAYLOR COLERIDGE

A79   A.L.s., Merton Col[lege, Oxford], March 18, 1817. To: Highgate, London. 3 pp.

Apologizes for not proceeding [as proposed by STC] on the translation of *Nemesius* since he cannot find a copy of the work. Has been reading Pindar, whom he does not find difficult, despite the many allusions. "Pindar may not unaptly be compared to a boy going to school, who picks every flower by the roadside, merely because his journey's end is unpleasant. Conscious that his subjects were deficient in permanent interest, he seeks to generalize them by introducing all the moral and political observations that can be deduced from them." Admires Aristotle's independence. Says he needs STC's help in logic and classics. Feels he needs but cannot afford a private tutor.

Quoted in full in *LHC*, pp. 14–15.

A80   A.L. (inc.), [25 Bedford Square, London], [September 1820]. To: Highgate, London. 4 pp. Letter is in a wrapper of folded paper with notation of contents and note "prob. July-August 1820."

A detailed account of the whole Oriel affair. Mentions harsh accusations in the letter from [John] Keble to John [Taylor Coleridge]. Feels "wrong'd, illiberally, ungentlemanly treated" but tries to present the affair as impartially as possible. Says undergraduate days were comparatively unrestricted in a liberal college where he made many undergraduate friends whom he defends. Says he was warned of the precariousness of his fellowship and, having been to "two passing parties," confessed his immorality. On the next day HC visited [John] Keble, who spoke reprovingly in language which "might have [been] addressed more properly to one who was hardly ever sober, than to one who had been occasionally tipsy." Says he then sought the advice of Rickards, a fellow-probationer, and sent off letters measuring "my expression by the strictest standards" which was regarded as proof of the truth of the charges. Laments "If a humble Christian, in his prayers, calls himself a miserable sinner – shall this be made a handle to accuse him of murder, or theft?" Says he saw [Richard] Whately and [John] Keble to no avail. Remarks that Dr. [Edward] Copleston spoke to him kindly.

Quoted in full in *LHC*, pp. 37–41.

A81 A.L.i., [25] Bedford Square, [London], October 2ᵈ, [1820]. To: Highgate. 4 pp. Letter is in a wrapper of folded paper with notation of contents and dates.

> A further account of the Oriel affair [see A80]. Presents case against him as it must have appeared to fellows of Oriel, adding "Now this, my dear Father, is a plain statement of *facts*, which may prevent your committing yourself by defending me on untenable points." Admits trying to help a young man "whose looks certainly indicated drinking" through school and realizes the damage this association has done to his reputation. "But yet all this, tho' it fully justifies their exclusion of me, is very far from even excusing the manner of it. Nothing I had done had affected my character as a Gentleman." "Above all, nothing that I can think of, can excuse . . . their attempt to send me over the wide Ocean with a blasted character to leave my name for a bie-word to my family – the one scabby sheep turn'd out of an immaculate flock – the sole jarring note in the concert of Coleridges." Promises to do what he can for "Ebony" [William Blackwood, of *Blackwood's Magazine*] – "A Romance in the first person, setting forth the manifest disadvantages of Ugliness . . . my signature Caliban." Mentions Mrs. [Ann] Gillman.

Quoted in full in *LHC*, pp. 41–44.

A82 A.L.i., [Oxford?], [December 1820]. To: [Highgate, London]. 1 p.

> Anticipates journey to London. Speaks of the difficulty in writing a letter to the Warden of Merton College [see A151]. Expresses anger at John [Taylor] Coleridge for believing the Oriel charges and alleging acquaintance with the Harrises "as proof of my love of low company." Defends conduct with Mary [Harris] and bites back—"Nor does this observation beseem one, whom I have heard charged with marrying a linnet without one gold feather in her wing." Sends love to Mr. and Mrs. [James] Gillman.

Quoted in full in *LHC*, pp. 55–56.

A83 A.L.s., 15 Clifford's Inn [Ambleside], Thursday afternoon [n.d., 1822]. To: [Highgate, London]. 2 pp. Letter is in a blue envelope endorsed "H. C. to S. T. C. | London 1822 | Ambleside school."

> "You must be aware, that the pain arising from the contemplation of a misspent past, is often the cause of continuance in misdoing even after the temptations which first misled have lost their powers, and when the sophisms which have long deluded, appear in their true deformity." Speaks of the difficulties in

72

recovering psychologically from what he has been through. Finds that a depressed state hinders his teaching. "Boys of 15 are harder to govern than men of twenty." Wishes "to make another trial of my talents in London," but "will not be obstinate." Promises to finish "Prometheus" forthwith. Mentions Robert [Jameson], Mr. [Basil] Montagu, Mr. and Mrs. [James] Gillman and Miss [Jane] Harding.

Quoted in full in *LHC*, pp. 74–76.
Quoted in full in *Memoir*, pp. xciii–xciv.

A84   A.L.i., Ambleside, March 12, 1824. To: Highgate, Near London. 4 pp.

Says he is "well in body, and prosperous in estate." Has been too busy teaching to make progress in "the works which we have spoken of together." Has been engaged to do an essay on poetry for *Encyclopedia Metropolitana* [the essay never appeared]. Gives a long defense of Derwent's character, admitting that Derwent is vain and intellectually impatient but expressing confidence, "with the faith of a Brother, and of a Christian, that the work of so many years, so many solemn thoughts, so many holy feelings, aided by all his happier recollections, all his early sympathies, cannot have been so effaced in a few months, that it will not outlast a momentary whim, or a few passing scruples." Mentions Dora Wordsworth [Quillinan], Sara [Hutchinson], Mrs. Wordsworth, John and Willy [Wordsworth]. Says Wordsworth has been translating Virgil [E. de Selincourt and Helen Darbishire, *The Poetical Works of William Wordsworth*, vol. 4, Appendix A, Oxford, 1958] "into a sort of confluent couplet—or if the phrase be not a ball, rhiming blank verses. It is certainly, from the sample I have seen, a powerful work, but between Wordsworth's republican Austerity, and the courtly pomp of Virgil, the contrast is so wide, that I doubt, whether the more perfect correctness of sense can atone in a translation for such disparity of Mode." Mentions [John] Williams, [Robert] Jameson.

Quoted in full in *LHC*, pp. 84–87.

A85   A.L.s., [n.p.], [n.d., 1820–1823]. 3 pp.

Says STC has just cause to wonder and be offended at him. "The truth however is best told, and tho' I am conscious that I have at least omitted the best means of preventing an occurrence, which end how it will must be a source of pain to my dear Brother, and has given so deep a wound to you, yet a plain confession of the folly, delusion, and Procrastination with which I have really acted, may perhaps prevent your readily attributing my disobedience to moral defects of a still more hopeless character." Cannot remember STC's giving him a note to deliver to Derwent [DC]. Though to say this is of no avail, "I did not see the affair in the same light that you did. I thought that Derwent was perfectly indifferent to Miss H[all] and therefore concluded, that her music, and the pleasure of displaying his abilities in poetical Reading induced him to pay her whatever degree of attention he might have shewn. In fact, I thought, that she probably liked to hear him and look at him as others had done, and would forget him as others had done, when he was out of sight." Intended to communicate STC's fears to Derwent, but procrastinated for fear of causing pain "till Derwent left Highgate for Cambridge." Bitterly reproaches himself, "the more so as no exertion on my part now can in the least repair the damage, which, unlikely as it was that any one should have forseen it in its present extent, I ought . . . to have guarded against." Castigates himself in bitter terms. "Nothing could be farther from my mind or tongue than the slightest palliation of Mrs. Chism's fault in the Business. ["and tho' as for Miss Hall, I did not correctly know" is struck through.] All that I did was to throw the blame of the whole upon her, certainly in a manner I should not have done after more mature consideration. . . . I cannot conclude this without expressing high praise for the self-command and prudence which D[erwent] shew'd on the occasion, however unguarded may have been the conduct on his part which led to it. I think I can also assure you, that you have nothing to fear from any attachment [?] on his part. On the other hand, the esteem which I certainly felt for Miss H[all] has been much diminish'd by her strange behavior." Will not ask STC to see him "till you could do it with composure." "I trust its [his fault's] consequences will speedily be at an end."

MRS. SAMUEL TAYLOR [SARA FRICKER] COLERIDGE

A86   A.L. (inc.), [n.p.], [n.d., 1820?]. To: [n.p.]. 2 pp.

Very similar in tone to entry A87. "That I have been the cause, I dare not say innocent cause, of much uneasiness to you, I have often had to lament, but never more keenly than today. . . . What I can do, I will, but I despair of ever becoming exactly the son you would choose. . . . To please you thoroughly, my inclinations must not only be govern'd, but changed." She [Mrs. STC] would have him change the most central parts of his very nature, and he protests that she expects too much. "You will know what I mean when I say that the blood in my veins is stronger than the example before my eyes. I may make my hands and my tongue obey, but not my mind." Quotes Mrs. STC as saying "that my nature would generally lead me right, if passion did not pervert, or indolence obstruct it." The letter breaks off with the words "but such is my temper that all controul is hateful to me, not because it . . . ."

A87   A.L.i., [Grasmere], [n.d., 1820?]. To: [Greta Hall, Keswick, Cumberland]. 5 pp. The letter bears no date or address of any kind. The watermark reads "John Dickinson & [Co., Ltd.] | 1815."

Feels that he is "not born to be happy" and that "happiness was not the certain concomitant of virtue." "I by no means assert that I am incapable of enjoyment. . . . But all that is human is bounded; our life is a fruitless effort to break the chain which only death can dissolve. . . . Therefore, when I say that I can never be happy, I mean that I require a larger area, or in other terms, a greater degree of liberty than is compatible with the condition of humanity. . . . There is a . . . character, that . . . would fain stand alone, neither influencing nor being influenced by any one. Such, at some times am I, but my disposition leading me to love, and therefore of course to a wish to be loved, prevents my long continuing so." The inward struggle he has described "produces an inward irritation," which breaks out in ways which upset Mrs. STC. God alone can alter him. "If I am to be happy at all, I must be happy in my own way; . . . no one can or shall prescribe to me the road I am to pursue to it. . . . To those whom I love, I will give up all, provided they ask it of my love. . . . I claim, and will maintain my claim, to be sole judge of what is my duty." Resolves to improve "whatever may be unpleasant in my temper or manners" and to throw off sloth. Similar in tone to entry A86.

Quoted in full in *LHC*, pp. 102–104.

A88   A.L.i., Ambleside, Nov. 2^d [1826–1829]. To: [Greta Hall, Keswick]. 3 pp.

The portfolio arrived, and he received the shillings yesterday. Has been hard at work on "Poetry" [for the *Encyclopaedia Metropolitana*] and hopes to have it transcribed so that he may keep a copy in order, "if it be allowable (by the way, I wish you would ask Uncle [Robert Southey] if it be allowable) that I may publish it separately in an enlarged state at some future time." Wonders what he will be paid for the article. Most encyclopedia articles are "copied verbatim or abridged. . . from other works." When he was in London, the former editor promised him 5 guineas a quarto sheet, so he should receive 40 guineas, though he expects 30. Expects to hear from both [William] Blackwood and A[laric Alexander] Watts [see A152, 153]. If The *Literary Souvenir*[, or *Cabinet of Poetry and Romance*, A. A. Watts, ed., 10 vols., 1825–1834] should be sent to Keswick, would she please send it to him along with all the spare sheets of Vindication [Robert Southey, *Vindiciae Ecclesiae Anglicanae: Letters to Charles Butler, Esq., comprising Essays on the Romish Religion and vindicating "The Book of the Church,"* London, 1826] "It is a delightful work. . . . How ignorant or dishonest a writer Butler must be" [Robert Southey's *The Book of the Church*, 2 vols., London, 1824, had prompted Charles Butler's *The Book of the Roman Catholic Church: in a series of letters addressed to Rb^t Southey . . . on his "Book of the Church,"* London, 1825]. Will return Uncle [Robert Southey]'s books. "I did mention to Mr. Stuart [HC's partner in the Ambleside school] what you said in your last — but his Creditors are very troublesome at fair times—I am truly sorry you were obliged to borrow from Aunt [Mrs. (Edith Fricker) Southey]. Asks for DC's and SC's addresses. Adds in a note that he was sorry to hear from Mr. Lyon that the young Duke of Buccleugh is "much disesteemed at Cambridge in a moral point of view . . . oh that horrid Cambridge! He has been spoiled there."

A89 A.L.i., [Grasmere], [n.d., 1829]. To: Greta Hall, Keswick, Cumberland. 7 pp. Note on address face "Forwarded by Rev. F. Aychbowm [sic]." The letter is mutilated.

Rejoices over Sara Coleridge's [whom he calls "Namput"] and HNC's coming marriage in August [September 3, 1829]. Gives his shell collection to Cuthbert [Southey]. Remarks upon his bachelor state. Assures Mrs. STC that her letters are either burned or put up. Says he "wrote the critique on the Pilgrim to Compostella" [*Blackwood's Magazine*, July 1829]. Has read, with Professor [John Wilson], Southey's *Colloquies on the Progress and Prospects of Society* [London, 1829], which he admires hugely. Is "constructing a long, laborious article upon Hogarth" ["Ignoramus on the Fine Arts, No. III," *Blackwood's Magazine,* October 1831]. Has had recommended to him "the *Court Journal* (which, by the way, seems to be very good .– for nothing –) as a channel for my communications, reserving my poor unworthy verses, which could confer no brilliancy on the *Gem*, to fill up the procession of the *Court Journal*. The *Court Journal* must pay uncommon well, before I will rank myself among its familiars." Speaks of [Thomas] Hood's starting the *Comic Annual* [1830]: "He is a man of real genius, and I wish him well." Speaks with deep regret of the death of his benefactress, Lady [Margaret Willes] Beaumont. Mentions Dervy [Derwent Moultrie Coleridge], Mr. [Richard] Townsend, Elleray [John Wilson's home], Mr. Alaric Watts, Mr. Marshall, and Mr. Aychbawm [private chaplain to Lord Grosvenor].

Quoted in full in *LHC*, pp. 98–102.
Fragment quoted in *Memoir*, p. xxix.

A90 A.L.i., Grasmere, Feb. 6, postmarked 1831. To: No. 1 New Square, Lincoln's Inn, London. 4 pp. Endorsed on seal and address faces by Mrs. STC "School 1831 | Big Boys | very interesting."

Feels he will never be a master as he cannot handle the boys. He has recurrent nightmares about being a small child persecuted by big boys. Has received £10 from the Professor [John Wilson] and assurances that the first ten pages [of "Ignoramus on the Fine Arts"] will be in the February number ["Ignoramus on the Fine Arts, I–III," *Blackwood's Magazine*, February, March, and October 1831]. Used the money to pay Mrs. [Dinah] Fleming [his landlady]. Mentions Miss [Dorothy] Wordsworth, Henry [HNC], Sir J[ohn] St. Aubyn, Derwent [DC], and Sarah Fox. Sara [SC] and babe [Herbert Coleridge] must make a delightful picture. Mentions verses to little Miss Fleming ["The Sabbath-Day's Child," *Poems*, Leeds, 1833]. "You probably saw the Tea-table in B[*lackwood's Magazine*, March 1830] but it does not look so well in print as it sounded when Elizabeth Warde listn'd to it." Mentions Uncle [Robert Southey], Edith [Southey Warter], Aunt [Mary Fricker] Lovell, [Sam] Archer, Wordsworth, Joanna Baillie, Hal [HNC], Mrs. Carter, Mr. [James] Brancker, and STC.

Quoted in full in *LHC*, pp. 127–130.

Quoted in part in *Memoir*, pp. xcviii–xcix.

A91 A.L., Rydal Mount, April 16, 1831. To: Hampstead, London. 4 pp. Signed only "I remain your dutiful son."

Writes of his unpaid bills to W. J. St. Aubyn, T[homas] Troughton, and a bookseller at Kendal. Miss [Dorothy] W[ordsworth] "was kind enough to send me a message, offering to pay any bill that might be pressing." Expects a remittance in May "which will set me entirely free from debt, except to yourself." Will send a list of needed clothes. Has received £20 for the two parts of "Ignoramus" ["Ignoramus on the Fine Arts, Nos. I–III," *Blackwood's Magazine*, February, March, October 1831]. Speaks playfully of Sara [SC]. "Dod-a-bless a little soul. Does it read Greek with its good man [HNC] of a night? Lord love it. You see she never grows any older in my imagination. But she is a sweet creature." Mentions Aggy Micchie [his late washer-woman], Owen Lloyd, Mrs. Carter, HNC, STC, Mrs. [James] Gillman. Says he has none of his father's works except *Aids to Reflection* [London, 1825], "which I rejoice to see a new [second] Edition of announced." Mentions Mr. Wordsworth, Dora [Wordsworth Quillinan] and William [Wordsworth].

Quoted in full in *LHC*, pp. 130–132.

A92 A.L.i., Grasmere, October 16, 1831. To: No. 1 Downshire Place, Downshire Hill, Hampstead, Near London. 5 pp. Page 5 is crosswritten on page 1. Endorsed on address face "Oct 31 | Feelings towards | his mother | Rebellion can alone prevent reform | Mr. Withington & Allan Bank."

Assures Mrs. STC of his love for her and excuses not having written and having missed her at Rydal Mount. [Mrs. STC visited the North for the last time in the summer of 1831.] Does not know what to say to Henry [HNC] about his Homer [HNC, *Introduction to the Study of the Greek Classic Poets*, London, 1830]. Mentions Professor [John] Wilson and Sotheby's translation [William Sotheby, *Polyglott Georgics*, 1827]. Thanks Mrs. STC for the clothes and papers she has sent. Feels the *Athenaeum* is well worth the two pence but the *Carlisle Patriot* certainly is not. Describes Mr. and Mrs. Withington and children, the present occupants of Allen Bank. Understands that "Sara [SC] and her spouse are gone to Ottery without the Bab[y, Herbert]. Hopes they have no trouble with rioters [the agitation preceding the passage of the Reform Bill]. "My own opinion is, that nothing but a rebellion can prevent Reform." Has written to [Thomas?] Hood. Has been paid £10 for "my last" ["Ignoramus on the Fine Arts, III," *Blackwood's Magazine*, October 1831]. Mentions the Wordsworths, P[rofessor John] Wilson, Miss [Dorothy] Wordsworth, Dervy [Derwent Moultrie Coleridge], Edith [Southey Warter], Kate [Southey], Bertha [Southey Hill], and the *Winter's Wreath* [1828–1832]. "I have contributed largely [between 1829–1832] and been paid in part only."

Quoted in full in *LHC*, pp. 132–135.

A93   A.L.s., [Grasmere], Feb. 17, postmarked 1832. To: No. 10 New Square, Lincoln's Inn, London. 4 pp.

Reviews the history of Mrs. STC's letters to him and is glad they have taken a more pleasant turn. Mentions Sara [SC]'s marriage, Derwent [DC]'s prospects, Miss [Dorothy] Wordsworth, Dora [Wordsworth Quillinan], Mr. and Mrs. Wordsworth, and Miss [Sara] Hutchinson. Writes at length on the health and character of Mr. [John] Dawes. Has mixed feelings about the Reform Bill. Mentions Dr. [Andrew] Bell [founder of the Madras system of education]. "Wish he'd left Uncle [Robert Southey] and Mr. W[ordsworth] more, and unincumbered with conditions. A few thousands in trust for me, would not have been amiss." [Bell desired that Southey and Wordsworth collect and edit his writings, but they never did so.] Has received D [DC]'s sermon [DC, *The Circumstances of the Present Times, considered with a view to religious improvement. An Advent Sermon*, London, 1831]. Mentions Mary [Pridham Coleridge], STC, the [James] Gillmans, Hal and Sal [HNC and SC], Mr. [Edward] Quillinan.

Quoted in full in *LHC*, pp. 135–138.

A94   A.L.i., Leeds, July 24, 1832. To: 1 Downshire Place, Downshire Hill, Hampstead, London. 4 pp. Endorsed on address face "First letter from Leeds."

Is slow acknowledging her parcel because "I have to write eight, nine, and ten hours a day to keep up with the press." Details his arrangements with [Francis Edward] Bingley, from whom he is to receive £20 for *Worthies* and £50 for *Poems*. Will assist in a magazine [*The Academic Correspondent*, 1832], the editor of which "is Mr. Fenton, Mrs. Green's Son in Law." Mentions Sara [SC]'s confinement with Edith [Coleridge], STC, Henry [HNC], and Uncle [Robert Southey]. Is comfortable with the Bingleys, who have a baby. "Don't be alarm'd. I am in less temptation at Leeds, where I know no *public house people*, than at Grasmere." Mentions James and Henry Gillman [sons of James Gillman].

Quoted in full in *LHC*, pp. 142–144.

A95   A.L.s., Leeds, Christmas Day, 1832. To: No. 1 Downshire Place, Hampstead, near London. 5 pp. Page 5 is crosswritten on page 1.

Sends his sympathy for Sara [SC]'s ill health. Is tied down working on *Northern Worthies*. Has signed a contract with [Francis Edward] Bingley. Despite reverence for clergymen is glad he is a layman. "I long to see Derwent [DC], John Wordsworth, and Owen Lloyd, with an excellent living apiece, and I think Derwent has the best chance of the three, if *he play his cards well*—but there's the rub." Will eat Christmas dinner with Henry Rawson, brother of George Rawson. Has met, at the Rawsons, [Thomas Babington] Macaulay. "I can't say I was smitten with him at all – he does not seem to be a Liberal of the right, i. e. of the Xtian philanthropic sort." Mentions Westmorland election. Is to move lodgings from Bingley's to Mrs. [Elizabeth Green] Mason's. Discusses finances briefly. Mentions Hal [HNC], John [Taylor Coleridge], Aunt [Edith Fricker] Southey, Mrs. Bingley, the Flemings, and Miss [Dorothy] Wordsworth. Adds in postscript that he was introduced to the Rawsons by Edwin Atherstone [author of *The Fall of Nineveh*].

Quoted in full in *LHC*, pp. 148–151.

A96   A.L.i., Leeds, [n.d., 1–28 September 1833]. To: No. 1 Downshire Place, Hampstead, London. 4 pp. Endorsed on address face "Letter with Poems. 1833."

Says he has no news. Feels sorry for Sara [SC] and asks how Henry [HNC] is taking her illness. Has heard of the death of the younger [Jane K. Fox] of Mrs. [Sarah] Fox's two daughters. Has published the first volume of *Poems* [Leeds, 1833] and promises to send a copy to Mrs. STC and STC. "The second, containing Prometheus &c. will come out pretty soon" [there is no second volume]. Had a week-end excursion to Hawksworth, where he met Mr. [James] Brancker's brother-in-law and Mrs. [Sarah] Fox's brother, John Hustler. Has read a paper before the Leeds Philanthropic Society. Has dined with Mr. Nevins and his daughter. Mentions Mr. [Francis Edward] Bingley.

A97   A.L.s., Grasmere, Oct. 7, 1833. To: No. 1 Downshire Place, Hampstead, London. 7 pp. Endorsed on address face in HC's hand "Favoured by Mr Woollam." Endorsed on address face "Mr. W's blindness | Not a convert to Mr W: Sent in package | 1834?"

Reproaches Mrs. STC for reproaching him on his quitting Leeds and details his financial standing with [Francis Edward] Bingley. Speaks of the kindness and good character of [James] Brancker. His clothes are on the road from Leeds and his books will come later. Speaks of Herbert and Edith [Coleridge] and Dervy [Derwent Moultrie Coleridge]. Gives a delightful sketch of Sara [SC] as a child. "I am constructing an article for the next Blackwood, which I hope will bring in £10." [HC's next article in *Blackwood's* is "What is poetical description?," *Blackwood's Magazine*, April 1839.] Mentions Aunt Eliza [Fricker] and Aunt Martha [Fricker]. Disputes the charge [in the reviews of *Poems, Quarterly Review*, vol. xlix, 1833] that he is deeply indebted as a poet to Wordsworth. Mentions Dora [Wordsworth Quillinan], Miss [Dorothy] Wordsworth, and says that Mr. Wordsworth "is all but blind." Love to Sara [SC]. Mentions the [James] Gillmans, Miss Janetta Smith, Mrs. [Sarah] Fox.

Quoted in full in *LHC*, pp. 154–158.

A98   A.L.i., Grasmere, postmarked Aug. 4, 1834. To: No. 1 Downshire Place, Hampstead, Near London. 5 pp. Page 5 is crosswritten on
page 1. Endorsed on address face "His Father's death— | for his life
1834."

> From Miss [Sara] Hutchinson's report had expected the announcement in
> Henry [HNC]'s letter of STC's death. Cannot really mourn as he feels STC's
> presence too strongly. "When we mourn for the dead, we mourn but for our
> own bereavement." Regrets the pain he has caused STC and wishes he could
> resolve "that my future life would be such as my Father's Spirit may behold
> with satisfaction." Includes poem "The silent melody of thought that sings"
> [included in *Memoir* in DC, ed., HC, *Poems*, London, 1851]. Mentions SC,
> HNC, a sonnet "on Sara's short lived twins" ["Twins," DC, ed., HC, *Poems*,
> London, 1851], and "The Rydal Mount Family."

Quoted in full in *LHC*, pp. 165–167.
Quoted in part in *Memoir*, pp. cix–cx.

A99   A.L.i., Grasmere, May 16, 1835. To: No. 1 Downshire Place,
Hampstead, London. 4 pp. The first page of this letter is half crosswrit-
ten. Endorsed on address face "May 19, 1835 | Interesting to me about
the childs books."

> Discusses at length "the sweet one's sweet little book" [SC, *Pretty Lessons for
> Good Children*, 1834]. Mentions numerous other books of beast stories, but
> concludes, "But I dare say all this is very uninteresting to you, who were never
> fond of critical discussion, or discussion of any sort at any time, and least of
> all when you are anxious for information of a more household interest." Speaks
> of lending his copy of SC's book to Mrs. [Louise] Claude, with whom he is
> studying German. "It was always my dear Father's wish that I should acquire
> German though I know there are those who wish he had never learn'd it him-
> self." Speaks of reviews of STC's *Table Talk* [HNC, ed., *Specimens of the
> Table-Talk of the Late Samuel Taylor Coleridge*, 2 vols., London, 1835] in
> *Edinburgh* [*Review*, lxi, 129] and *Quarterly* [*Review*, xciii, 1]. Speaks of
> Southey's pension [granted by Peel in 1835]. Has dined with Mr. and Mrs.
> Wordsworth at Rydal. Mentions Miss [Sara] Hutchinson; Dora [Wordsworth
> Quillinan]; Miss [Dorothy] Wordsworth; William [Wordsworth, son]; John
> [Wordsworth], and his wife [Isabella Curwen] and daughter Jane. Discusses his
> wardrobe. Mentions [Francis Edward] Bingley. Says Mr. [James] Brancker
> promises to help him get copyright for *Poems* [Leeds, 1833]. Does not
> know what to write on for *Quarterly* article.

Quoted in full in *LHC*, pp. 172–175.

A100   A.L.s., Grasmere, Saturday – I don't know what, [September,
1835]. To: No. 1 Downshire Place, Hampstead, London. 4 pp. En-

dorsed by DC on address face "The Wordsworths | His wardrobe | The Quarterly."

Writes news of the Wordsworths. Mrs. Wordsworth is visiting her son and daughter-in-law. Mr. Wordsworth is well. Dora [Wordsworth Quillinan] is in good spirits and Miss [Dorothy] Wordsworth "is grown fat, but her memory is gone." Details condition of his clothing. "They say every one has a pet part of their body – and I confess, if I could be conceited of any thing about my ugly little carcase – it would be of my little feet. At least they prove that I am not stunted or runted, that I am as big as ever Nature intended me to be." Refers to HNC's review of *Worthies* in *Quarterly Review* [liv, September 1835]. "If he had been rather less brotherly, or cousinly, or call it what you will, it would have been all the better. He lets the cat out of the bag. It looks like a family concern." Refers to [Dr.] Thomas Arnold's *Thucydides* [which appeared in three volumes between 1830-1835]. Mentions Henry [HNC], Sara [SC], Emily [Frances Gillman Coleridge], Mrs. [Sarah] Fox, and Mrs. [Dinah] Fleming.

Quoted in full in *LHC*, pp. 176-178.

A101   A.L.i., Grasmere, August 21, [1836]. To: 21 Downshire Place, Hampstead, London. 5 pp. Page 5 is crosswritten on page 1.

Mentions his sore heel, blistered by ill-fitting shoes. Had breakfast with John Taylor Coleridge at Rydal, where things are "more in *status quo* than we would wish." Mentions Mr. and Mrs. Wordsworth, Dora [Wordsworth Quillinan], Mr. [Edward] Quillinan, Willy [Wordsworth], and John [Wordsworth], "(not the Rev. but Ap. Richard.)" Speaks of Southey's *The Doctor &c.* [London, 7 vols., 1834-1847]—"And yet, it is possible, that poor Uncle finds a relief in writing happy nonsense. He says he cannot now bear to write serious poetry." Generalizes on the paradox that humorous works are often written by men in great distress and mentions STC, Wordsworth, Southey, and Shakespeare. Comments on Wordsworth's last volume [William Wordsworth, *Yarrow Revisited, and Other Poems*, London, 1835]—"I think I perceive . . . a decided inclination to the playful, the elegant, and the beautiful; with an almost studied exclusion of the profound feeling and severe thought which characterized the offspring of his middle age." Hopes HNC and family are safe and well in Devonshire. Mentions Sara [SC], Herbert and Edith [Coleridge], and Mrs. Woollam. Remarks on getting accustomed to John Taylor Coleridge as a judge. Mentions Frank [Francis George Coleridge] and Derwent, Mary and Emily [Coleridge]. Intends to send article on Macbeth directly to [John Gibson] Lockhart [see "Schiller's Translations of Macbeth," DC, ed., HC, *Poems*, London, 1851]. Sends news of Mr. and Mrs. Parry, Mr. [James] Brancker, and Mr. [John] Dawes. Asks to be remembered to Mr. and Mrs. [James] Gillman.

Quoted in full in *LHC*, pp. 195-197.

A102   A.L.i., Rotha Some place – Oct. 28, [1836]. To: Downshire

Place, Hampstead, London. 4 pp.

Mentions the Judge [John Taylor Coleridge] and Henry [HNC]. Has begun an introduction for a second edition of STC's *Biographia Literaria* [HNC and SC, eds., STC, *Biographia Literaria*, 2 vols., London, 1847], but "I do think, that an introduction from the 'Rev. Derwent Coleridge, M. A., Head Master of Helston School, etc., etc., etc.,' would have more weight than plain Hartley Coleridge." Encloses a poem for possible inclusion in the edition [the sonnet, much altered, is published as "To S. T. Coleridge," DC, ed., HC, *Poems*, London, 1851]. Mentions Mrs. Woollam, Katty Woollam, Mrs. [Louise] Claude, Owen Lloyd, his clothes, Mrs. [Dinah] Fleming, and Paddock [Mrs. Fleming's youngest granddaughter]. Says he has nearly finished "a volume of Sonnets on Scripture Subjects" [not published until DC, ed., HC, *Poems*, London, 1851]. "My Essays . . . would make at least two Octavos" [DC, ed., HC, *Essays and Marginalia*, 2 vols., London, 1851]. Mentions his "Mince Pie" [*Blackwood's Magazine*, February 1828]. "I am provoked that you should be tormented by this evocation of evil spirits by D[e] Q[uincey], [Joseph] Cottle, [Edward Thomas] Allsop, and Co.," Mentions Joanna [Hutchinson], Dora [Wordsworth Quillinan], Sir C[harles] Bell, Sir B[enjamin] Brodie, and Cuthbert [Southey].

Quoted in full in *LHC*, pp. 198–201.

A103 A.L.s., Grasmere, Nov. 6, 1836. To: Hampstead, London. 3 pp. Endorsed on the address face in HC's hand "Favoured by Mrs Woollam." Note on address face "1836 Alsop' book."

Speaks of visit to Rydal. "I do not now see Miss [Dorothy] Wordsworth, but I hear her, which I had rather not, for to be anywise witness to distress one cannot relieve is unprofitable pain." Mentions bad weather, sickness, Mrs. [Jane Moss] Brancker. Says Mr. [James] Brancker has been a father to Mrs. [Louise] Claude's children. "Perhaps I have some knowledge of what it is practically to be without a father." Condemns Allsop [Edward Thomas Allsop, *Letters, Conversations and Recollections of S. T. Coleridge*, 1836] in round terms. "But I owe Master Allsop a licking. To be sure, he has the excuse of idiocy, which De. Q[uincey] could not plead." Promises to retaliate in print for a direct attack in Allsop "upon my cousins, the Judge [John Taylor Coleridge] and the Bishop [William Hart Coleridge], and an implied one on my Uncle [Robert Southey] and Mr. Wordsworth. I cannot undo what is done, but I think it incumbent upon me to shew that I do feel for the honour of my family and my friends, and it is only prudent to let the bags know that we are not to be st[ung] with impunity." Says his German is improving. Mentions Mr. and Mrs. Woollam and Sara and Henry [SC and HNC]. Signs the letter with the Greek letters for "Snouderumpus-son" ["Snouderumpus" was Hartley's nickname for Mrs. STC].

Quoted in full in *LHC*, pp. 202–204.

A104 A.L.s., Grasmere, Dec. 26, 1836. To: Downshire Place, Hampstead, London. 4 pp. Note on seal face "Came in this state to Highgate. | T. H. Dunn."

Thanks Mrs. STC for parcel and is cheered by note from Sara [SC]. Says the severe winter has been hard on old people like Mr. [John] Dawes. Intends to keep Christmas day, "Christmas day, *de jure*, being Sunday," with Mr. [James] Brancker. Speaks of his clothes. Acknowledges "Remains" [HNC, ed., *Samuel Taylor Coleridge, Literary Remains*, vols. i, ii, 1836; vols. iii, iv, 1838]. "I am, in the whole greatly pleased with them. . . . Some of the marginal notes can barely be intelligible to any but those who are familiar with the books in which they were written, and a few contain certain opinions not strictly consonant with my father's later judgement. But Henry has performed a laborious task, with infinite care, industry, and skilfulness." Plans an essay on STC "as a Poet, a Critic, and a literary Man" [fragments published in *PMLA*, December 1931]. Returns to the problem of clothes. Sends love to Sara [SC] and HNC. Mentions the Parrys, Frank [Francis George Coleridge]'s and Edward [Coleridge]'s children, the late Miss [Sara] Hutchinson, Dinah and Mrs. [Dinah] Fleming. Adds that he has been invited by James Spedding to contribute to a memorial volume [ed. Lord Northampton, *The Tribute*, 1837] for the family of Edward Smedley. Has had a previous letter on the subject [see B233]. Intends to send some translations [but never does]. Mentions Mrs. [Louise] Claude, Aunt [Frances Taylor] Coleridge, Uncle S[outhey], Mr. Wordsworth, Derwent [DC], and Mary [Pridham Coleridge].

Quoted in full in *LHC*, pp. 204–207.

A105 A.L.s., Grasmere, Jan. 13, 1838. To: No. 10 Chester Place, Regent's Park, London. 4 pp.

Discusses his clothes, which he finds adequate. Says Mr. Wordsworth's eyes are improved. Sends news of John Wordsworth. There is a new master in Ambleside, Monsieur Galippe. "I cannot thoroughly understand the principle on which so many of the affluent entrust their sons, and still more their daughters, to Foreigners." Mentions Robert Southey's *Voyage to Moscow* [London, 1813]. Speaks of Aunt [Edith Fricker Southey]'s "melancholy close" [16 November 1837]—"Never knew I a Being – in whom a pure and benevolent Spirit was so little joyous." Says he has "on the anvil" two or more volumes of essays, a volume of sonnets, two or three articles, and "Prometheus." "I do not think it would have been possible for my father to have continued Christabel, had his health been ever so joyous, and the reception of the poem ever so encouraging. . . . I never knew a work, in which there was any continuity at all, that was succssfully continued." Asks for clarification from Hal [HNC] on the copyright of *Biographia Borealis*. Mentions Mrs. [Eleanor] Richardson and baby, Mrs. [James] Greenwood, Kate [Southey], Mr. [John] Dawes, Mr. Wordsworth, Mr. [Thomas] Poole, Mr. [James] Brancker, Aunt Edward [Anne Bowden Coleridge], Uncle Edward [Coleridge], Mary [Pridham Coleridge] and Derwent [DC].

Quoted in full in *LHC*, pp. 218–221.

A106 A.L.i., Sedbergh, May 25, 1838. To: 10 Chester Place, Regent's Park, London. 4 pp.

Offers a number of excuses for not writing. Talks at length about his cold. Says he will write Henry [HNC] about STC's books when he feels better. Mr. [the Rev. Isaac] Green "could not be chosen Head–master – The school is in the gift of John's Col[lege] Cam[bridge]." Speaks of the deceased Mr. Wilkinson [the master whose place HC is filling], who has left a widow and eight children. Sends regrets on Sara [SC]'s ill health and comments on the difficult pregnancy of Mrs. [Isaac] Green. Speaks of clothing needs. Regrets death of Mary [Pridham Coleridge]'s mother. Love to Sara [SC], Henry [HNC], and Kate [Southey]. Mentions Bertha [Southey Hill], and Uncle [Robert Southey] and Herbert [Coleridge].

Quoted in full in *LHC*, 222–224.

A107 A.L.i., Rydal Mount, March 13, 1840. To: No. 10 Chester Place, Regent's Park, London. 4 pp.

Intends to turn over to Mrs. STC his payment from [Edward] Moxon [for *The Dramatic Works of Massinger and Ford*, London, 1840]. Feels his work on *Massinger and Ford* ends too abruptly; had made notes for more, but was rushed. Discusses the state of his clothing and mentions Mrs. [Eleanor] Richardson. "Mr. Barron Field (a friend of Lamb) is at Mr. Wordsworths," as are Miss Joanna Hutchinson, H[erbert] Hill and Whately. Mentions Derwent [DC] and his wife [Mary Pridham Coleridge]. Sadly misses Mrs. [Louise] Claude, who has left for good. Grasmere is not itself without Mrs. Carter and Mrs. [Sarah] Fox. Mrs. [James] Brancker is mortally ill. Wishes to proceed on his essay on STC [fragments published in *PMLA*, December 1931].

A108 A.L., Knabbe [Cottage, Rydal], August 18, 1841. To: No. 10 Chester Place, Regent's Park, London. 7 pp.

Is up early to write and "the cool light on the hills gleams silvery through the bridal veil of mist." There is to be a wedding in Rydal between Miss Roughsedge, a friend of Dora Wordsworth Quillinan's, and the Rev. E. Hornby. Has written to [Edward] Moxon but has not yet had a reply. John Cross, the Leeds bookseller, is selling HC's *Poems* [Leeds, 1833] with a new label and title page "to avoid the awkward appearance of Vol. 1, when no Vol. 2 was forthcoming." [James] Brancker and [Thomas] Troughton and Mrs. Nicholson [Ambleside booksellers] have ordered copies of *Poems*. Would Mrs. STC care to buy the rest from [John] Cross? Mrs. [Jane Moss] Brancker has died and is much lamented by Mr. [James] Brancker in his own quiet way. Owen [Lloyd] has also died. "Seldom have I known a man so generally lamented." Mentions Mr.

and Mrs. [Isaac] Green; Bertha [Southey Hill], Herbert, and Baby Hill; Dr. and Mrs. [William] Fell; Mary [Pridham Coleridge]; Derwent Jun. [Moultrie Coleridge]; and Herby [Herbert Coleridge]. A woman was injured in front of Nab Cottage when her "car" turned over, and she has been confined at Nab for a fortnight. Mr. [James] Brancker's Ambleside home, Croft Lodge, is for sale. Sends news of the Claude family and the Briggs family. Mentions Miss Harden and her spouse, Mr. Barker, who "is 6.5 in height, uglier if possible than your humble servant – at least on a much larger scale." "Mrs. Wordsworth entered her seventy second year on Monday" and is well. "Miss [Emmeline] Fisher, the young Poetess, is at Rydal Mount." Asks for a copy of Sara [SC]'s *Phantasmion* [London, 1837] and sends Mrs. [Eleanor] Richardson's love. Adds that he has seen Mr. Kennard, "uncle to Papa's Godson [Adam Steinmetz Kennard, son of John Kennard] to whom he wrote that beautiful letter" [First published as "Address to A Godchild, *Saturday Magazine*, No. 138, 30 August 1834, p. 78; "Letter to a godchild," HNC, ed., STC, *The Literary Remains of Samuel Taylor Coleridge*, London, 1836–1839]. Has dined with Mr. Brians, whose "brother-in-law, a Clergyman, seems the most intelligent Coleridgian I have ever met." Mentions [Richard] Townsend and Mr. Carter. Signed "Your truly affectionate Brat."

A109   A.L.s., [Nab Cottage, Rydal], April 13, 1842. To: [No. 10 Chester Place, Regent's Park, London]. 4 pp.

Has just recovered from a long series of winter colds. Mentions [Dr. William] Fell and Bertha [Southey Hill]. "No Coleridge, having attained maturity, has died within the last thirty years but at a ripe age – for even our dear Father, could not be call'd a short lived man." Asks Mrs. STC to thank Sara [SC] for the Phantasmion [SC, *Phantasmion*, London, 1837], which he has given to Mrs. [James] Greenwood. Has lent his own copy to Miss Taylor, who was "much pleased with it." "I wonder that it is so grudgingly praised in certain quarters. But they certainly are not liberal of praise – though I have no right to complain, as I am told." Intends to have his copy of Burton's *Anatomy of Melancholy* [from STC's library] put "into decent attire." Fanny [a former servant of the Wordsworths'] has been widowed recently. Mentions Mrs. [Eleanor] Richardson, Derwent [DC] and Mary [Pridham Coleridge], John Wordsworth and family, Kate [Southey], the [Herbert] Hills, Katey [Hill], and Owen Lloyd. [Edward] Moxon has declined to publish a volume of poems, but "will be glad of Essays."

A110   A.L.s., Ambleside, May 7, 1842, postmarked June 8, 1842. To: No. 10 Chester Place, Regent's Park, London. 3 pp.

Intends to "send [Edward] Moxon a larger parcel of essays soon; and then await his ultimatum." Speaks of "trowzers," his washing bill, and Mrs. Wordsworth. Asks about Derwent Jun. [Derwent Moultrie Coleridge]'s fractured leg. Assures Mrs. STC of his sympathy for her: "I have thought more of you than of the actual sufferers [SC and HNC]. That for a time I forgot you, at least that your image was at one time no very welcome visitor in my memory's chambers, is most true. But think not it is so now. Grey hairs have brought me, if not wisdom and reflection, at least retrospection." Says he dreams almost nightly of her or Derwent [DC]. Says Bertha and Herbert [Hill] are as well as can be expected and adds "Their Chicks!—Oh that you could see the Darlings. It would rejoice your old heart."

Quoted in full in *LHC*, pp. 254–255.

A111 A.L., Bertha's Thursday Night, [January 1843]. To: No. 10 Chester Place, Regent's Park, London. 4 pp. Endorsed on address face by Mrs. STC "From Bertha's just about the time of our great loss." Endorsed by SC "On the Death of dear Fanny Patteson."

Has received news from Mary [Pridham Coleridge] of the terminal illness of Lady [Frances Duke Coleridge] Patteson. "Now sickness reduces her to the common condition of humanity." Expects to complete within a few days the volume for [Edward] Moxon [not published during HC's lifetime]. Speaks of Dora [Wordsworth Quillinan]'s fortitude in the face of her ill health. Includes twelve lines on Bertha [Southy Hill]'s three children: "The prattling tongue – and two meek silent faces" [unpublished]. Asks if anything he could write would amuse "*him*" [HNC]. Mentions SC's essay on the disadvantages of beauty [unpublished], and says he could write "with more and better knowledge on the disadvantages of cleverness." Says Mr. [James] Brancker has "wooed and won a Miss Simmons." [This is the second Mrs. Brancker; the first was Jane Moss.] Mentions Mr. Wordsworth, Mrs. I[saac] Green, and Rotha Quillinan.

A112 A.L.i., Knabbe [Cottage, Rydal], Jan. 28, postmarked 1843. To: No. 10 Chester Place, Regent's Park, London. 4 pp. With note on inside of accompanying envelope. Endorsed on address face "On the Death of Dear Henry!"

In the main a letter of condolence to Mrs. STC and SC on the death of HNC [26 January 1843]. Hopes SC's children "though they must needs increase her anxiety, . . . will prevent her sinking into herself in moody retrospect." Includes ll. 9–12 from "The Fourth Birthday" [DC, ed., HC, *Poems*, London, 1851], written to Edward Green. Asks about SC's children, Herbert and Edith [Coleridge]. Mentions Mary [Pridham Coleridge], Mrs. Wordsworth, Mr. and Mrs. [Isaac] Green, Miss [Emily] Trevenen, Derwent [Moultrie Coleridge], and Derwent [DC]. Adds a note on the [Herbert] Hills, Herby, Kate, and Bertha [Southey Hill], Aunt [Mary Fricker] Lovell, Cuthbert [Southey] and his wife.

Quoted in full in *LHC*, 259–261.

A113 A.L., Knabbe [Cottage, Rydal], May 15, Going to rain, postmarked 1843. To: No. 10 Chester Place, Regent's Park, London. 8 pp. Letter and sheet folded to form envelope have narrow black borders. Endorsed on address face "very interesting | after his visit to | Keswick and the | Funeral of his—— | beloved Uncle–R Southey."

Discusses his wardrobe. Speaks of Sara's Phantasmion [SC, *Phantasmion*, London, 1837], "I have been a little mortified at the dullness of some folks with regard to Phantasmion, which I think, sets her [SC] above all female writers of the age – except Joanna Baillie." The news from Keswick is not good. Missed the funeral [Robert Southey died 21 March 1843] but is not really sorry. "It would have been painful to see persons by the grave side equally related and equally dear to the departed, who would not so much as speak to each other" [Southey's second marriage, to Caroline Bowles on 4 June 1839, occasioned a bitter family quarrel]. Mentions Aunt [Mary Fricker] Lovell, Kate [Southey], Cuthbert [Southey] and describes Cuthbert's wife, whom he much admires. Sends news of Mrs. Joshua [Mary Calvert Stanger], Mr. Thomas Spedding, Miss Dinglinson, Miss [Eliza?] Lynn, Mr. [James] Lynn, William Denton, Sara Denton, Margaret Muckle, [Joshua] Stanger, Edith [Coleridge], Mrs. Isaac Green, John and [Isabella Curwen] Wordsworth, Mr. Wordsworth, Dora [Wordsworth Quillinan], Miss [Isabella] Fenwick, and Mrs. [Eleanor] Richardson. Love to Sara [SC], Edith [Coleridge], and the Judge [John Taylor Coleridge]. Signed "I am your plague."

Quoted in full in *LHC*, pp. 263–266.

A114 A.L.i., Ambleside, Nab [Cottage, Rydal] Feast of Crispian, October 25, 1843. To: No. 10 Chester Place, Regent's Park, London. 5 pp.

Hopes the sovereign his mother sent Mrs. [Eleanor] Richardson has not been lost and will come with the expected parcel. Speaks of Sara's essay "On Rationalism" [HNC, ed., STC, *Aids to Reflection*, London, 1843. Volume II, Appendix C., pp. 335–556]. The essay "is a wonder. I say not a wonder of a woman's work—where lives the man that could have written it? None in Great Britain since our Father died. Poor Henry [HNC] was perfectly right in saying that she inherited more of her father, than either of us; and that not only in the amount but in the quality of her powers." Comments on the probable questionable reception of the essay, "to a large portion both of the high and low church the very word Reason is so terribly odious, that I verily suspect that they think it was invented by Tom Paine." Speaks at some length of his reunion with Derwent [DC] [their first meeting since 1822]. "The quantity of French phrases wherewith he tambours his conversation would have made Papa blaspheme outright without reverence to the cloth." Praises Derwent as a clergyman and regrets their visit was so brief. Supposes [Edward] Moxon wants more material to make a volume. Wishes he could get out a volume of sonnets before the New Year. Mentions Herbert [Coleridge], Dervy Junior [Derwent Moultrie Coleridge], Christabel Rosa [Coleridge], Fanny [Frances Coleridge Patteson], [William Lisle] Bowles, Mr. [John] Dawes, Mr. Marsden, "the Rydal family," Mrs.

B[enson] Harrison, Herbert White, Mrs. [Eleanor] R[ichardson], Miss S[ara] Briggs, Juliet Fox, Sarah Fox, Joanna [Hutchinson] and Mrs. W[ordsworth]. Adds Mr. and Mrs. J[ohn] Wordsworth have gone off this cold morning for Listian.

Quoted in full in *LHC*, pp. 267–269.

A115 A.L., [Nab Cottage, Rydal], [n.d., 1843]. To: [No. 10 Chester Place, Regent's Park, London]. 4 pp. Endorsed at end by Mrs. STC "1843."

Thanks Mrs. STC for the parcel she has sent him and discusses the clothing it contained. The coat required letting out, though "I am not, however, quite a Falstaff yet." Is obliged to Dr. Jennings "for the interest he appears to take in me" and does not mind Dr. Jennings' advice. "I do not take a certain degree of bluntness amiss – if it is not mingled with contempt, the appearance of which made me very refractory to the well meant rebukes of Mrs. [James] Gillman." Mentions the [William] Richardsons, Mr. Crabbe, and Miss Barker. Is very worried about the health of Mrs. STC, Sara [SC], and Derwent [DC]. Mr. Wordsworth is well, and the [Edward] Quillinans are remaining over the winter.

A116 A.L. (inc.), Rydal, Jan 14 or 15, 1844. To: No. 10 Chester Place, Regent's Park, London. 4 pp.

Thanks Mrs. STC for Edith [Coleridge]'s drawing of a cat and mentions "The Raffaelle of Cats," [Gottfried] Mind [1768–1814]. [This drawing and several others by Edith Coleridge are in the Humanities Research Center, The University of Texas at Austin.] Describes a gift from Mrs. [Edith Southey] Warter, [Doctoris Felicis Hemmerlini, *Opuscula et Tractus*, Strassburg, 1493–1500] from the library of Robert Southey. Details the condition of his clothing and mentions Mrs. [Eleanor] Richardson, [William] Fell, and Mr. [James] and Miss Greenwood. Cannot believe "Miss [Harriet] Martineau's tale of Mesmerism," yet "Would that our dear Sara [SC] could be mesmerised to health." [SC turned, for a time, to mesmerism as a possible cure for the breast cancer which eventually killed her.] Mentions STC, Mrs. [James] Gillman, Miss Brent, and Miss Penelope Brice of Asholt. Mr. [John] Dawes is now over eighty. "He is still cheerful and Kind as ever – a stout Whig and a hearty abuser of Bishops and Puseyism, of which you may suppose he knows very little." Has read Dr. [Thomas] Arnold's Life [Arthur Penrhyn Stanley, *The Life of Dr. Arnold*, London, 1844]. "Highly as I always thought of him, I think much more highly of him now." Mrs. Fletcher has given Mrs. [Thomas] Arnold a copy of HC's "On the Late Dr. Arnold" [DC, ed., HC, *Poems*, London, 1851]. Mentions his defense of Wordsworth in a newspaper [this defense is unidentified], three proposed monuments to Southey, and Edward [Southey].

Quoted in full in *LHC*, pp. 270–272.

A117   A.L.s., Nab [Cottage, Rydal], Feb. 7, 1844. To: No. 10 Chester Place, Regent's Park, London. 9 pp., continued on inside of accompanying envelope.

Is sorry about SC's psoriasis. Says DC "has no fault but a certain measure of, I will not call it presumption but assumption, probably owing in part to his habits of command and a little to the worship universally paid to him – which is greater than either his father, or W[ordsworth] or S[outhey] obtained at his age." Mentions [John] Moultrie's address to DC [in Book III of John Moultrie, *The Dream of Life*, London, 1843]. Speaks of Herby and his sister [Herbert and Edith Coleridge]. Is not fond of bluestockings. "So very bad my taste, that I preferred Jane Butler to the then Miss Poole, who – I see as Mrs. John Sandford—is a mighty authoress. . . . Her sentiments are good enough, but her style is inflated and American." Mentions John Priorley and the poetess Miss Shelton. Comments on DC's manners. Says his bust has been taken at the request of Cornelius Nicholson. [There is no record of this bust.] Feels that he does not resemble STC at all. "Sara is the inheritrix of his mind and his genius. Neither Derwent nor I have much more than the family cleverness." Mentions his amanuensis, Sara Briggs. Asks if he may spare Sara's eyes by correcting the sheets for the Selections [STC, *Poems*, London, 1844?]. Mentions the difficulties of being nearsighted, SC's sleeplessness, and Kate [Southey]'s trials. Sends news of Mr. Wordsworth, Mrs. Wordsworth, Dora [Wordsworth Quillinan], and Mr. [Edward] Quillinan, whom he likes hugely. Cannot understand why they call little Dora Hill [daughter of Herbert and Bertha Southey Hill] Georgina.

Quoted in full in *LHC*, pp. 273–276.

A118   A.L.i., Ambleside, postmarked May 30, 1844. To: No. 10 Chester Place, Regent's Park, London. 4 pp. Envelope is endorsed on seal face by SC "Full of personality goodnatured as to | particular persons caustic as to generall reflections."

Is sending Mrs. STC a package by Miss [Isabella] Fenwick. Mrs. [Eleanor] Richardson is very ill. Appreciates the newspapers, the *Spectator* and the *Record*, Mrs. STC has sent. Mentions Kate [Southey]. Has heard Cuthburt [Southey] is a good clergyman. "This I have learned from sources on which I can depend—for as for what is said to parents about their children or to children about their parents . . . it is generally either flattery or malice – often the latter under the guise of the former." Asks about the outcome of the booksale [of Robert Southey's library]. Mentions "My excellent Quaker Friend Crosfield," Derwent [DC], Errol Hill, the Wordsworths, and Dora [Wordsworth Quillinan]. Speaks of Derwent [Moultrie Coleridge] and Herbert [Coleridge]. "Whether they will be poets or not is little matter. I'm glad Herbert [has] taken to Chemistry." [Herbert Coleridge became a distinguished philologist.] Mentions Sara [SC].

A119   A.L.i., Friend Fell's [Ambleside], August 19, 1844. To: [No. 10 Chester Place, Regent's Park, London]. 4 pp.

Has received the parcel of clothes and comments on the shirts. Has visited Appleby and intends to write Sara [SC] all about it. Spends a page and a half on what he would have written to Sara, had he written her. Mentions the Rev. John Richardson and his pretty wife; their children, Edith and Charley Henry [Richardson]; armor belonging to George Clifford, Earl of Cumberland; his life of Lady Anne Clifford; the chapel which has been ruined by remodeling; the vicar and his wife; "a pretty little poetess, whose proof sheets I helped to correct, who is well and wealthily married to Mrs. J[ohn] Richardson's brother"; and "a sweet river place . . . call'd the Vale of Tempe, to the sore perplexity of an unclassical Country Town." Goes into detail on the death of Miss [Sara] Briggs, his amanuensis. A post mortem by Dr. [John] Davy and [Dr. William] Fell revealed the brain tumor which caused her death. HC is much distressed by the loss of his young friend. Remarks on the health of Mr. [John] Dawes and on the feminine nature, mentioning Madame de Staël. Mentions Mr. Wordsworth; "his brother the Doctor" [John Wordsworth]; Dora [Wordsworth Quillinan]; John and Isabella Wordsworth; Mrs. Wordsworth; Mr. [Edward] Moxon; Cuthbert [Southey]; Mr. [James] Brancker; Herbert [Coleridge]; and Sarah, Elizabeth, and Thomas Hutchinson.

A120   A.L.s. (inc.), Ambleside, postmarked Jan. 15, 1845. To: No. 10 Chester Place, Regent's Park, London. 2 pp.

Has received Derwent [DC]'s pamphlet [?] from Mary [Pridham Coleridge]. Mentions Herbert [Coleridge], Edith [Coleridge], and Sara [SC]. "I will not say much about the Essays, but be hopeful – I must try to make a far better year of 1845 than any since I left Leeds." "A cool Gentleman of the name of Cleksel [?], whom I never saw or heard of, but who states he is an ardent admirer of my Father's" wishes HC to send him letters, records of conversations, and recollections of STC's for publication in the Durham University Magazine. "I have given him his quietus with civil brevity, for I don't like University Mags that pay nothing. A Lady, Mrs. Mil[ner], wife to the Vicar of Appleby made a somewhat similar request but with perfect delicacy, that she might print my father's letters to his god–son in the Christian Mother's Mag. which she edits. I could see no objection and sent her some verses for she is good woman."

A121   A.L.s., [Nab Cottage, Rydal], May 15, [1845]. To: [No. 10 Chester Place, Regent's Park, London]. 7 pp. Endorsed on back of last page "Verses on ——— | Dr. Arnold – 1847? - | (note to poem)."

Thanks Mrs. STC for shirt and spoon brought by Miss [Isabella] Fenwick. Discusses domestic arrangements with Mrs. [Eleanor] Richardson, Robinson [a tradesman], and Mrs. Wordsworth. Promises to send verses on Dr. [Thomas] Arnold ["On the Late Dr. Arnold," DC, ed., HC, *Poems*, London, 1851] and admires the biography [Arthur Penrhyn Stanley, *The Life of Dr. Thomas Arnold*, London, 1844]. Mrs. Arnold's "eldest Son [Matthew Arnold] has obtained a fellowship – at the same election [March 1845] and college [Oriel] as the Judge [John Taylor Coleridge]'s Son [Henry James Coleridge]." Speaks of the character and death of Mr. [James] Greenwood. Dr. and Mrs. Briggs's youngest daughter "has died in a state approaching to mental alienation," leaving six children, the youngest of whom has been brought to the Briggses by "its Aunt Mary Jane [Briggs] [see B30]." Talks of D. [DC] and M[ary Pridham Coleridge] and the christening of their "Thampet" [Henry Nelson Praed Coleridge, b./d. 1845]. Identifies his essays in *Janus* as "Antiquity," "Pins," and "Preface – which may serve." Mentions Aubrey de Vere, Sara [SC], Edith [Coleridge] and Herbert [Coleridge].

Quoted in full in *LHC*, pp. 279–281.

A122 A.L.i., [Nab Cottage, Rydal], [n.d., late summer, 1845]. To: [No. 10 Chester Place, Regent's Park, London]. 4 pp. The letter bears no date or address of any kind. It is the last known letter from Hartley to his mother.

Hopes the arrangement of his bills is not troublesome to Mrs. STC and Mrs. Wordsworth. Mentions the daguerreotype likeness in which he looks like an old man of eighty. [This daguerreotype is in the Humanities Research Center, The University of Texas at Austin.] Says he will be very happy to meet Aubrey de Vere [SC's friend]. Mr. [John] Dawes has died [August 1845] leaving no will. He gave £500 to Mrs. [Louise] Claude's only son [Louis] before he died. His funeral was largely attended. "In fact, I never saw so many self invited attendants at any funeral except Owen Lloyd's. He was much beloved." Mentions the death of "my little Nephew" [Henry Nelson Praed Coleridge]. "There is a great party to night to celebrate the majority of Mr. M. B. Harrison [son of Benson Harrison and Dorothy Wordsworth Harrison], eldest son of my some time flame, *Chucky Doro*. Mr. Wordsworth and Miss [Harriet] Martineau are to be there." Mentions Sara [SC].

Quoted in full in *LHC*, pp. 281–282.

A123 A.L.i., [n.p.], [n.d., possibly as early as 1833, but the handwriting appears to be that of a much later period]. To: No. 10 Chester Place, Regent's Park, London?]. 2 pp. A fragment of a longer letter.

Complete fragment reads "the family so kindly assembled. How awfully affecting yet how beautiful must have been your sacramental communion. . I am glad the Biographia [*Borealis; or, Lives of the Distinguished Northerns*, Leeds, 1833] pleases Dr. James [Gillman?]. I happened to be looking it over when

91

your letter arrived – I cannot think so highly of it, and was amazed at the awful array of typographical errors which [Francis Edward] Bingley would not let me correct or advertise in an errata. Considering how discrepant some opinions must be to his, I consider the compliment great, *if* – it was not intended to please you. One merit the book has – and that I divide between Papa's exhortations and Mr. [John] Dawes' instructions – it is good English. Whatever you may think of the sentiments they were sincere at the time. I could alter the one sincerely now—but should another Edition ever be called for, I would expunge many expressions, some that savour of levity, and others – really censurable for over vehemence. But dear Mammy I haven't left space for more than H.C."

MRS. S. T. COLERIDGE
AND SARA COLERIDGE

A124 A.L.s., postmarked Leeds, No. 19, 1832. To: Downshire Place, Hampstead, London. 3 pp. Endorsed on address face "after the 2nd number of the Worthies 1832."

Has had a bad cold. Is sorry about Sara [SC]'s health, "but it is a sad thing that she should have such Frickerish nerves. . . . My own nerves from seventeen till after twenty were dreadfully weak, in fact I was a martyr to the Blue Devils in my youth." Has just finished "The Lives of Lady Anne Clifford, Roger Ascham, Bishop [John] Fisher, [William] Mason, Sir Richard Arkwright. Tomorrow, God willing, the first sheet of Prometheus will be put to press with a dedicatory sonnet to my Father" ["Prometheus" was first published in DC, ed., HC, *Poems*, 2 vols., London, 1851. The "Dedicatory Sonnet" was published in *Poems*, Leeds, 1833]. Mentions Hal [HNC], Sara [SC] and their children.

Quoted in full in *LHC*, pp. 147–148.

A125 A.L., Grasmere, Jan. 18, 1836. Raining Cats and Dogs. To: No 27. Downshire Hill, Hampstead, Middlesex, Europe. 4 pp. Endorsed on address face "Brancker | the copyright 1836."

Nearly faints, fearing something has happened to Mrs. STC or SC, when he received Henry [HNC]'s letter with black seal and edges [HNC's father, Colonel James Coleridge, died 10 January 1836]. "Independent of the judgement to come, death seems to me at the worst a bore, like the breaking up of a merry Saturday night's party by the uninvited intrusion of the Sabbath, and to the great majority of mankind, the best thing that could happen." Will send details of arrangements with Mrs. Parry's parcel or "with the article for the Q[*uarterly*

Review] which, D. V. shall be ready in three weeks at the farthest" [see "Schiller's Translations of Macbeth," DC, ed., HC, *Poems*, London, 1851]. Writes with joy that "by the kind offices of my excellent, though radical friend [James] Brancker, I am quite disentangled from all engagements with [Francis Edward] Bingley." Discusses at length Mr. Brancker's political differences from the rest of the Branckers and the parallels between Brancker's position and his own. Says that though STC "could not have much admired little Johnny Russell's unprecedented piece of stupidity and blundering, call'd 'the Reform Bill,' " he [STC] did admit the necessity of reform. Describes at length the kindness of [James] Brancker in freeing him from Bingley. Mentions Mrs. [Jane Moss] Brancker and Lady [Margaret Willes] Beaumont. Speaks of Uncle [Robert Southey]'s always being held up to him as an example. "It is an extraordinary proof of the loveliness of Southey's character, that though his name was rife in every objurgation and every admonition I received, I never could help but love him." Sends news of Rydal. Dora [Wordsworth Quillinan] and Miss [Dorothy] W[ordsworth] are much the same. Defends Wordsworth's last volume [William Wordsworth, *Yarrow Revisited and Other Poems*, London, 1835] against Derwent [DC]'s charges of poverty and degeneracy, though he does wish Wordsworth "had not call'd poor old Lady Lonsdale a *Nymph* ["Lines written in the album of the countess of_____.," *Yarrow Revisited*, p. 237]. Speaks of Edith [Southey Warter] and her child [Edith Frances Warter]. "I cannot imagine that queen-like creature having any thing to do with clouts, nightcaps, and other unsightly and anti-aristocratic utensils which are entailed upon maternity in the lower and middle orders." Mentions Miss Senhouse, Squire Pocklington, Mrs. E. Carlton, the Revd. Bates, Miss North, the Misses White, Mr. [John] Dawes, and Giles, his tailor.

Quoted in full in *LHC*, pp. 182–187.

WILLIAM FELL

A126 A.L.s., Leeds, 16 October, [1832]. To: Ambleside, Westmorland. 5 pp. "Favoured by Mr. T[homas] Green".

Encloses "a copy of the first number of the Yorkshire Worthies" [containing the lives of Andrew Marvell, Dr. Richard Bentley, Thomas Lord Fairfax, and James Earl of Derby]. Expects the second number, containing "the lives of Anne Clifford, Countess of Pembroke, Roger Ascham, Bishop Fisher (these are all printed) Mason the Poet and Sir Richard Arkwright," should appear on the first of November. "I cannot say that Biography is just altogether my forte, for I dont at all excel in plain statement. Neither, in the haste with which the work is to be got out, is it possible to hunt out for original facts, or collate original documents, even were they accessible, which is far from being the case. Moreover there is nothing in the world so difficult as to write good plain prose, in a style which attracts no notice for itself, but sets of[f] the sense to the best possible advantage. For myself, I find it easier to write simply in verse than in prose. When I compare Southey's Biographical style with my own, I confess I am almost driven to plunge myself over head and ears in the slough of despond." Wordsworth and [Sam?] Archer would say "that magazine writing spoils a man for everything else." HC thinks "a good syle would do as well for a magazine as a bad one. The truth is, that simplicity is a great gift, and the imitation of simplicity is the worst of affectation." Speaks at length on the imitation of simplicity. "But here is no occasion to make this letter a translation of Cicero *de Oratore* interlarded with St Augustine's confessions." Is comfortable with the [Francis Edward] Bingleys, who have a new baby, "my fondness for babies making amends in the eyes of Mothers, for a multitude of sins." Knows few people in Leeds. Reports election news. Heard Mr. [Michael Thomas] Sadler speak. "I really cannot say that it at all came up to my preconceptions of Sadler as a high-minded philanthropist, and a philosophic politician." Sadler defended his opposition to the Reform Bill [and lost the election in December to Thomas Babington Macaulay by 1,596 votes to 1,984]. Has heard two women preach "and though I would not gladly [see] any woman I cared much about turn preacher, I do heartily rejoice in that perfect freedom which allows all to preach, and compels no one to listen." Mentions Mr. [James] Brancker, Herbert White, "Mrs. White, and Mrs. [Louise] Claude and her little ones." Will try to spend a week with the Fells at Christmas.

Quoted in full in *LHC*, pp. 144–146.

MRS. CHARLES [SARAH HUSTLER] FOX

A127 A.L.s./copy in unidentified hand, Grasmere, Feb. 21, 1832. To: Perran, near Truro, Cornwall. 4 pp.

Greets her as Dear Freundlin. "I know but two words of German, and I cannot dispose of them better than to give you one of them. Indeed, you are quite welcome to both, but the other being Der Teufel which means *Apollyon*, is not worthy of your acceptance." Freundlin is hers by twofold right. [She is a Quaker.] Engages in a bit of linguistic speculation and thanks her for her sweet letter. Had not known that Mary [Pridham Coleridge] was ill or he would have written Derwent [DC]. Has since had a few lines from Derwent. "Pray do persuade him to sacrifice beauty to legibility if he cannot unite the two – for the sake of my soul – for I am very apt to say naughty words when I am puzzled with an interesting letter. I am happy, however, that his spirits are relieved, of which the said letter gives satisfactory proof, not only by its microscopic caligraphy which denotes dry eyes and a steady hand, but by a P.S. in defense of the German Heresy of Polly – Homerism." Mentions [Friedrich August] Wolf, "a capital name to pun upon" [see A30], whose theories he intends to demolish in an article [?]. Is glad Derwent can think of such things and wishes Mary were out of her difficulties, "for there are cruel apprehensions that she may have to endure a mother's pains without a mother's joy." [No births are recorded between 1828 and 1835.] Should like to see his nephews [Derwent Moultrie Coleridge and Herbert Coleridge], of whom his mother [Mrs. STC] sends great reports, and hopes to have nieces soon. Mentions Juliet and Guinea Kitty [Fox], her mother [Mrs. William Hustler] and Dale-end [the Fox Ambleside home]. Describes the beautiful Grasmere scene. Mentions "Friend Samuel," and *The Winter's Wreath* [1828-1832] to which he has contributed a sonnet to Wordsworth ["There have been poets that in verse display"?]. Also mentions Mrs. Fox's husband [Charles] and Miss [Dorothy] W[ordsworth], who "is slowly convalescent." Would send her his copy of *Winter's Wreath*, but "I fear it would be like M[rs] Bow's letters from the Dead to the Living, which surely were not worth the price of postage." [The irrepressible Tom Brown, with whose works HC was familiar, published *Letters from the Dead to the Living* in 1702.]

A128 A.L. (inc.)/copy in the hand of Mary Pridham Coleridge, [Grasmere], 17th or 18th of January, [1836]. To: [n.p.]. 4 pp. Accompanied by a typed copy. See also A129.

Gracefully apologizes for not having written, quoting "Tom Brown the third's [Thomas Brown, 1663-1704] paraphrase of some Latin." Remembers well the miserable day she left Grasmere. Hopes to be in her vicinity, for he wishes to visit his brother [DC, who is at Helston, Cornwall] and his little ones [Derwent Moultrie and Emily Gillman Coleridge]. The passing years have taught him the value of family ties. He and Derwent were "perpetual quarrellers" in their boyhood. While others thought him a great tyrant he was in fact Derwent's slave. He was jealous of Derwent's accomplishments, looks, and bearing. "He had a ready, open, winning address–I was excessively clumsy, slow, and embarrassed —spoke and acted like one who has been conning a pompous speech which he has more than half-forgotten. He was never out of temper for he had no need. Smiles greeted him everywhere." Derwent even wrote "sweet and beautiful verses" before HC produced so much as a couplet worth preserving. "I did not love him the less for all this, but combined with a very strong tendency to admonition (which he will find useful in his pastoral office) it made me, at times, feel more pain than pleasure in his society." All this has now passed away, "for I have outlived the ambition of shining where he eclipsed me," and Derwent "now devotes his powers to nobler objects." When they meet, however, they must agree to a truce on politics and ecclesiastical establishments, for Derwent's opinions on those topics are quite set. The *Quarterly* article [HNC's review of *Biographia Borealis* in the *Quarterly Review*, liv, September 1835] has prompted [Francis Edward] Bingley to invite HC to continue the work, but Mrs. STC disapproves of his returning to Leeds, and he could not accept Bingley's terms, in any case. At HC's request [James] Brancker has secured his release from Bingley [see Appendix], and he is now free to find the best market he can for the second volume of *Poems* [none published].

A129 A.L.s. (inc.)/copy in the hand of Mary Pridham Coleridge, [n.p.], [n.d.]. To: Perran, near Truro, Cornwall. 2 pp. Although the typist (probably EHC) of the preceding letter treats A128 as a separate letter, it is more likely the first section of this letter. The fold of note paper on which A128 is copied bears the number 1; the fold on which A129 is copied bears the number 2.

Mentions the marriage of Miss Carlton to the Reverend Bates and the impending marriage of Miss Carlton's brother to Miss North. Has received a letter from his brother-in-law [HNC, see B102] announcing the death of his father [Colonel James Coleridge, 10 January 1836] and sending news of [SC], their mother [Mrs. STC] and the Brats [Edith and Herbert Coleridge]. Asks if she has seen Sara's second edition [SC, *Pretty Lessons in Verse, for Good Children*, London, 1835. Second Edition, with woodcuts]. The article "on Churchgoers" [?] will appear shortly. Kindest regards to her husband [Charles Fox] and love to Juliet [Fox] and Aline [?].

A130 A.L.s./copy in the hand of Mary Pridham Coleridge. According to the copyist, the original was postmarked Ambleside, Ap. 9, 1842–5 [1844]. To: [Perran, near Truro, Cornwall]. 4 pp.

In the geologic past, of which he professes ignorance, there was a long period of frost during which "the groanings, and moanings, and whinings of the Mastodons, Maegatherions, and other extinct monstrosities were congealed to silence." So it has been with him and he sends her "my first drop of thaw." There has been no real change in the scenery, but the mountains are not the same to him "as they were when you had your little boat on Grasmere Lake and could laugh at my awkwardness in handling the oars." Speaks of his changing attitude toward and conception of the physical world. "In riper youth I thought of them [mountains, snow, and ice] as Powers in all their beauty and all their ruggedness witnessing and authorizing a kindred power in myself. An imagination, that as it enabled me to make one beauty of all the uncountable beauties great and small that were asserting themselves around me. . . . might enable me not to create – for that is a word not applicable to any effluence of the human mind – but to generate a correspondent world in which the images derived from outer things should be not causes but emblems of the things within – and Love itself – a sacrament of that love divine which merges itself in its objects. Now the mountains are to me but mighty monuments – of what has been – and what might have been and might be yet had I living objects of love enough – but no matter." Wished she and Juliet [Fox] had been there yesterday to see the celebration of the Bard's 74th birthday [William Wordsworth was born 7 April 1770]. Three hundred little children were there. "I never saw the old Poet look so magnificent in his quietitude." There was fiddling and a dance of which not even William Penn would have disapproved. Will send her a Kendal *Mercury* containing some verses upon which he wants her opinion. Sends a sonnet, "Now the old trees are striving to be young, "[DC, ed., HC, *Poems*, London, 1851]. Kind remembrances to her husband [Charles Fox] and dearest love to Juliet [Fox].

Quoted in part in *New Poems*, p. 33.

MRS. JAMES [ANN] GILLMAN

A131   A.L.s., Knabbe [Cottage, Rydal], near Ambleside, Dec. 9, 1840.
To: Highgate, near London. 3 pp.

"Do not be surprised–The hand was once familiar to you – you have look'd on it, I flatter myself, with pleasure, e'en now, and though it can never again be look'd on with the same hope and happiness as heretofore, yet I trust, you will not turn away from it, when it assures you, that you and yours have not been forgotten though my gratitude has been silent for so many years." Speaks of the dark cloud over him, the deaths of STC and James Gillman, his own un-worthiness as an author, and his gratitude to the Gillmans. Mrs. STC often speaks of Mrs. Gillman, "but her last letters have told too much of her in-creasing infirmities. As if she had not enough trouble Derwent [DC]'s affairs come at the eleventh hour. I always thought he was prospering at Helston, and this reverse has almost brought tears from an eye unused to flow." [EHC notes "There must have been some obscurity in the way in which this movement of his brother's was communicated to Hartley. D.C. came to London from Corn-wall to better his fortunes."] Advice does more harm than good. "I believe I should myself have been a better and a happier man, had I been let alone." Mentions James [Gillman, son] and "my little Niece and Nephew" [Edith and Herbert Coleridge]. Reports on his twice teaching in the Sedbergh school. "I acquitted myself to the satisfaction of Masters and Pupils." Loves to teach but hates to enforce discipline. "How is my old Pupil Henry [Gillman, son]?"

Quoted in full in *LHC*, pp. 245–246.

THE REV. ISAAC GREEN

A132   A.L. (inc.) Lumber-room general, Grasmere, Sept. 26, 1836.
To: [Sedbergh]. 2 pp.

Thanks Green for the sermon he has sent and promises to do all he can for the good work Green proposes [rebuilding the chapel at Sedbergh?]. Mentions Mr. [Charles?] Kingsley. "Perhaps it would not be amiss to mention the cal-culation of Professor Lilienstein, a devout and erudite German, who demon-strated, as far back as 1820, to his own perfect satisfaction, that the Milennium is to commence in 1836." Discusses, in the remainder of the letter, the possibility of a millennium, Biblical prophecies of such an event, and the history of such predictions.

A133   A.L.s., Grasmere, Feb. 1, 1837. To: Sedbergh. 2 pp.

Doubts that his intended volume of sacred sonnets "will be much to the taste of the Clerical Reviewers." Feels that regular prayers for Parliament should be dropped lest people, seeing Parliament "getting if possible worse and worse . . . begin to doubt the efficacy of prayer *in toto*." Sends news that Mr. [James] Brancker intends to stand for Liverpool rather than Kendal, "but I do not think, between ourselves, that he really wishes for a seat in the Pandemonium at all." Mentions Green's sister-in-law and her son Daniel. Has had a dream that Mrs. Isaac [Green] is angry with him. Sends regards to Mrs. Isaac and love to [erased and written over in unknown hand, "Edward and the Fairy"]. Adds that he picked up a paper which fell from an Irish emigrant's pocket. The paper had "a cross and divers papistical, cabalistical characters – some words in Irish – Tempus venit in Latin – and these verses in English,

1605
It was tried, but did not thrive.
1837
We'll give the dogs a hoist towards Heaven."

A134   A.L.s., Grasmere, Good Friday—or rather Saturday—a fine night, [n.d., April 1838?]. To: Sedbergh. 2 pp. Endorsed on the address face "forward by Mrs. Hodges." Endorsed at top of first page "April 1838."

Regrets the death of Mr. Wilkinson [Headmaster in the Rev. Isaac Green's school at Sedbergh], who has left a widow and eight small children. Mentions Master Bouske, the death of the elder Mrs. Greenwood, Mrs. Dodgin, Mrs. [Isaac] Green, his goddaughter [Caroline Green], Mr. Upton, and Mr. Wilkinson of Howgill. "Had your house been in a less busy and agitating state I think I should have paid you a visit, as I might possibly have helped you in the school; but under existing circumstances I am afraid I should be in the way." [Hartley does go to Sedbergh to serve as Headmaster until midsummer vacation.]

Quoted in full in *LHC*, 221–222.

A135   A.L.s., postmarked Ambleside, A[ug?], 1840. To: Sedbergh Yorkshire. 4 pp. Letter is in a wrapper of folded paper endorsed by EHC "Hartley Coleridge | To the Revd Isaac Green | (Aug. Sixth.) 1840. | Purchased for Maggi Dulles for Two guineas by me as a Christmas gift 1912 of Francis Coutts, now Lord Latyner [Francis Burdett Thomas Coutts-Neville became 5th Baron Latymer 15 July 1912.]

Describes the weather, both good and bad. Attended services at Rydal Chapel, but his mind wandered far afield. Dined at Mr. Roughsedge's "and saw that most interesting of all sights, a pair of youthful lovers, whose loves were blessed with parental approval." Speaks of the beauty of Miss R[oughsedge] and the excellence of her father's port. Mentions Mr. Sandford, Mr. Jeffries, Mrs. Lawrence, Miss Hanna Ward, Mr. [Thomas] Blackburn [a former pupil of HC's in the Sedbergh school]. Speaks of the birth and death of SC's and HNC's daughter [Bertha Fanny, b. 13 July 1840, d. 24 July 1840]. Will send Green a copy of his second volume of poems. [The intended second volume was not published.] Mentions Mrs. [Isaac] Green, Mr. Upton, the Misses Upton and Wilkinson, and Mr. and Mrs. Evans.

Quoted in part in *Memoir*, pp. cxvii–cxviii.

MRS. ISAAC [CAROLINE IBBETSON] GREEN

A136 A.L.s./copy in unidentified hand, [Sedbergh], [n.d., 1843]. 4 pp.

"Once I would have called you My dear Caroline but now I must call you Madam or M^rs_____ Well my dear fill up the blank as your feelings direct." Her sister-in-law, whom he regards almost as "an elder sister" since her mother [Mrs. Green of Grasmere] was almost a mother to him, has said that she wishes a letter from him to enliven her. Does not feel at all lively, but will try. "The first topic which the English break out with is the weather, the next may be politicks or books —— or their Neighbors —— the last is self." Proceeds to comment pointedly and at some length about the weather, beginning "Look out and about you – Green is the universal colour" and stressing the word "green" throughout. Mentions Isaac [Green] and includes eight lines of verse on the weather, "Like a winter wind that has lost its way." She must have heard of "Mr. Wordsworth's accession to the vacant laureateship." [Wordsworth became Poet Laureate in 1843.] "No Laureate ever attained the wreath under more propitious circumstances. The Queen was delivered of a Daughter. The Duke of Sussex died." [Queen Victoria gave birth to a daughter, Alice, 25 April 1843. Augustus Frederick, Duke of Sussex, died 21 April 1843.] Includes 26 lines of "pastoral dialogue of alternate Lamentation and rejoicing," beginning "Why Damon, why in sable suit today." Hears that she, Isaac, and his God daughter [Caroline Green, Jr.] are expected at Pavement End [Grasmere].

Quoted in part in *New Poems*, pp. 96–97.

LILLY GREENWOOD*

A137 A.L.s./copy in unidentified hand, Grasmere, August 1st [n.d.].
To: [n.p.]. 2 pp. Probably addressed to Lilly Greenwood.

She must not be alarmed at the sight of an unknown hand, for it is the hand of
"a little Gentleman" who once carried her about in her father's garden. Loves
her very much and hopes she is attentive to her duties at school and at home.
Misses her when he goes to the Wyke, but she is in school for her own good.
Sends her a poem for grace at dinner [noted as "Sweetest Lord that wert so
blest," DC, ed. HC, *Poems*, London, 1851].

A138 A.L.s./copy in unidentified hand, [Nab Cottage, Rydal], June
14, 1842. To: [n.p.]. 4 pp. Probably addressed to Lilly Greenwood.

Describes Louisa Claude's birthday picnic, which was held in Mr. [James]
Brancker's garden. Mr. [John] Dawes said grace. Louisa Claude looks well,
"very tall and stout." Mentions Papa and Mama and Miss Heap, who is good
natured enough to laugh at his witticisms. Advises her always to laugh at the
jokes of an old gentleman from whom a legacy may be expected and sends
much humorous advice on how to do so. Concludes that this is a nonsensical
vein for an old man with no legacy to leave and sends twenty lines of poetry,
"In Holy Books we read how God hath spoken." Best respects to Miss Wilson
"and best what you please" to Miss Higgins.

CHARLES LAMB
FOR WILLIAM WORDSWORTH

A139 A.L.s., Merton College, [Oxford], May 16, 1815. To: Temple,
London. 3 pp. On internal evidence this letter would seem to be written
to Mr. Wordsworth, but it is clearly addressed to "Mr. Lambe." A note
[not in Hartley's hand] on the face reads "for Mr. W."

Recounts his first days at Merton College. Has been examined, matriculated;
has gone to chapel and to lectures. Asks about London. "I hope you have
procured commodious lodgings, and that you had no difficulty in getting them."

*This is one of many names which appear in the correspondence under variant
spellings. In this instance I have perhaps arbitrarily chosen Hartley's spelling over
that of correspondents who spell Lilly with a single *l*.

Describes difficulties in writing Latin verse. Speaks of Sunday spent with "My Cousin" [the Rev. William Hart Coleridge] at Cowley. Describes WHC's parsonage there. "Give my kindest remembrance to Mrs. Wordsworth whose health has not, I hope, suffered by the fatigues of Travelling." Speaks of debt to Sir George and Lady Beaumont. Sends regards to Mr. and Miss Lamb, Mr. Montagu and Basil, and Cousin John [Taylor Coleridge]. Mentions William Jackson and [Thomas?] Cookson.

Quoted in full in *LHC*, pp. 11–13.

OWEN LLOYD

A140 A.L. (inc.), [n.p.], [n.d., 1831?]. To: [n.p.]. 4 pp. Accompanied by envelope addressed in unknown hand to "The Rev. Derwent Coleridge, St. Mark's College, Chelsea." and postmarked Sept. 15, 1851. Endorsed on envelope by DC "Hartley to Owen Lloyd."

Has expressed himself to Lloyd "with a very foolish degree of vehemence" and writes to explain. Was "irate at the sneering manner in which Mr. B[enson] H[arrison?] spoke of [Richard] Whately [Archbishop of Dublin] and [Dr. Thomas] Arnold." The mention of Whately's name brings back painful memories of the Oriel affair, "wherein the conduct of Whately [Dean of Oriel College] . . . was strongly contrasted to that of other and it may be, more orthodox personages." Says he is "much more a Tory than a Whig, and least of all a Democrat." Discusses his belief in the separation of church and state. "My conclusion, therefore, is that neither Kings nor Parliaments . . . can alter the essence of the Almighty, or prescribe the issues of his grace, that they confine their legislative activities to matters within their own compass." Says that Lloyd says Christianity lies at the root of all civil obligations. Does not deny this, "But I cannot see any good reason for consecrating any particular duty more than another." No man has the right to make "any indifferent action a sin or a duty by express act or vow." The marriage vow "does not constitute, but removes a prohibition." "The Man who never loved knows not what chastity is. . . . Better to suffer any agony of soul, to know that providence has decreed one 'single to live, and unlamented to die,' to be aware as I am, that nature has let the Devil set his cloven foot upon your face, and made you the abhorrence of every sweet and lovely [woman], or that Fortune has thrust you into such an uncomfortable corner, that any man . . . would rather die for love in the said corner by himself, than tempt any poor female to half starve in it with him . . . ."

Quoted in full in *LHC*, pp. 124–127.

EDWARD MOXON

A141   A.L.s., Grasmere, Nov. 15, [1839]. To: [n.p.]. 1 pp.

A report from HC on his progress on Massinger and Ford [HC, ed., *The Dramatic Works of Massinger and Ford*, London, 1840]. "I will do everything in my power to recompense you for any inconvenience you may have suffered by delay [see A49]. "You may exercise your discretion upon the notes–the long one about Massinger's religion I am rather afraid of–perhaps it had better be printed as a post-script under the head, Was Massinger a known Catholic, as it might be extended to an Essay." Mentions Shakespeare, [Richard] Crashaw, Pope, Wordsworth and Mr. [Robert] Southey.

THOMAS POOLE

A142   A.L.s./copy in the hand of Ernest Hartley Coleridge, Merton Coll. [Oxford], Nov. 16, 1817. To: Nether Stowy, Somerset. 3 pp.

Thanks Poole for his hospitality in Stowey. Was most kindly received by Captain and Mrs. King. Several of STC's Bristol friends, including the poet [Joseph] Cottle, have asked after Poole. Has seen Miss O'Neil [Eliza O'Neill, later Lady Eliza Becher] in Mrs. Oakley [Mrs. Oakley in George Coleman the elder's *The Jealous Wife*, 1761] and in Belvidera [in Thomas Otway's *Venice Preserv'd, or a Plot Discover'd*, first acted in 1682]. Includes criticism of her performances, that of the entire company, and of Mr. Acraman's [Rudolph Ackermann] collection of pictures. Admires the madonna of Carlo Dolci [1616–1686] but finds the Savior of Dominchino [Domenico Zampieri, Il Domenichino, 1581–1641] "wanting in expression." "We are of course all in mourning for the princess [Princess Charlotte died 6 November 1817], and I believe the day of her funeral will be solemly kept here, with prayers and fasting—her loss is indeed a severe national calamity, and a most remarkable circumstance, that the direct line of the royal family is likely to be soon extinct, though its members are more than was ever known since the conquest." [For some interesting reasons, see Ida Macalpine and Roger Hunter, *George III and the Mad-business*, New York, 1970.] Sends regards to Mrs. R[ichard] Poole, Elizabeth [Poole, daughter of Thomas Poole's deceased brother, Richard], Mr. and Mrs. Ward, and Susan and Ann Oddity. Mentions the Baby and Mr. W[ordsworth]'s nephew Dan[iel], who is studying with Mr. Stephens of Wadham [College, Oxford]. Sends respects to Mr. and Mrs. Acland, Captain and Mrs. Clifton, Mrs. Buller, Mrs. Francis Poole, Miss Harris, Jack, Edward, and the Parrot. Adds a note to give his love "to Daddy and Mammy Rich."

Quoted in full in *LHC*, pp. 16–18.

THE PROVOST [EDWARD COPLESTON]
AND FELLOWS OF ORIEL COLLEGE

A143 A.L., [25 Bedford Square, London?], [between October 15 and 19, 1820]. To: The letter was presented by STC to Dr. Copleston when they met in London on Friday, 20 October 1820. 2 pp. See Introduction for an account of the Oriel affair. Accompanied by a 5-page draft "Protest" in the hand of STC.

As the time is approaching for the confirmation of probationary fellows, HC wishes to tell Dr. Copleston "how far I plead guilty to the charges alleged against me." Does not wish to retract his previous confession [of occasional intemperence, omission of some college duties, and friendship with certain undergraduates]. "So far as these facts are the ground of your decision, I have nothing to object to it: it lies in your own bosoms." Denies intemperence on more than two or three occasions and that his companions were anything other than Gentlemen. "Permit me then to protect against the charges of *habitual* intemperence, irregularity as a *consequence* of such intemperence, and love of improper society." Thanks the Provost and Fellows for past favors and friendly advice.

Quoted in full in *LHC*, pp. 48–49.

THE REV. JOHN
RICHARDSON OF APPLEBY

A144 A.L.s./copy in unidentified hand, [Nab Cottage, Rydal], Sat^y August 17 [1844]. To: [n.p.]. 6 pp.

Is as lonely as [Thomas] Campbell's last man ["The Last Man," *The New Monthly Magazine*, London, 1823]. Has he seen Tom Hood's parody of Campbell's last man ["The Last Man," *Whims and Oddities*, London, 1826]? "Then I will say with Wordsworth 'as lonely as a crow on the sands.' " Is in a room "not big enough to whip a cat in" and the hour is late. Quotes Shakespeare and Burns and mentions Dr. Browning's [Sir J. Bowring's] translations from Lettish, Finnish, Magyar, Volkynian, and Servian ("how far *from* few can decide"). Mentions the Ojibbeway Indians and Jeffery the Interpreter, "the Hermes Tris Megistus of the Iowaw Indians" [?]. Is himself as unilingual as if he had lived before the building of Babel. He and William [Richardson, the Rev. John Richardson's brother] met with no adventure between Kendal and the Nab. The rain is incessant, but the English are better off than the people in Poland and America.

Schwetz, at the confluence of the Vistula and Schwetzwasser, was entirely under water. Had he been a priest in the Middle Ages, "I would neither have worn a cowl nor a helmet. Motley had been my only wear. I should have made a capital fool. I hope among other proposed revivals that useful and by no means sinecure office will be restored to its medieval honors." Has Richardson seen "The Ideal of a Christian Church" by the Revd. W. G. Ward, Soc. Bal. [William George Ward, *The Ideal of a Christian Church*, etc., London, 1844]? Comments on Ward's ecclesiastical views. The Bishop of Norwich has been staying at Mrs. [Thomas] Arnold's. Dr. C[hristopher] Wordsworth, "ex master of Trin. Col. Cam. (the unholy Trinity, never in unity)" is visiting his "Brother at the Mount" [William Wordsworth]. Mentions two clerks, Old England, William Green, Kate Wilson, Mr. Bellas and Edith and Charley Richardson. Will Mrs. Richardson locate and send Miss Hopkinson's album? Will send the verses composed at Mr. Eubank's in his next. Kind remembrances to Captain Bennett, Rougate Miller, Mr. Hill, Mr. Addison, and Mr. Hollinshed. Love to Mrs. Bell, Mrs. H. and her sister, and little Mary. Dates the letter. Concludes in a note, "it is not certain that Mrs Lutwitch is enceinte. The Country are happily relieved from their sympathy with the Queen." [Prince Alfred was born 6 August 1844.]

ELIZABETH SCAMBLER

A145   A.L.s./copy in unidentified hand, [n.p.], [n.d.], 1830. To: Ambleside. 2 pp.

Sends fourteen lines for Bessie's fair friend. "All Ladies are fair by prescriptive right as all clergymen . . . are Reverend, all M.P.'s . . . gentlemen, all ambassadors . . . are Excellencies, and all Lawyers . . . are learned counsels." Mentions Henry Hunt and Talleyrand. The enclosed sonnet is not a translation from Petrarch but an imitation from memory. The original may be found in Veronie's grammar. [Upon Giovanni Veneroni's *Le Maître Italien*, 1702, was founded Romauldo Zotti's *Grammaire Françoise et Italienne*, 1800.] He would have known what would suit the "fair friend" had he seen her, or even had contact with things which were hers, "or felt the lightest touch of her fingers in the dusk – a touch far more quickly withdrawn than that wherewith she elicits the most evanescent half note from that instrument whose happy keys have privilege to kiss her lily hands (happy the Elephant that dying bequeathed its tusks to such voluptuous honour)." Thinks he has managed fairly well, nevertheless, for the poem is "Foreign, Italian, Petrarch & Laura. There are birds and flowers and mournful music and grief and love and religion and a ghost and if all this won't do the D——l is in it." Hopes to see Bessie during her holidays.

A146   A.L.s./copy in unidentified hand, Grasmere, August 26th 1837.

To: [George Town, St. Vincent Island, British West Indies]. 6 pp. A reply to B237.

Was agreeably surprised and flattered to receive her letter and is delighted that her expatriation has not affected her "naturally lively spirits." Has hesitated to reply as he is the worst newsmonger in the world and good news is very scarce in Europe. Moreover any news must suffer during the three month voyage from him to her. "What is still more perplexing, that which is true at this present of mine, i.e. August 26th 1837 may become false before your present i.e. the period when my scrawl will reach you. It might puzzle a grammarian to determine in what tense to write intelligence to be honoured three months after date whether the present indicative or the future potential. . . . The Modern Poet which is now all the go may be quite forgotten, the present ministry may be kicked to the Devil (as they deserve) and even our fair and youthful Sovereign may be overwhelmed with abuse from the very quarters that are now drenching her with praise." [Queen Victoria ascended the throne 20 June 1837.] Dinah Fleming, HC's Grasmere hostess, died while he was at Sedbergh assisting Isaac Green, who has been ill. Mrs. Fleming died of a relapse of influenza, and had never recovered properly from nursing her husband during his protracted illness. Is lodging with William and [Eleanor] Richardson, who are very civil, but "another Dinah is not to be expected." She will be surprised that after his past experience [HC taught school in Ambleside ca. 1823–1827. See A90] he would undertake teaching again, but he succeeded better than he expected. "The head master was sole Disciplinarian and there were no Mamas to pry and dictate. Age . . . has blunted the keeness and acerbity of my temper." Isaac Green is married to Miss [Caroline] Ibbetson. Has been depressed but endeavors to be more cheerful. Mentions her mother [Mrs. Scambler], Alice [Scambler], Jane [Scambler], Doll [Dorothy Scambler], William Dawes, George Simpson, [Frederick] William Faber, and the late Mr. Kingsley. Is about to print some poems, etc. [not published during HC's lifetime] and will contrive to send her a copy.

A147 A.L.s./copy in unidentified hand, Knabbe. According to the copyist, the original was postmarked Nov. 5ᵗʰ 1840. To: [Chalkside House, nr Wigton]. 4 pp.

Begins with an affectionate sonnet to Bessie, "I fear you think (when friends by fate are parted", and expresses his gratitude to her for their friendship. Death has been very busy among their old friends. "Of the Lads with whom I grew up I am almost the sole survivor," and most of her friends, too, are gone. Sends six lines of poetry beginning "They lived awhile that we and all might see." Sophy White, Marianne Newton, Eliza Dickson, Jane Green, Alithea North, and Mary Carleton have all died young. He was much affected by her mention of John [Scambler], whose "earthly trial was short." Sends news of Mr. Carr, Miss E[liza] D[owling], William Fell and his wife [Hauchen Reckam Fell]. Mentions Alice, Jane, Doll, Tom, and Henry [Scambler] and sends thanks to her mother. Adds a note on Knabbe, the Islands of Rydal, Helvellyn, and the weather. Edward Lloyd has brought news of Owen [Lloyd]. Miss Harden is now "The Revd Mrs Barker."

Quoted in part in *New Poems*, pp. 76–77.

A148   A.L.s./copy in unidentified hand. According to the copyist, the original was postmarked Ambleside, Sept. 4, 1842. To: [High Street, Annan, Dumfrieshire]. 2 pp.

> Replies to her request for a "newsy" letter. He lives at the Nab "(I have named it Knabbe, so mind if ever you should vouchsafe me another letter) and the Nab is an Island like Kerguelen's Land (vide Map) so far divided from the Human Earth that I really think Mr C—— and Miss Eliza (you know the lovely creature who grows not less lovely every day) might be married at the Independent Chapel (only it is not licensed for that purpose) and I know nothing about it." Sends eighteen and a half lines of "Not such a Marriage as in Paradise" on the wedding of Miss O.

ROBERT SOUTHEY

A149   A.L.s., Coleorton, March 4, 1807. To: Greta Hall, Keswick Cumberland. 3 pp. Endorsed on seal face "From Hartley Coleridge, aged 10 years and six months, | to Robert Southey, written his first attempt at verse: | – given to me by Kate Southey, Sunday evg, July 8, 1855. | D[erwent] C[oleridge]."

> Sends Southey his first poem, "Poetry to an Ass." Says his father has smoothed the meter and "helped me to the Moral," which reads
>
> > And now to say a Word by Way of Moral
> > As I would gladly win the Laurel
> > My Tale shews that Cowards fear not more the
> > brave Man's Eye
> > Than brave Men loath the Coward's Cry.
>
> Sends love to his mother, brother, sister, two friends, aunts, Edith [Southey] and Herbert [Southey].

Quoted in full in *LHC*, pp. 4–5.

JOHN TAYLOR

A150   A.L.s./typed copy, Kensington, December 29, 1821. To: [n.p.].
1 p.

Having been at Kensington, has overlooked Taylor's kind note until now. "At
this interval of time, it is perhaps better that the article [HC's] respecting my
father, hastily as it was written, and containing little more than blank assertion,
should not appear" [in *The London Magazine,* edited by John Taylor 1821–
1824]. Hopes his article on mythology will appear, though he fears it was submitted too late.

THE WARDEN OF
MERTON COLLEGE

A151   A.L. (inc.), [25 Bedford Square, London?], [December 1820].
To: [Merton College, Oxford]. 4 pp. The letter is apparently a draft,
for it is interlined in the hand of STC. Letter is in a wrapper of folded
paper with endorsement of contents and the note "prob. June 1820" by
EHC. See Introduction for an account of the Oriel affair.

Feels it is his duty to lay before the Warden a full account of his conduct from
the time he left Merton to the time of his dismissal from Oriel. Feels that the
Warden knows his conduct at Merton "was not sullied by any such glaring or
frequent aberations from duty as to distinguish it to my disadvantage, from
that of other Undergraduates." Undoubtedly his past conduct was examined
carefully before his election to Oriel. Feels the charges against him are forged
calumnies. "You will remember that I consider the Provost and Fellows not as
my accusers, but as my judges, acting on the reports of my accusers." Reviews
the conduct expected of him as a Fellow of Oriel. Was warned first by Mr.
[Richard] Whately and then by the Provost [Dr. Edward Copleston]. "I did not
follow it as was doubtless expected; nor make Oriel my home, but still continued in the same society, I had kept during my latter years at Merton, and
with much the same habits." Defends the principles and reputations of his associates [Richard] Battiscombe, [Edward] Wilson, [Anthony] Chester, [George]
Sandby, [Henry] Neech, and [Robert] Monro, "several of whom had behaved
towards me with such kindness, while I was Academically their equal, that it
would have been base ingratitude to have deserted them when I was advanced."
Had St. Aubyn as a pupil and spent much time helping other undergraduates.
On two or three occasions "I drank somewhat too freely," but not so freely as
to be deprived of his mental or physical powers. The stranger for whose com-

pany he has been much blamed had just taken his Master of Arts at the College. "Whatever I drank myself – was solely from compliance with what I conceived to be politeness; in fact, my offence was, the not having fortitude enough even to tacitly reprove another [the stranger]." Refers to his conversation with Mr. [Richard] Whately.

Quoted in full in *LHC*, pp. 317–320.

ALARIC ALEXANDER WATTS

A152   A.L.s./typed copy. According to the copyist, the original was postmarked Kendal, Oct. 2, 1826. To: Care of John Andrews, Esqre., 167 New Bond Street, London. 1 p.

Sent the packet of his contributions [to *The Literary Souvenir, or Cabinet of Poetry and Romance*, A. A. Watts, ed., 10 vols., 1825–1834] from Kendal on the first of September by the New-times Coach. Perhaps the packet has not been delivered because he addressed it to Regent Place rather than Regents Park. Will dispatch a second packet. Had he not misunderstood Watts's terms, his contribution would have been larger. Has communicated, via Professor [John] Wilson, Watts's request to Mr. [Thomas] De Quincey who is now at Edinburgh. If Watts will direct the *Literary Souvenir* along with Mr. [Robert] Southey's copy, perhaps half the expense may be saved. "N.B. The Coach arrives at the Bull and Mouth Inn in the city."

A153   A.L.s./copy in the hand of Sara Dustautoy, Grasmere, May 3, 1829. To: [n.p.]. 4 pp.

Gratified as he was at the opportunity to contribute to the *Literary Souvenir* [*The Literary Souvenir, or Cabinet of Poetry and Romance*, A. A. Watts, ed., 10 vols., 1825–1834] and "flattered with the prospect of shining on your delicate paper, reposing betwixt your ornate covers, associating with the beauty and fashion of your most lady like embellishments," he was most distressed to find that two successive packets of his manuscripts have been lost. Is now open to charges of slighting the offer and violating his own engagement, but is willing to send further contributions if they would still be acceptable. Expects the same remuneration afforded to others of his standing and suspects prose is more in request than verse. [HC's only known contribution to the *Literary Souvenir* was "Address to Certain Gold Fishes," which appeared in 1830.] Adds a postscript in praise of Watts's poems.

Quoted in full in *LHC*, pp. 96–98.

A154 A.L. (inc.), [n.p.], [n.d.]. To: [n.p.]. 4 pp. The paper is water-marked "G R | 1817."

"It is one of the highest excellences of our constitution at least in its Ideal, that the Praerogatives of the King, are, when properly understood, the Privileges of the People." As a symbol of the state, "the regal office" is invested "with a certain sacredness." The subject's security lies in the idea of the constitution toward which, for ages, the physical constitution has been moving. The king keeps the law from becoming "a murderous letter at variance with its maker's spirit." The love of the people for the king is insured by his power to save them "from the clutches of the Letter." "If the Romans, while lamenting over the slaughter'd at Cannae, came forth in their garb of mourning to wellcome the flying Consul, because he had not despaired of the Republic, far more will the nobler English, tho' harassed by a thousand difficulties, and smarting with a thousand, hail with acclamations and joyful tears, that Sovereign, who shew'd by a timely extention of pardon that he despair'd not of human nature." Recalls that during the French Revolution the British people had an almost fanatical aversion to "everything under the appearance of Republicanism." The cry of the mobs was "Church and King," and "the Church and King Mobs were . . . at least as ferocious as the Radical ones of the present day." "Much may doubtless be said, in defense of the Execution of Charles [I], but there is one answer that outweighs it all — it was a stab to the moral sense of the nation." Despite his weaknesses, Charles was loved by the People; "It was a Parricide." The worst detractors of monarchy are its pretended friends. Quotes a passage from "a letter published in your paper," concerning a criminal, Hammett [?], who applied to a barrister to secure a pardon from the king. The barrister's reply was that the king could not pardon without the consent of his advisers, and the barrister refused to seek a pardon and thereby cause a pang "to the sensitive, the already too outraged feelings of . . . his benevolent Sovereign." "Let us reflect a moment on the injury herein committed upon the royal dignity." Not only has the subject been deprived "of the benefit and the King of the glory of pardon," but "the bright gem of mercy" is "torn from the crown." The King is not bound to the opinion of "councellours." To let the decision rest with "a Secretary for the home department" is to deprive the King of his prerogative and the people of their source of appeal. It is to set a "great gulf" between the people and the throne.

RECIPIENTS UNKNOWN

A155 A.L.s./typed copy, Merton Coll., March 2, 1817. To: [n.p.]. 1 p.

Encloses the certificate "fill'd up as directed." Thanks his correspondent for "the trouble you have taken on my behalf, which has procured me a sum tho' small acceptable." Spent the vacation in Cumberland. Mentions Mr. and Mrs. [Robert] Southey, Sara [Coleridge] and Edith [May Southey].

A156 A.L. (inc.)/copy in the hand of Mrs. STC, [n.p.], Decr 2nd 1820. To: [n.p.]. 3 pp.

His father has been at Oxford and has spoken with Dr. [Edward] Copleston [Provost of Oriel College] who, while in some ways complimentary, reiterated charges, "which my father & all my friends *believe*, and I *know* to be false." Copleston defended the way in which Probationers are investigated. Never, before HC left Oxford, had he any idea of the extent of the charges against him. Has told his correspondent in former letters the worst he knows of himself, but has had a warning to keep such contrition for his maker and not to be "over free with it to the Fellows of Oriel." STC secured from Dr. Copleston a memorandum of the charges, much the same as those contained in Keble's letter [John Keble, Fellow of Oriel, to John Taylor Coleridge, 19 June 1820]. After returning to Highgate STC had another meeting with Copleston at which he presented HC's "protest containing my acknowledgements of my *real* delinquency and solemn disavowal of whatever else has been alleged beyond it." The Provost repeated the charges and added that HC had been "Picked up *dead drunk* in the street which, so help me God, *I never was in my life!*" Copleston repeated to STC his previous offer that HC "should accept from the College the sum of £300 *and let the matter be hushed up.*" His friends, the Wordsworths, Mr. [John Hookham] Frere, the [James] Gillmans, all feel that accepting the money would convince the world "that I was even such as they have named me." Of what use is Copleston's promise of silence? "The more mystery they make about the matter the worse it will be for me." Quotes the reply STC made in his name refusing the offer. Will write to the Warden of Merton College [see A151], to Sir G[eorge] B[eaumont, see incomplete letter to Lady Beaumont, A2], and to Uncle Edward [Coleridge], giving them a true account of the case and copies of the papers "necessary to the elucidation of the affair."

Quoted in full in *LHC*, pp. 49–51.

A157 A.L.s./copy in unidentified hand, [Grasmere], Decr 23 (1838). To: [n.p.]. 2 pp. Begins "Dear Mademoiselle."

"Though I cannot flatter myself with the hope that the notes of my Lyre will operate on the Autocrat as those of Orpheus are recorded to have effected the Potentate of another gloomy Empire or even that they will put any more serviceable votes in the pockets of the distressed Poles yet your request is too agreeable to my Vanity to say nothing of my radicalism to be refused." Is afraid he will be the only Lake Poet to contribute, for "the Conservative bards would I doubt not gladly assist an individual Pole with regard to politics but a donation to the refugees in general they would consider a bounty on rebellion." Had he known of the scheme earlier, he would have composed something more suitable, but for the moment, "the song must serve." Mr. I[saac] Green has a sore throat. Mrs. [Caroline Ibbetson] Green has made a beautiful sketch of the condemned Chapel at Howgill. She has done a lithograph of the Church and School at Sedbergh. Describes the new Chapel at Howgill and Mr. [Stephen] Sedgewick's Chapel, the consecration of which was attended by the Bishop of Ripon. "Though I met him more than once I could not overcome the fear with which I always regard persons in superior stations." Regards to her sisters and to Dr. [W.] Briggs and Mrs. [Anna Maria] Briggs.

A158   A.L.s./copy in unidentified hand, Knabbe, November 30, 1840. To: [Lancaster]. 3 pp.

Wishes he could give her young friend something better for her "Museum" than "the pothooks & hangers of a poor hack scribbler!" Perhaps it is well for him that she knows no more of him than that he is STC's son and dwells among the Lakes "whose names Wordsworth has made as familiar as Parnassus and Tempe." Sometimes it is better to know things only at a distance. Perhaps romantic lovers on the Moon gaze upon the earth and think it a paradise of peace and innocence, etc. They know nothing of the sickness, wars, etc., "the Eastern Question, of Municipal elections, and the hitherto unabolished slave-trade, of Newgate or Norfolk Island, or Sierra Leone, or the Pontine marshes." Writes on the presumption that her friend is female, for he detests male autograph hunters. Describes the November landscape. Supposes Lancaster has celebrated the birth of the Princess [the Princess Royal, Victoria Adelaide Mary Louisa was born 21 November 1840]. "What an unaccountable creature a royal Babe must be."

A159   A.L.i., Nab, July 14 [1848?]. To: [n.p.]. 4 pp. Begins "Dear Kate."

Will, reluctantly, comply with her request to destroy her letter. "I assure you no eye save my own has seen the inside of it, and to shew my obedience I will only read it once more, and I will offer it up as a pure offering . . ." Kissed her letter once or twice "when no one was in the Kitchen." Has forgotten what was in the sonnet written on the night of their parting. "But nothing could be further from my thought and belief than to attribute to you the reckless levity of 'toujours gai,' a character I neither envy nor very particularly respect. Our brief acquaintance did not furnish many themes of solemn import but I saw quite enough to be convinced that you could both think and feel (the feelings of those who cannot or do not think are ever hollow or insincere) and I deemed your apparent joyousness rather the results of quick sympathy with the enjoyment of others heightened by the participation of 'Nature's joy' amid beautiful scenes continually varied by 'a glad and tricksy atmosphere' than of mere constitutional light heartedness." Quotes four lines from Cowper [William Cowper, *The Task*, I., "The Sofa," ll. 493-496, London, 1785] and comments that man, as a reflecting being, cannot be as gay as the lark. "The past is a sea full of wrecks as well as pearls." Some memories, even of past troubles, are sweet, "but the memory of broken friendships of disappointed love, of taunt and oppression and unkindness, above all of forfeited esteem and eyes turned away in sorrow or fixed in stern rebuke or mere afflicting pity that once glowed with delight with your appearance is never sweet and needs more than human aid to render it salutary . . . ." Trusts she is unacquainted with this last evil, "but you cannot be without some bitter drops in your cup. I have sometimes been half afraid that you might consider me as a hard eyed jester, too merry for a world of woe and trial – but I can be serious and in solitude have need of self watchfulness, energy and divine assistance to preserve me from despondency." Has conducted no young ladies to the waterfall, though there are two school-mistresses at the Nab. W[illiam] Brancker is expected. "I can't bear to think of Croft Lodge passing into other hands, but so I suppose it must be." [After Croft Lodge failed to sell in 1840–41, it apparently was withdrawn from the market and sold in 1848.] Respects to her mother and to "the infant who does not appear very infantine to see." Would she be so kind to transcribe the enclosed verses and send him a copy.

A160 A.L.s./copy in unidentified hand, [n.p.], [n.d.]. To: [n.p.]. 1 p. In the hand of the copyist, "Copy of Letter accompanying 'The Angel of the Rose' " [DC, ed., HC, *Poems*, London, 1852]. Salutation: Dear Lady.

"As Mr. G. S. *the Usher of the Black Rod*" has told him that she claims the promise he made her two years ago, he has here redeemed it to the best of his ability. "I have sometimes observed a mysterious crimson flitting across your cheek but never could divine so agreeable a solution for the phenomenon as the little German supplies." Sends Grasmere news of Mr. Withington, Mrs. Ashworth, two ladies staying at Mary Fisher's. Mentions *Peter Bell* [William Wordsworth, *Peter Bell, A Tale in Verse*, London, 1819.], Richardson [a lecturer], the Lune, and her sisters and brother.

Letters to
Hartley Coleridge

A. FRIEND

B1   A.L.s., [n.p.], 29 Sep^r, 1847. To: [Nab Cottage, Rydal]. 3 pp.

Sends a leaf from Edward Johnson's *Nuces Philosophicae* [Ipswich, 1842]. Urges HC to read the book and reply to the arguments and attacks therein.

ANNE ADDISON

B2   A.L.s., Regent Terrace, Newcastle, Novr 9th, 1846. To: [Nab Cottage, Rydal]. 3 pp.

Has just received the portfolio which she left with friends at Kendal for HC to write in. Thanks HC profusely for his poems and that of his "Friend" [William Charles Bonaparte Wyse, see B264].

MRS. THOMAS [MARY PENROSE] ARNOLD

B3   A.N.s., Fox How [Ambleside], July 26th, 1842. To: [Nab Cottage, Rydal]. 1 p.

Asks if one of her sons may borrow HC's copy of Homer's *Odyssey* for two or three weeks. Will see that it is safely returned.

B4   A.N.s., Fox How [Ambleside], Sept. 27, [n.d., 1845]. To: [Nab Cottage, Rydal]. 2 pp.

A note of condolence on the death of HC's mother.

113

JOANNA BAILLIE

B5   A.L.s., Hampstead, April 28th, 1842. To: [Nab Cottage, Rydal]. 1 p.

Humorously and gracefully thanks HC for his sonnet ["To Joanne Baillie," DC, ed., HC, *Poems*, London, 1851] conveyed to her by Mrs. Fletcher.

EDWARD BAINES, JR.

B6   A.L.s., Leeds, January 28th, 1841. To: Rydal, nr. Ambleside. 2 pp.

A young lady of Lancaster, Miss Eleanor Dawson, possessed a poem of HC's in his own hand, which she valued highly. While on a visit to Leeds, she lent it to Mrs. Edward Baines, who accidentally destroyed it. Asks HC to rewrite the lost lines, which were originally sent to Miss Crossfield of Lancaster. Quotes a few lines from memory to identify the poem. Please send the poem to him along with an autograph line for Mrs. Baines, who likes autographs.

MARY HARRIS BARNARD

B7   A.L.s., Sheering, near Sawbridgeworth, Herts., March 31st, 1835. To: [Grasmere]. 3 pp.

It will be a surprise to HC to receive this letter, undertaken at the request of her father, Mr. Harris. Assures HC of their affection for him and desire to see him again. Many changes have occurred since 1820. Her father has suffered a paralytic seizure. Her sister Susan is in bad health. Speaks of old times at Oxford, mentioning Mr. Griffith; Mr. Radford, now Rector of Lincoln; and Miss Stockford. Regards from the whole family.

B8   A.L.s., New Road, Oxford, Jan[y] 26th, 1836. To: Grasmere near Ambleside, Westmoreland. 4 pp.

Was glad to receive his letter, which was forwarded to Oxford, where she is staying with her father. The family circle has been reduced—by the deaths of her mother and sisters Elizabeth and Susan—to her father, Mr. Harris, and her sisters Martha and Kate. Alludes to STC's death [25 July 1834]. Invites HC to visit them in the spring or summer. The cats Mosse, Trudge, and Jack have all died since HC left Oxford. Charles Swann has died, leaving only a daughter, Emma. Miss Jones has maried Mr. Cleoburey. Considers their [the Cleobureys'] proceedings absurd (they have separated twice). Sends more news of Frank Demainbray; Captain Stockford of Cowley; Anna Finch; Miss Towsey; and Mr. Radford, the Rector of Lincoln, who is marrying Miss Stockford after an eighteen-year engagement. Supposes HC has seen Robert Montgomery, whom she finds difficult to read. Would like any of HC's books he would send her. Is returning to Sheering, near Sawbridgeworth, Hertfordshire, on February 18th.

MARGARET BARTON

B9   A.N.s., Rather Bank, September Seventh, [n.d.]. To: [n.p.]. 1 p.

Note enclosed with muffetees for HC.

THOMAS BLACKBURNE

B10   A.L.s., Dalton Square, Lancaster, Sepr 11th, [1847]. To: [Nab Cottage, Rydal]. 1 p. Letter is written on inside of paper bordered in black and printed with a two–page memorial poem [by Thomas Blackburne] to "Eleanor Blackburne, died Sepr 2nd, 1847, Aged 22 years." The back of the letter bears notes in HC's hand on Charles I and others.

The dead girl was his favorite sister. His father, being ill of the same disease, dysentery, missed the funeral. Describes the funeral. Has two sisters left; three are dead.

B11   A.L.i., 8 Beaufort Terrace, Seacomb nr Liverpool. Sep. 25, [n.d.]. To: [n.p.]. 4 pp.

Writes to end a half-year silence. Makes fun of his own elevated style. Refers to the black year he has just passed through and hopes the next will be better. Cannot decide what to do, and fears oppressive systematization if he takes orders. Has been reading Maurice's Kingdom of X [Frederick Dennison Maurice, *The Kingdom of Christ*, London, 1838]. Is interested in medicine. Needs encouragement. Says it is a blessing to have a hero like Charles Lamb. Sends a book.

B12 A.L.s., Burcher Court, Kington, June, postmarked 13, 1842. To: Rydal, near Ambleside. 10 pp.

A long letter filled with general remarks on life and religion. Thanks HC for the lines on Owen Lloyd ["A Schoolfellow's Tribute to the Memory of the Rev Owen Lloyd," DC, ed., HC, *Poems*, London, 1851] and the addition in reference to her [?]. Reminisces about their childhood visits to the gardens of Old Brathay. Lectures HC at some length on the need to reform himself.

ISABELLA BRADSHAW

B13 A.N.s., [n.p.], [n.d.]. To: [n.p.]. 1 p.

Should HC walk out this morning, she would feel obliged if he would call on her. Asks him to excuse the liberty she is taking.

JAMES BRANCKER

B14 A.L.s., Liverpool, May day wet & cold, postmarked May 1, 1835. To: Grasmere, Ambleside. 3 pp.

Thanks HC for his amusing letter. Discusses local politics. Advises HC to take no steps in the Leeds matter [with Francis Edward Bingley] at this time. Has been busy preparing a townhouse on Duke Street [Liverpool]. Will come to Grasmere in three or four weeks, and Mrs. [Jane Moss] Brancker may stay until Christmas. Asks about HC's work. Speaks of a man called "Kitty" [?] who would sacrifice everything for Beauty and is going to America. Sends regards to his friends at Grasmere, mentioning Allan Bank and "Old James" [Greenwood?] and his wife.

B15 A.L.s., Liverpool, January 16th, 1836. To: Grasmere, Ambleside. 3 pp.

Encloses a letter [from Francis Edward Bingley, see Appendix, 4] releasing HC from the clutches of his Leeds bookseller [Bingley]. Does not believe Bingley is quite honest about the London house's wishing to purchase HC's copyrights. To be in the hands of a reputable London bookseller might be the best thing for HC. Suggests HC consult Mr. Wordsworth on his next move. Speaks of local politics, mentioning [William] Eward and Landon. Love from Mrs. [Jane Moss] Brancker, who is ill. Mr. Brancker [father] is also ill. Hopes to see HC in late April or early May. Love to Dinah [Fleming].

B16   A.L.s., [n.p.], [n.d.]. To: The Nab [Cottage, Rydal]. 1 p.

His lady is made anxious by the delay of her epithalamium ["Second Nuptials," DC, ed., HC, *Poems*, London, 1851?]. They will "exhibit" in the church the next day, and HC is invited to dinner. Has seen [William] Fell, [Herbert] White, and Mr. and Mrs. [James] Greenwood.

B17   A.L.s., Otterspool Cottage, Tuesday Octr 8, 1844. To: [Nab Cottage, Rydal]. 4 pp.

Was glad to hear from HC and sends greetings from his daughter and Mrs. [Miss Simmons] Brancker. Mentions Wordsworth's opposition to railroads and concludes that better transportation will enable even more people to enjoy nature. Mrs. [Louise] Claude, "Doodle," and Anna Marie [Briggs?] are here. Doodle is going with the Whites to Plymouth. Kate [Brancker, a daughter] sends her love. Mentions Mr. Clay, Mrs. King, and Mr. [John] Dawes.

MISS ANNA MARIA BRIGGS

B18   A.N.s., Ambleside, Saturday, Sept. 21 [1839?]. To: [n.p.]. 1 p.

Invitation for Monday to meet Mrs. Hughs, her nephew Charles Hemans, Miss Braves, and Miss Bellasis.

B19   A.L.s., Ambleside, Wednesday evening, Oct. 23, [1839?]. To: [n.p.]. 4 pp.

Reminds HC of his commitment for Miss Graves's historical meeting, which is to be held November 5th at the Briggs' house. The time is short; is sure HC won't fail her. He has less than a fortnight to write the history of England as it would have been had Guy Fawkes been successful. HC should suggest to Mr. [Owen?] Lloyd a topic for a paper. Her mother [Mrs. Anna Maria Briggs] begs HC to plan to spend the night. Is sorry HC did not meet Mr. [Richard Rawlinson?] Vyvyan.

117

B20   A.L.s., Ambleside, Jany 2, 1840. To: [Grasmere?]. 1 p.

Invitation for dancing on 8 January. Miss Bellasis will come. He is to come
before dark and her mother [Mrs. Anna Maria Briggs] begs that he plan to
spend the night. Has just heard of the death of John Wordsworth of Cambridge [31 December 1839; nephew of William Wordsworth's].

B21   A.N.s., Ambleside, Tuesday morning, April 27, [1841?]. To:
[n.p.]. 1 p.

Invitation to dinner tomorrow at 5 o'clock to meet Edward Lloyd.

B22   A.L.s., Ambleside, Saturday evening, April 2, [1842?]. To: [n.p.].
1 p.

Heard HC say he would have sent verses to town by Mrs. [Thomas] Cookson
had they been ready. Is going to London on Wednesday and offers to take the
poems. Wants some copies herself to take with her. Hopes he received his book
safely.

B23   A.L.s., Lis [?], May 12, [n.d.]. To: [n.p.]. 3 pp. Back bears ink
and pencil notes in the hand of HC.

Asks what has become of Mr. and Mrs. John Gisborne, who were friends of
SCT's. HC can send answer through her mother [Mrs. Anna Maria Briggs].
Asks how HC likes the verses of [Francesco] Redi [1626-1698] which she
copied out and sent him [James Henry Leigh Hunt, *Bacchus in Tuscany, A
dithyrambic poem from the Italian of Francesco Redi*, 1825?]. Will also send a
less widely known sonnet.

B24   A.L.s., Pisa, Jany 9, 1846. To: [Nab Cottage, Rydal]. 4 pp.

Thanks HC for his letter, although his hand is very difficult to decipher. Alludes to the death of Mrs. STC [24 September 1845]. Is pleased with the stay
in Pisa, unlike that in Leghorn, which is filled with Jews and Greeks. Sees
[John and Isabella Curwen] Wordsworth, who are here with Mr. Woodcock.
Speaks of Edward and Willy Wordsworth [John Wordsworth's children], Mr.
Angus Fletcher, and Mr. and Mrs. Sloane whom she praises highly. Describes
the Christmas festivities at a friend's house.

MARY J. BRIGGS

B25 A.L.s., Low Nook, Ambleside, Feby 24th, 1847. To: [Nab Cottage, Rydal]. 4 pp.

Heard from Jane Claude that HC has the fifth number of Dombey [Charles Dickens, *Dealings with the Firm of Dombey and Son Wholesale, Retail and for Exportation*, London, 20 (as 19) monthly parts from October, 1846]. Would like to borrow it when he has finished with it. He has not visited them for a long time. Her mother and father [Dr. and Anna Maria Briggs] have been confined to the house. Her nephews will enjoy their holidays.

SARA BRIGGS

B26 A.L., Ambleside, Thursday, Octr. 22nd, [n.d.]. To: [n.p.]. 2 pp.

Reminds him of his promise to produce a copy of Southey's lines on Lodore ["The Cataract of Lodore. Described in Rhymes for the Nursery," Robert Southey, *The Complete Poetical Works of Robert Southey*, vol. II, Boston, 1880]. Would be glad to receive them before the end of next week, when she is going to Worcestershire. Regards from Dr. and Mrs. Briggs.

[DR.] W. BRIGGS

B27 A.L.s., Thursday, 19th June, postmarked Ambleside, 1845. To: [Nab Cottage, Rydal]. 2 pp.

Knows HC's fondness for young children. Now has the infant of their late daughter Margaret [see A121]. Asks HC to have lunch and see the child.

MRS. W. [ANNA MARIA] BRIGGS

B28 A.L.s., Ambleside, Jan^{ry} 14, [n.d.]. To: [n.p.]. 2 pp.

Asks HC to dinner the next day at 5 o'clock. Her son and her nephew, Frank Maude, are now home. The family has had much illness. If the day is unfavourable will HC come the next day.

B29   A.L.s., Ambleside, Thursday Even^g, Jan^ry 18th, [1838]. To: Grasmere. 3 pp.

While she was ill, she decided upon a certain plan. Having heard that HC, when he leaves his friends late, sometimes shelters in a shed or outhouse, she has quietly engaged for HC a bedroom at Mrs. MacKaneth's for the remainder of the winter. He can occupy it any time he finds it convenient. Begs him to say what he thinks. Her daughter Margaret has a new baby boy named Herbert. Owen Lloyd is gone to Kendal. Miss Dickenson is marrying Mrs. Plunkett. Her son is returned to Liverpool. Her daughter Anna Maria is at Holly Hill. Dr. [Thomas] Arnold will occupy the pulpit at Rydal for three weeks.

B30   A.N.s., Ambleside, August 14th, [1848]. To: [Nab Cottage, Rydal]. 1 p. Note on back in HC's hand, "I dined with the good *Doctor* on the 15*th*. On the 16*th* he was taken from us."

Invites HC to dine with them the next time he is in Ambleside. Wants to consult him about a motto for a sun dial.

CHARLOTTE BRONTË

B31   A.L., postmarked Bradford, Yorkshire, De. 10 [1840]. To: Knabbe, Rydal, nr Ambleside, Westmoreland. 4 pp.

Is almost as much pleased to get his letter as she would have been to get one from Professor [John] Wilson containing a passport to Blackwood['s *Magazine*]. HC does not flatter her but writes like an honest man and a gentleman. Thanks him for his reply. Thinks she will give up on her Percy-West romances [see "Charlotte Brontë and Hartley Coleridge, 1840,, Brontë Society *Transactions*, vol. X, no. 1, 1940]. Feels she could have persevered like a Richardson and spun the tale out to thrice the three volumes HC estimated it would fill. Speaks at some length of Samuel Richardson and his characters Sir Charles Grandison, Miss Harriet Byron, and Miss Lucy Selby. Describes the pleasures of creating an imaginary world filled with characters who are like Melchisedies [Melchizedek, priest-king, *Hebrews* 7:1–3]. Some of the created characters are ugly, some so beautiful as to startle their own creator much as Pygmalion must have been startled by his statue. Wishes she had been born in time to contribute to

120

the Lady's Magazine [1770–1832], which she used to read with so much pleasure before her father burnt them. While she is tempted to apply to a publisher, she thinks it would be best, on the whole, to lock up this manuscript and apprentice herself to some trade. Discusses the politics of her romance. Since HC could not decide from her previous letter whether she was male or female, she will let him continue guessing. He should not draw any conclusions from what he calls ladylike tricks in her style—Richardson and Rousseau write like old women and Bulwer, Cooper, Dickens, and Warren like boarding school girls. Thanks him for his kindness and frankness in dealing with a correspondent who would identify herself by no more than the initials C. T. [Several of Charlotte Brontë's stories of this period were written under the name "Charles Townshend."]

Quoted in full in "Hartley Coleridge and the Brontës" by Fran Carlock Stephens. *TLS*, 14 May 1970.

B32   A.L.s., The [?]. June 16, [18]47. To: [Nab Cottage, Rydal]. 2 pp. Similar letters were written to Thomas De Quincey, Alfred Tennyson, William Wordsworth and John Gibson Lockhart. Signed "Currer Bell."

Her relatives Ellis and Acton Bell have joined her in a volume of poems [Charlotte, Emily, and Anne Brontë, *Poems by Currer, Ellis, and Acton Bell*, London, 1846]. As the publishers warned her, the book has not sold well. Before giving the remaining copies to the trunkmakers, she has decided to distribute a few copies. Begs HC to accept one in acknowledgement of the pleasure they have received from his writings.

Quoted in full in "Hartley Coleridge and the Brontës" by Fran Carlock Stephens. *TLS*, 14 May 1970.

MR. AND MRS.
WILLIAM C. BROOKS

B33   A.E., with calling cards of Mr. and Mrs. William C. Brooks, Rusholme. 2 cards and envelope.

FANNY BRYANT

B34   A.L.s., The Holme, Regent's Park, London, [n.d.]. To: [n.p.].

3 pp.

Met HC on a visit to her brother, Mr. Bryant of Belfield. Had written Mr. Field to get autographs of Wordsworth and Southey, but he could not oblige. Asks HC for these two autographs plus his own and STC's. Looks for the new book of poems HC said was in progress [unpublished during HC's lifetime].

MARY BURTON

B35   A.N., [n.p.], [n.d.]. To: [n.p.]. 1 card.

Card to HC with Mary Burton's kindest regards and best wishes.

GEORGE MOIR BUSSEY

B36   A.L.s., 17 Frenchwood Street, Preston, Lancashire, 9th of August 1848. To: [Nab Cottage, Rydal]. 2 pp.

Though HC may have forgotten him since his residence in Kendal as editor of the Mercury, will take advantage of his son's trip through the Lake District to send HC his regards. Hopes HC is well and writing more poetry and prose to elevate the moral character even among the workers. Asks if the Worthies [HC, *Biographia Borealis; or, Lives of the Distinguished Northerns*, Leeds, 1833] is to be continued.

ANTHONY CHESTER

B37   A.N.s., [n.p.], [n.d.]. To: [n.p.]. 1 p.

Is sorry HC was not at home. Would have liked to have introduced his wife and daughters to HC.

WILLIAM BROWNSWORD CHORLEY

B38 A.L.s., St. Anne Pl. Liverpool, 14 Sept^r, 1834. To: [Grasmere]. 3 pp.

Has a pleasant memory of their correspondence before *The [Winter's] Wreath* [1825-1832] was given up. Was pleased by HC's volume [HC, *Poems,* Leeds, 1833] and is glad to hear it is to have a successor [unpublished during HC's lifetime]. Encloses a volume [W. B. Chorley, trans., *The Lyre and the Sword of C. T. Korner,* London, 1834]. Has always been interested in [Carl Theodor] Korner [1791-1813] and has sought to make him more widely known in England. Hopes HC is well and occupied. Alludes to STC's death [24 July 1834]. Is afraid HC has given up plans to visit Liverpool.

JAMES SMITH CLARKE

B39 A.L.s., Rockdale, 27 May, 1848. To: [Nab Cottage, Rydal]. 3 pp.

Has heard Mr. Cameron, of Wakefield, read some lines of STC's at a lecture. Was unable to find the lines in Pickering's edition [STC, *The Poetical Works,* London, 1835?] in the Rockdale library. Could not locate Mr. Cameron. Thanks HC for answering his letter to the [*Manchester*] Guardian. Has already memorized the poem [?]. Gratitude and compliments to the author of "The Worthies of Yorkshire" [HC, *Biographia Borealis; or, Lives of the Distinguished Northerns,* Leeds, 1833]. Has ordered the 1844 edition of STC's poems [STC, *Poems,* London, 1844].

JANE CLAUDE

B40 A.L.s., [36 Faulkner Street, Liverpool], 9th December, postmarked 1841. To: The Knabbe, Ambleside. 3 pp.

Has been deputized by Louise [Claude] to thank HC for his letter. Discusses Louise's slowly improving health. She hopes to be able to read without difficulty by the time HC's essays come out [not published during HC's lifetime]. Speaks of the [William] Fells' baby [Jeanetta] and Mr. William Dawson and his nieces and nephews. Asks if the emblem [?] is Mr. [John] Dawes's, and will HC please write some more. Describes Louis [Claude]'s job on a ship. Asks HC if he saw the notice Mary [Claude] sent the Fells. It offered to reward anyone caught and convicted of stealing the turnips or breaking the fences of William Pearce. Love from all.

MRS. LOUISE CLAUDE

B41   A.L.s., [36 Faulkner Street, Liverpool], Sunday, [n.d., January, 1836]. To: Grasmere. 2 pp.

Sends HC a message from [James] Brancker. Brancker expects to settle HC's affairs with [Francis Edward] Bingley in a week. HC should not interfere in any way [see Appendix]. Mrs. [Jane Moss] Brancker is again very ill. Mr. Brancker's father is so ill that he is not expected to live through the winter. Brancker is in very bad spirits.

B42   A.L.s., [36 Faulkner Street, Liverpool], Sunday, [n.d., January, 1836]. To: Grasmere. 2 pp.

A letter from [James] Brancker tells her that HC's Leeds affairs [with Francis Edward Bingley, see Appendix] are settled. Hopes this will cheer HC and that he will rouse himself and publish. Mrs. [Jane Moss] Brancker is very ill, but old Mr. Brancker is better.

B43   A.L.s., [36 Faulkner Street, Liverpool], [n.d., probably January-March, 1839]. 4 pp. including a two-page transcript of a poem in the hand of Mary or Louise Claude. Address sheet is bordered in black. "Favoured by J[ames] Greenwood, Esq."

Mary [Claude] especially looks forward to seeing HC when the Claudes return to their home in the Lake District. Speaks of the dead Annie [Claude]'s long illness and its effects on her sisters and brother. Describes Louis's progress at school. Mentions Helen Edmunds and Margaret Toves. Would like to show some of HC's translations to Mr. Migault. Love from the children.

B44   A.L.s., [36 Faulkner Street, Liverpool], Sept. 21st, [n.d.]. To: Grasmere. 3 pp.

Was never out of news when writing from Westmorland, but since HC has no interest in Liverpool, she will write about the family. The girls are happier since their cousins [the Adolph Claude children?] arrived. Mary [Claude] will be the last to adjust to town life. Jane and Louise [Claude] like to walk in town and see new things. Louis [Claude] is in school six hours a day and is reading a great deal on his own. Wishes she had a pocket edition of HC's poems to carry about in her bag. Sends Schiller's poems. Asks him to put the book in a conspicuous place where it will constantly remind him of the Claudes.

B45   A.L.s., [36 Faulkner Street, Liverpool], [n.d., early spring, before 1840]. To: Grasmere. 9 pp. "Favoured by [James] Brancker, esq."

Thanks HC for his long and interesting letter. Reports on the health of each of the children and their dislike of Liverpool. Describes two soirées at the Royal Institution. Mentions Dr. Reynolds and the [Richard] Rathbones. Describes the scientific exhibitions at one of the soirées. Compares the schooling of Louis [Claude] and Jones [Greenwood], mentioning Louis's Latin teacher, Mr. Thomas. Discusses some of Mr. [Benjamin Robert] Haydon's theories of art. Delights in the company of her children. Mary [Claude] has been of great assistance to her in managing Louis. Speaks of Louis's great admiration for Jones [Greenwood]. Says Mr. [John] Dawes has written Louis a very kind letter. Mentions Mary's singing and Mrs. [James] Greenwood.

B46   A.L. (inc.), Falkner St. 36, Fbr. 27th, [18]40. To: [Grasmere?]. 4 pp.

Has not heard from HC for a long time. They have been very anxious about both Mrs. A[dolph] Claude and Miss Reckam. Her brother-in-law [Adolph Claude] has gone to New Orleans, and his wife, Minna, grieves for him. Hauchen [Reckam] pines for her lover [William Fell]. The girls [Louise, Mary, and Jane Claude] are delighted at Hauchen's and Fell's engagement. Louis [Claude] was shocked that they kissed in his presence. Has had letters from the Briggses and Mary Ann Harrison. Mentions Mr. Dobson. Mrs. [Jane Moss] Brancker is no better. She will see no one, and Mr. [James] Brancker will see very few. Has to go to Brancker's Duke Street office if she wants to see him. Ann Brancker came from Oxford to Liverpool in mid-December and left on 26 February, having seen her brother [James Brancker] only once. Reports on the health of each member of the family.

B47   A.L.s., Dulwich, 1st June, 1840. To: [Nab Cottage, Rydal]. 6 pp.

Gives long descriptions of each of the Withington children, Alice, Fanny, Arthur, Florence, and Lilly, who are all delicate. Describes the village of Dulwich and Mary [Claude]'s disappointment at the song of the nightingale [see A18]. Mrs. Withington, who lives with her father, has few friends, most of her own having left and most of her father's being too old. Was delighted with the National Gallery. Also saw at an exhibition Miss Gillies's portrait of Mr. Wordsworth and thinks it not very like him. [In 1840 Margaret Gillies painted a miniature for Mr. Moon the publisher; Miss Gillies made three copies.] Is miserable to think of [James] Brancker's selling Croft Lodge [his Ambleside home]. Speaks of Mrs. [Jane Moss] Brancker's failing health. Louis [Claude] is going to spend his holidays with Mr. [John] Dawes, but she is afraid the rest of the family will not get to Ambleside this summer. Has not seen HC's Massinger and Ford [HC, *The Dramatic Works of Massinger and Ford*, London, 1840]. Asks HC to send poems, including the "Prometheus." Has not done much sight seeing, as she is still weak. Mentions Mary, Jane, and Louise [Claude] and Mrs. A[dolph] Claude. Intends to remain in Dulwich until 12 September. [HC's letter A12 is, however, clearly directed to the Liverpool address.]

B48 A.L.s., Faulkner St. 36, [Liverpool], 5th August, 1840. To: [Nab Cottage, Rydal]. 5 pp. Page 5 is crosswritten on page 1.

Thanks HC for his welcome letter. Comments at length on the younger generation. Complains that all girls want now is to be married. Feels relations are too shallow among the young men and women. Louis and Louise [Claude] have returned from Ambleside [see A12]. Describes the children's reactions to the visit. Louis is going to King's College, London, for two years. Is concerned about SC's health and approaching accouchement. [SC's daughter, Bertha Fanny Coleridge was born 13 July 1840 and died 24 July 1840.] Mentions Edward Jeffries. Asks if HC has ever heard a story about Wordsworth's having been the means of stopping a plan to drain Grasmere Lake. Mentions Mr. [Frederick] Faber. A friend of hers, Mrs. Richard [Hannah Mary Reynolds] Rathbone proposes to publish a collection of poems on childhood. Mrs. Rathbone asked her to ask HC if she might use his "Sabbath's Child" and two or three others [HC, "The Sabbath Day's Child," "The First Birthday," "Primitiae," and "To K. H. J.," in Hannah May Reynolds Rathbone, ed., *Childhood*, 1841]. Best regards.

B49 A.L.s., [36 Faulkner Street, Liverpool], [n.d., September, 1840]. To: [Nab Cottage, Rydal]. 4 pp.

Asks HC to let her know whether Mrs. R[ichard (Hannah Mary Reynolds)] Rathbone may use some of HC's poems for her book [*Childhood*, 1841]. They went on a tour of Wales with the A[dolph] Claudes, who sail on Wednesday for Valparaiso. Is pleased with the effects school [King's College, London] is having on Louis [Claude]. Mentions Mr. Hodgson, a tutor at King's College, with whose wife Louis talks of Windermere. Speaks of a Mr. Ryan who has manuscript copies of some of HC's poems. Mentions Mrs. [Jane Moss] Brancker and Croft Lodge [the Brancker Ambleside home].

B50 A.L.s., [36 Faulkner Street], Liverpool, 9th September, 1840. To: The Nab [Cottage], Rydal, Ambleside. 8 pp.

Mrs. Richard [Hannah Mary Reynolds] Rathbone will be much pleased if HC will let her use the poem on Katey Jones and they will all be delighted to see something new from his pen [HC, "The Sabbath Day's Child," "The First Birthday," "Primitiae," and "To K. H. J.," in Hannah Mary Reynolds Rathbone, ed., *Childhood*, 1841]. *Childhood* will also contain some of Mrs. Rathbone's own poetry and some of her daughter's. Mrs. Rathbone, whose oldest child is twenty, had another child, twelve years after the last. Is afraid the child will be quite spoiled. Describes at great length their trip to Wales. Is disappointed that, with the exception of Westminster Abbey, works of art and science make little impression on the girls. Louis [Claude]'s letters have been full of his troubles and longings for home. He is at King's College, London. Discusses her choice of schools and Louis's weak scholastic background at length. The deciding factor in sending Louis to King's College was that Mr. Withington's last request was that Arthur [Withington] be sent there. Mr. [James] and Mrs. [Jane Moss] Brancker are going to C[roft] L[odge, Ambleside] in a fortnight. Discusses Louis's character. Mary [Claude] is ill and Jane [Claude] has broken a darning needle in her foot. Gives a detailed account of the surgeon's futile efforts to extract the needle. The Adolph Claudes left [for Valparaiso] on the second. Saw them aboard and met the captain. Will miss them very much, especially the children. Regards to Mrs. [James] Greenwood.

B51   A.L.s.,Woodcroft, 6th October, [1840]. To: [Nab Cottage, Rydal]. 4 pp.

Sends Mary [Claude]'s thanks for HC's letter [A13?]. She and Mary are at the Richard Rathbones' to keep Margaret [Rathbone] company while her parents go to fetch another daughter who is ill. Mary [Claude] fell ill just after their arrival. Jane and Louise [Claude] have returned to town [Liverpool]. Sends news of Mr. [James] Brancker's political activities and Mrs. [Jane Moss] Brancker's improved health. Is sorry to hear [William] Fell has been ill. Mentions Mr. Withington, his daughters Fanny and Alice, and discusses Louis [Claude]'s progress at school. Describes Margaret [Rathbone], who is a great friend of Mary's. Jane [Claude] had broken a needle in her foot, but the needle is out and the foot healing. Sends regards to "Hauchen" [Mrs. William Fell] and [William] Fell.

B52   A.L.s., [36 Faulkner Street, Liverpool], Friday, 20th Nove, postmarked 1840. To: The Knabbe, Rydal Water, Ambleside. 6 pp.

Thanks HC for his letter [A19?]. He must not take any trouble about Mr. [Frederick] Faber's poems, as she can send for the volume from London [Frederick William Faber, *Cherwell Water Lily and Other Poems*, London, 1840]. Describes Mary [Claude]'s reaction to Faber's poems, about the beauty and excellence of which she is not sanguine. [For HC's estimate of Faber's poems see A19.] Asks if HC is really working on a second volume of poems. Wishes HC could visit Liverpool while Alice and Fanny [Withington] are there; there would be bed for him on Duke Street [James Brancker's townhouse]. Tells him of a friend of Mary's whose admiration for him knows no bounds. Writes at length of the Richard Rathbones and Mrs. [Hannah Mary Reynolds] Rathbone's projected book "Records of Children" [*Childhood*, 1841]. Margaret [Rathbone] has copied HC's sonnets from an album belonging to Louise and Jane [Claude]. Mary refused to show Margaret HC's sonnet about SC's twins ["Twins," DC, ed., HC, *Poems*, London, 1851]. She has sent Mrs. Rathbone the copy Mrs. [Margaret Harrison] Jones sent her of the lines to Katey ["To K. H. J.," Hannah Mary Reynolds Rathbone, ed., *Childhood*, 1841]. The elections have gone much against the reformers. Due to the death of W[illiam] W[alker] Currie, there were two elections, William Rathbone losing both. Louise had a tooth extracted and is now cutting her wisdom teeth. One sentence each [signed] from Mary and Jane gives HC their feelings about Louise's precocity. Mentions Mr. [James] and Mrs. [Jane Moss] Brancker and Croft Lodge [the Brancker Ambleside home]. Love to the [William] Fells.

B53   A.L.s., 1 Brighton Road, Waterloo, near Liverp'l, Sunday, 18th April, [1841]. To: [Nab Cottage, Rydal]. 9 pp. Page 9 is crosswritten on page 5.

Has come to the seaside for Louise [Claude]'s health, about which she is much concerned. Mary and Jane [Claude] are to join them tomorrow, and Louis [Claude] is already here. Knows HC will be shocked by Mrs. [Jane Moss] Brancker's death. Only Ellis had realized the danger. Mr. [James] Brancker will see no one but his brothers, and she supposes he has now gone to Croft Lodge [the Brancker Ambleside home]. Hopes HC will see him soon and write her. Thinks Brancker could bear to see only HC and Mr. [John] Dawes. Has had a letter from Mrs. Withington, who is much upset. A case concerning some property of Mrs. Withington's father is now to be decided in the House of Lords. Speculates at length about the Fells' new baby and asks HC to write about it. Mary would be delighted to have either Mr. [Frederick] Faber's poems or HC's. Discusses Mary's reading, mentioning "The Wren" by Mr. [Frederick] Faber ["The Wren of Rothay," *Cherwell Water Lily and Other Poems*, London, 1840]. Says HC would be delighted by Faber's letters to Louis. Mary is one of the baby [Fell]'s godmothers and will go to Ambleside for the christening. The baby is to be called Janette. Speaks of Louis's character and improved behavior. Louise's illness and other considerations have made their move most agreeable. They would welcome letters from HC. Has not given HC details of Mrs. [Jane Moss] Brancker's last days partly to spare him pain and partly because he has probably heard as much as he wants from [William] Fell.

B54   A.L.s., [36 Faulkner Street, Liverpool], 3rd September, postmarked 1841. To: The Knabbe, Rydal Water, Ambleside. 6 pp.

Describes in the greatest detail Louise [Claude]'s illness. Louise cannot eat or sleep, has headaches, and suffers from any noise or light around her. Mentions John Brancker, Hauchen [Mrs. William Fell], C[roft] L[odge, James Brancker's Ambleside home], [James] Brancker, and Mrs. R[ichard (Hannah Mary Reynolds)] Rathbone and her daughter Margaret. Was much amused by "Les amours de Monsieur Vieux Bois" [French caricatures], of which Jane will send HC some copies if she finishes them. Asks if HC has seen "Lord Bateman" [*The Loving Ballad of Lord Bateman*, George Cruikshank, illus. An adaptation by W. M. Thackeray of the traditional ballad. Notes by Charles Dickens. London, 1839]. A friend of Mrs. Rathbone's has written a sequel, "Lord Bateman's Daughter." They have been pleased with Miss [Harriet] Martineau's *Deerbrook* [3 vols., London, 1839] and *The Settlers at Home* [in *The Playfellow. A Series of Tales,* 4 vols., London, 1841]. Describes Louis [Claude]'s activities, mentioning Mr. Ryan, his private tutor in London. Hopes HC will visit the [James] Branckers. Describes the disposition of the property of Mr. Miller, an uncle from whom Mr. Withington had had great expectations.

B55   A.L.s., [36 Faulkner Street, Liverpool], 7th November, 1841. To: The Knabbe, Rydal Water, Ambleside. 7 pp.

Louise [Claude]'s health is worse. The doctors wished her to go to Mr. Jones in Milnthorpe, but they are unable to do so. Urges HC to publish. [James] Brancker often comes to see them, and Louis [Claude] is frequently at the Branckers. Mentions Miss Briggs and Mr. [Frederick] Faber. Sends five of Louise's emblematic verses, one of them on Margaret Rathbone. Asks HC to send an emblematic verse for some precious stones. Adds a note on Yates Greenwood and Louis.

B56   A.L.s., [36 Faulkner Street, Liverpool], 23rd January, [18]42. To: [Nab Cottage, Rydal]. 4 pp.

Would have reproved HC for not writing had she not supposed him busy correcting proofs on the Essays [unpublished in HC's lifetime]. Reminds him of their question about the emblematic meanings of the precious stones [see A16]. Has been unable to get Lady Blessington's Book of Gems [Marguerite Power Blessington, *Gems of Beauty*, 1838?]. Gives an account of Louis [Claude], mentioning Mr. [James] and Mrs. [Jane Moss] Brancker, Jane Horcefall [?], and the Misses Brancker. Mr. Brancker visits the Claudes' two or three times a week. Mentions the Tom Dawsons. Discusses at length Louise [Claude]'s ill health, mentioning her doctor, Mr. Day. Mentions the Prits family. Asks HC about the essays and poems, mentioning Mr. [Edward] Moxon [who declined to publish them]. Thanks him for trying to write an emblem on her.

B57   A.L.s., Harrogate, 3rd July, 1843. To: The Knabbe, Rydal Water, Ambleside. 4 pp.

Mary, Louise, and Louis [Claude] have been ill all winter, and Jane [Claude] has been in London. Writes at length of the children's health and Harrogate. Hears HC is going south [HC does not go]. Mentions DC, Mr. [James] Brancker, Croft Lodge [the Brancker Ambleside home], and Mrs. [Miss Simmons] Brancker, whom they all like. Asks for news of Mrs. STC and SC when

HC has seen them. Describes the only time she saw Katey Jones. The Adolph Claudes have lost a son [Willy?]. Her brother-in-law Charles [Claude] has made a trip to New Orleans. Mentions [Herbert] White, Mrs. White, and Emily [White]. Love from the children.

B58 A.L.s., [Broadlands, Ambleside?], Wednesday, 6th January, [1847]. To: [Nab Cottage, Rydal]. 3 pp.

The wedding [of Louise Claude to John W.] is to be on the 14th, and they would be happy to see him at breakfast as well as dinner. Expects Charles [Claude] and Louis [Claude] on the 12th and Mr. [James] Brancker on the 13th. Hopes he is not ill.

B59 A.L.s., [Broadlands, Ambleside?], [n.d.]. To: [Nab Cottage, Rydal?]. 4 pp.

Asks HC to tea on Tuesday to see Mrs. [John?] Davy, Miss [Harriet] Martineau, and others. If he is engaged Tuesday would he come on Thursday to meet their new neighbors Mrs. Joseph Green and her two daughters, the [John] Crossfields, and the [Herbert] Whites. Alice Withington is to be married to Alfred Eeles on Tuesday. Mentions Louise [Claude] and John [W., her husband].

B60 A.N.s., [Broadlands, Ambleside?], Tuesday, [n.d.]. To: [Nab Cottage, Rydal?]. 2 pp.

Old Mr. Brancker died quietly in his sleep Sunday night. Mentions Allan Bank and Mrs. [Miss Simmons?] Brancker.

B61 A.L.s., Dulwich, 15th March, [1847]. To: [Nab Cottage, Rydal]. 8 pp.

HC has probably heard from Mr. [William] Fell that her children [Louise Claude and her husband John W.] sailed on 9 March. Had a letter from Louise and John this morning. The pilot was leaving them and they were picking up fair winds. John says Louise, unlike many of their fellow passengers, is not seasick. Gives further details from John's letter and describes John and Louise's departure. John is in charge of 104 soldiers and looked quite magnificent in his uniform. Mary is exhausted after their journey first to London and then to Dulwich. Mentions Mr. Harding, Mrs. Withington, and Fanny Withington. Love to the [William] Fells. Remembrances to Mr. and Mrs. [John] Crossfield.

B62 A.N.s., [Broadlands, Ambleside?], Monday, [n.d., 1848]. To:

[Nab Cottage, Rydal]. 2 pp.

Mary [Claude] would like to borrow HC's Tennyson. She will send for them. Hopes to see HC before they leave for Rampside. Mentions Mary and Louise [Claude].

B63   A.N.s., Westfield Cottage, Rampside, 23rd August, [1848]. To: [Nab Cottage, Rydal]. 2 pp.

Louise [Claude] became the mother of a little girl on June 20. John [W., her husband] wrote that both mother and child are well. Mary [Claude] sends thanks for the Tennyson.

LOUISE CLAUDE W.*

B64   A.L.s., Liscard, August 6th [n.d.]. To: [n.p.]. 6 pp.

Is very sorry to have mislaid one of HC's papers. Gives a long account of her journey from Liverpool to Liscard. Louis [Claude] has been a frequent visitor to Liscard, as an attractive Miss Lloyd, a cousin of the [Charles] Lloyds, has been staying with the Prits and the Edward Lloyds. Is going to Aigburth on Saturday. Hopes to see the [James] Branckers and their little girl. Mentions the extraction of a tooth and hopes her health will improve.

B65   A.L.s., Faulkner Street 36, [n.d.]. To: [n.p.]. 4 pp.

They have long been expecting a letter from HC. Have had letters from Valparaiso [the Adolph Claudes]. Jeanetta [Claude]'s letter to Jane [Claude] asked about Mary Agnes Nicholson's mother, who was ill when the [Adolph] Claudes were in Ambleside. Speaks of Jennetta Fell, Mr. [James] Brancker, Mrs. Ecklin, snowdrops [flowers], and the [Herbert] Whites. Love to everybody.

B66   A.L.s., Harrogate, 19th May, postmarked 1842. To: The Knabbe, Rydal Water, Ambleside. 4 pp.

Hopes HC will forgive her for not writing. Does not like being away from her family and her home. Delights that they will all be together again there soon.

*See footnote under Louise Claude W., in correspondence from Hartley Coleridge, A group.

131

Is glad the [Herbert] Whites have settled in Ambleside. Mentions the Prits, Catherine Prits, Louis [Claude], and Mr. [James] Brancker. Wishes HC could see some of Mary [Claude]'s poetry, for Mary discounts all praise from the family. Mentions Baby [Jeanetta] Fell.

B67 A.L.s., 19 Arundel Street, Strand, 6th March, [1847]. To: [Nab Cottage, Rydal]. 6 pp.

Mrs. [Louise] Claude and Mary [Claude] are in Parliament Street having Mrs. Claude's picture made. If the picture turns out well, she [Louise Claude W.] will take it to India with her. She and John [W., her husband] had their pictures made yesterday; hers was so clear that you could even see her brooch with the two children on it. Jane [Claude], John [W.] and Fanny Withington have all gone to the ship. There are 19 passengers and 104 soldiers. Describes John's preparations for the journey. Louis [Claude] is with them. Mentions Mrs. Claude's plans to go to Dulwich, Mr. Harding's health, and her hopes for a letter from HC.

B68 A.L.s., Subathoo [Subathu, on the present Himachal Pradesh–Punjab border, India], May 13th, 1848. To: [Nab Cottage, Rydal]. 8 pp.

His long, kind letter arrived at just the right time. John [W., her husband] has been dangerously ill and she was much distressed at conflicting advice from different doctors. Although it is very hot, they are happy here among the mountains. Reports of insurrections in Punjab make her fear the 2nd Europeans will be moved. John tells her she is a very poor soldier's wife. She fears the sun more than battle. Describes the drought and longs for the rainy season. Even the natives are suffering and John is very busy. The thunderstorms make her quite ill. Describes electrical phenomena. The loneliness and strangeness of the station have made her so nervous that she is afraid of her own servants. Dreamed of Rydal and Ambleside last night; such rare dreams are always a delight. Fears they will live and die in India. Please write again.

MARY S. CLAUDE

B69 A.L.s., [36 Faulkner Street, Liverpool]. Thursday, 18th [n.d., probably October, 1838]. To: Grasmere. 3 pp.

Thanks HC for the letter and the sonnet [HC, "To the Reverend Frederick Faber," *LHC*, p. 225]. Is glad HC thinks so well of Mr. Faber [see A22]. Their three months' residence here has not at all reconciled them to living in town. Mentions Louis [Claude] and Jones Greenwood. Describes a visit to an art exhibition which included many pictures of the queen. Adolph and Jeanette [Claude] come every morning to work on their English. Miss [Hauchen] Reckam, Aunt Minna [Mrs. Adolph Claude]'s sister speaks English very imperfectly. Mentions Willy [Claude, Adolph's son]. They went with Mr. [James] Brancker to see the steamer *Liverpool*, which she liked much less than the American packets. Mrs. [Louise] Claude has gone to York. Love from Jane and Louise [Claude].

B70   A.L.s., [36 Faulkner Street, Liverpool], Nov. 3ʳᵈ, 1840. To: The Nab, Rydal Water, Ambleside. 4 pp.

Thanks HC for his letter and the lines [on Katey Jones] for Mrs. Rathbone [HC, "To K. H. J." and others, Hannah Mary Reynolds Rathbone, ed., *Childhood*, 1841]. Mrs. [Louise] Claude sent the lines to Mrs. H. [Margaret Harrison] Jones, who asks that only initials be used. Recommends and discusses Humphrey's Clock [Boz (Charles Dickens), *Master Humphrey's Clock*, 88 weekly pts., 20 monthly nos. from April 1840]. Mentions the [Herbert?] Whites, Broadlands [the Claudes' Ambleside home], Louis [Claude], Mr. [James] Brancker, and Croft Lodge [the Branckers' Ambleside home]. Asks how HC could think of coupling Mr. [Frederick] Faber's name with Mrs. Cousins and demands that he do penance by sending them Faber's poems forthwith [*Cherwell Water Lily and Other Poems*, London, 1840]. Mentions Mrs. [William] Fell, Jane [Claude] and her art teacher Mr. Barber, and says Mrs. Claude wishes to go to Southport. Louise [Claude] had a tooth pulled. The family, Margaret Rathbone, and another girl are all learning parts of Schiller's *Turandot, Princess of China* [A. T. Gurney, trans., Frankfort, 1836]. Mrs. [Jane Moss] Brancker is looking well. Describes a new card game introduced by Jane. Love from all.

B71   A.L.s., [36 Faulkner Street, Liverpool], Saturday, 24 July [1841]. To: [Nab Cottage, Rydal]. 4 pp.

Was glad to receive HC's letter. Louise [Claude] is still very ill. Liverpool is crowded with 60,000 strangers who have come for the Cattle Show and the meeting of the Agricultural Society. The German Opera is in Liverpool; Louis [Claude] and Yates Greenwood are going to see it tonight. Mentions Hauchen [Mrs. William Fell]'s Baby [Jeanette], little Dobson, Croft Lodge [James Brancker's Ambleside home], [Bell and Jane] Horsfalls, and Mr. Carr. Love to HC and the [William] Fells.

B72   A.L.s., [36 Faulkner Street], Liverpool, Feb. 25ᵗʰ, [n.d.]. To: [n.p.]. 4 pp.

Mentions a sonnet Mrs. Claude's friends in Berlin want. Thanks HC for writing; she will deliver his message to the [James] Branckers the first time she sees any of them. Describes at length the [Brancker] baby she saw at Aigburth.

Louise [Claude] is with the Whites at Devonport. They often hear from Jeanette Claude [Adolph Claude's daughter], who is very studious. Has heard that her godchild Jeanette Fell is clever but not very amiable. Dr. Feick, who once lived in Grasmere, is now professor of German at the Mechanic Institute. He visits the Claudes often. He hoped to teach HC German so that he could translate Schiller. Speaks of the ignorance of city children of snowdrops and other common plants. Love from Mrs. Claude and Jane [Claude].

B73 A.L.s., [36 Faulkner Street, Liverpool], Tuesday, 8th, Dec., [1840]. To: [Grasmere]. 3 pp.

Thanks HC for sending the poems [HC, *Poems*, Leeds, 1833?]. Can't think of taking his own copy and will take good care of it until they return to Ambleside in the spring. The Withingtons leave Liverpool on Christmas Eve. Mentions Alice and Fanny [Withington], Louis [Claude], Mr. [James] Brancker, Mr. [John] Dawes, and Mamma [Mrs. Louise Claude]. They are going to see three Carracci paintings [Annibale Carracci, Italian painter, 1560–1609]. Tonight they will hear Mr. [Hugh] MacNeile preach on the Jews [see *Popular Lectures on the Prophecies relative to the Jewish Nation*, 1833]. Mentions Mr. Sheppard. Love from Mamma, Jane, and Louise [Claude], and Alice and Fanny Withington.

B74 A.L.s., Broadlands, [Ambleside], Thursday evening, [n.d., 1847?]. To: [Nab Cottage, Rydal]. 4 pp.

Her books [*Little Poems for Little People*, London, 1847?] have come, and she sends him two copies. Is shocked at the illustration for one of the poems. Sends two or three of Mr. [Herbert] White's translations for HC to send to *Blackwood['s Magazine]*. If HC wants to look them over, she will write them out properly. Wants to copy HC's essay [?] before he sends it away to Kendal. Mentions Mr. [John] Crossfield, Rothay Bank [the Crossfield home], and Louise [Claude] and her husband John [W.].

B75 A.L.s., Broadlands, [Ambleside], March 7th [1848]. To: [Nab Cottage, Rydal]. 4 pp.

Since HC said he would have helped her prepare her "Little Poems" [*for Little People*, London, 1847] for printing, would he help her with some tales [*Twilight Thoughts*, London, 1848] which she intends to send Chapman [and Hall, her publishers]. Says he will find her punctuation and grammar improvable, and she has left him plenty of blank paper for comments. Mr. [Herbert] White has gout; Mrs. White is well. Uncle Charles [Claude] is going out to Valparaiso. Louise [Claude] and her husband [John W.] are enjoying India.

B76 A.L.s., Broadlands, [Ambleside], Saturday, [n.d., 1848]. To: The

Knabbe, Rydal. 3 pp.

Is sending Robert with the "Little Whirlwind" and the end of another story for
HC to look at. Intends to send the tales off [to Chapman and Hall, her pub-
lisher] next week. There is good news from India. John [W., Louise's husband]
has been appointed to serve with the 2nd Europeans at Subathu. Louise is well
and will soon join John. Mama [Mrs. Louise Claude] is in Liverpool.

B77   A.L.s., Broadlands, [Ambleside], 16th March, [1848]. To: [Nab
Cottage, Rydal]. 2 pp.

Chapman and Hall [her publishers] are ready to see her tales [*Twilight
Thoughts*, London, 1848]. If HC will send her some of them, she will get them
copied out. Asks HC what he thinks of the proposed title; she doesn't like
Chapman's titles. Mr. [Herbert] White is better. Mrs. Louise Claude has gone
to Bowness to see Mrs. White. The hot house plants at Croft Lodge [James
Brancker's Ambleside home] are to be sold.

B78   A.L.s., Broadlands, [Ambleside], Saturday, [n.d., 1848]. To:
[Nab Cottage, Rydal]. 2 pp.

Her publisher [Chapman and Hall] has just sent the proof sheets for the twelfth
tale. Would like HC to look at it before she sends it back. Jane [Claude] has
left. They are going to hear [John] Wilson [1800–1849] sing at Bowness. The
bears and monkeys have delighted the [William] Fells. Clara is the prettiest of
the Fells.

B79   A.N.s., [Broadlands, Ambleside], [n.d., 1848]. To: [Nab Cottage,
Rydal]. 1 p.

Asks if he will be in Ambleside the next day or Sunday. She would like to consult him about the proof sheets [of *Twilight Thoughts*, London, 1848] that
Chapman [and Hall, publishers] has sent her.

DERWENT COLERIDGE

B80   A.L.s., Helleston, Cornwall, 14th Oct., 1835. To: Mrs. Flemings',
Grassmere n^r Ambleside, Westmoreland. 4 pp.

Wishes very much to see his brother. Gives a long account of his children

[Derwent Moultrie and Emily Frances Gillman Coleridge]. Young Hopwood overestimates his preaching, which falls far short of what he wishes due to the fact that he is so busy with his school. Discusses at length what happens to a dead infant's soul. Continues the letter on Sunday evening, 18 October. Disagrees with HC's estimate [see A45] of *Table Talk* [HNC, ed., *Specimens of the Table-Talk of the Late Samuel Taylor Coleridge*, 2 vols., London, 1835]. While the conversations printed are fragmentary, they may be useful. Describes STC's conversation and the difficulties of reporting it. Hal [HNC] was present when HC's last letter arrived. HNC had just reviewed the Worthies [HC, *Biographia Borealis; or, Lives of the Distinguished Northerns*, Leeds, 1833] in the Quarterly [*Magazine*, September, 1835] and is so interested in HC that Derwent was loth that anything coming from HC should give him pain. Says to tell Mrs. Charles [Sara Hustler] Fox that Mr. Robt Fox and Caroline [Fox] spent the evening with them. Love to Juliet [Fox]. Love to all at Rydal Mount. Mentions Mr. [John] Dawes.

B81   A.L. (inc.), 1 New Bank Building, London, Monday 28th Dec., 1840, 10 pm. To: [Nab Cottage, Rydal]. 4 pp.

This is the tenth letter he has written today and the hour is very late. Has been ill since he left Cornwall. One of the ten letters is addressed to William Wordsworth, and HC can get all the news from that, since he does not feel inclined to repeat it in another letter. Has failed to write not because he had too little but because he had too much to say. Has *thought* many letters. Goes on at length about how unsatisfactory his imaginary letters were. Continues on Tuesday morning. Speaks of his poor friend [Zachary?] Macaulay, who was quite a talker. Writes at great length on the Missionary Society, its methods, and its relation to clergymen.

B82   A.L.s., Stanley Grove, Chelsea, 19th August, 1842. To: [Nab Cottage, Rydal]. 1 p.

Encloses a pamphlet [see A34]. Derwent [Moultrie Coleridge] is rapidly recovering from his broken leg. He [DC] and Mary [Pridham Coleridge] are well.

B83   A.L.s., St. Marks College, Chelsea, 22nd Aug., 1842. To: [Nab Cottage, Rydal]. 4 pp.

Can write only a little to acknowledge HC's letter, as the family is leaving for Frome in Somersetshire to place Derwent [Moultrie Coleridge] as a private pupil with his uncle-in-law Dusautoy. Shrewsbury did not agree with young Derwent, and he did not agree with Shrewsbury, though [Dr. Benjamin Hall] Kennedy [Headmaster at Shrewsbury] is a good friend of DC's. Says HC is often in his thoughts and he would be glad to see him. Perhaps he will visit the north. Reminds HC of his past transgressions and says that if for once HC will behave like an ordinary middle-aged gentleman, they will get on well. Discusses church matters and church-men. Mentions HC's poem on [Dr. Thomas] Arnold ["On the late Dr. Arnold," DC, ed., HC, *Poems*, London, 1851], whom DC criticizes severely. Asks to be remembered to Herbert White, who gave him a Horace and a Knox. He reads the Horace and looks at the Knox. Mae Ann Acker has been with them for a visit. She and Sara [SC] are well, but Henry [HNC] is quite ill.

B84 A.L.s., St. Mark's College, Chelsea, 25th Jany, 1843. To: [Nab Cottage, Rydal]. 1 p.

Informs HC of the birth of a new niece, Christabel Rose [Coleridge]. HC may write a poem to her at his earliest convenience. The women are behaving like characters in *Tristram Shandy*. Looks forward to seeing HC soon, as he plans to visit the north during the next vacation.

B85 A.L.s., St. Marks College, Chelsea, 9 April, 1845. To: [Nab Cottage, Rydal]. 3 pp.

Writes to announce the birth of a second son, whom they think of calling William Hartley [Henry Nelson Praed Coleridge, b./d. 1845]. Mrs. STC will write at more length. Asks HC to take this news over to the Wordsworths. Regards to the [William] Richardsons.

B86 A.L.s., St. Mark's College, Chelsea, 25 Aug., 1845. To: [Nab Cottage, Rydal]. 3 pp. Written on stationery headed "National Society's TRAINING INSTITUTION FOR SCHOOLMASTERS."

Says HC will have learned from Mrs. STC's last letter that their infant son has died [Henry Nelson Praed Coleridge, b./d. 1845]. He is buried in a cemetery opposite the college gates, though DC would have preferred a country churchyard. Does not like London churchyards. The family has been at Herne Bay, in Kent, a few miles from Margate. The vacation has been good for them all. Writes at length about Christabel [Rose Coleridge]. Is glad he saw Mr. [John] Dawes when he did [on DC's visit to HC, autumn, 1843]. Love to all friends.

B87 A.L.s., St. Mark's College, Chelsea, 10 October, 1845. To: [Nab Cottage, Rydal]. 4 pp. One page of the paper is bordered in black. Accompanied by a two-page extract in the hand of Mary Pridham Coleridge.

Describes Mrs. STC's funeral, listing family members present. Gives a summary of the passing of Mrs. STC, giving thanks that she died full of years, with undimmed powers, and without pain [see A63]. Speaks of her at length as a just and true spirit, always giving of herself, etc. Sara [SC] is very saddened by her two losses [HNC and Mrs. STC] and her ill health. Alludes to the death of a child [Henry Nelson Praed Coleridge, b./d. 1845]. Mentions Mary [Pridham Coleridge], Christabel [Rose Coleridge], and Derwent [Moultrie Coleridge]. Will write of business matters when the Judge [John Taylor Coleridge] comes to town.

B88   A.L.s., St. Mark's College, Chelsea, 28 Sept, 1846. To: [Nab Cottage, Rydal]. 6 pp.

Hears HC has set fire to his bedclothes. Mrs. [Eleanor] Richardson must be paid and precautions taken to lessen the danger and the alarm HC's housemates must feel. Feels he must counsel HC as a friend. Some people regard HC as a child, some as a lunatic, some as both. Should have written HC long ago, but feared, lest he should make bad worse. HC's behavior has cut him off from friends and family. DC cannot possibly visit HC in his present condition—circumstances prevent it, not to mention the fact that the misery of seeing HC so would doubtless cause DC's health to give way. Thinks that only physical labor at some mechanical occupation can save HC. He must turn water drinker with [Dr. William] Fell's advice. Sympathizes with HC.

MRS. DERWENT [MARY PRIDHAM] COLERIDGE

B89   A.L.s., Helleston, Cornwall, Aug[st] 15th, 1834. To: Grasmere, Westmoreland. 4 pp., including a 1-page note from DC. Paper has narrow black borders.

A letter of condolence on the death of STC [25 July 1834]. Speaks of closer ties between the brothers, HC's letter, and DC's dyspepsia. Is troubled to be writing to HC without ever having met him. Sometimes hears of HC from Miss [Emily] Trevenen's northern relatives. Is adding to the house and asks HC to visit in the spring. Mentions Dervy [Derwent Moultrie Coleridge], Sara [SC], James Coleridge, and Mr. and Mrs. Ion [?], who have gone to Switzerland with Juliet [Ion?].

DC assures HC of his love. Is now unable to write at length but promises to do so soon. Mentions a letter from Henry [HNC].

B90   A.L.s., St. Mark's College, Stanley Grove, Chelsea, Oct. 7th, [1842]. To: [Nab Cottage, Rydal]. 4 pp

Has made a mistake in sending HC the newspapers from Mrs. STC and he will receive them late. Regrets she has never met HC and he has never seen their boy [Derwent Moultrie Coleridge], who is close to manhood. Speaks of DC's plans for St. Mark's College. Mrs. STC has visited them. Henry [HNC] is so ill that DC has little hope he will recover.

B91 A.L.s., Stanley Grove, Chelsea, Novr 21st, postmarked 1842. To: The Knagge, nr Rydal, Ambleside, Westmoreland. 4 pp. With accompanying envelope.

DC will answer HC's letter soon. Accounts from Chester Place [on HNC's illness] are much more cheerful. HNC is better. Speaks of Mrs. STC's fortitude. Edith [Coleridge] is with them at Stanley Grove. Wishes HC could see Dervy, Herby, and Edy [Coleridge]. HNC, his family, and the Judge [John Taylor Coleridge] all received communion from Dr. [James Duke] Coleridge.

B92 A.L.s., [Stanley Grove, Chelsea], Decr 5, [1842]. To: [Nab Cottage, Rydal]. 4 pp.

Tells HC of the death of Lady [Fanny Coleridge] Patteson. Discusses Lady Patteson's character and death and remarks how much SC will miss her. DC saw Henry [HNC] and says [Sir Benjamin Collins] Brodie told SC not to despair. Sends family news, mentioning Dervy [Derwent Moultrie Coleridge], and Herbert and Edith [Coleridge]. Chides HC for not writing. Love from DC. Tomorrow is their fifteenth wedding anniversary.

B93 A.L.s., [Stanley Grove, Chelsea]. Jan^{ry} 19, [1843]. To: [Nab Cottage, Rydal]. 5 pp. Page 5 is crosswritten on page 1.

Henry [HNC] was very ill and thought to be dying for some hours yesterday. HNC refuses to see anyone but Sara [SC]. Mrs. STC is also ill. Sends news of Derwent [DC], Edith [Coleridge], Herby [Herbert Coleridge], and Dervy [Derwent Moultrie Coleridge], whom they are thinking of sending to Charter House. Sara [SC] is holding up well. Asks HC to write.

B94 A.L.s., Stanley Grove, Chelsea, Jany 25th, postmarked 1843. To: The Knagge, n^r Rydal, Ambleside, Westmorland. 3 pp. With accompanying envelope.

Henry is worse [HNC died 26 January 1843]. Sara [SC] is always by his side. Is also anxious about the health of Mrs. STC. Hopes her sad letters do not worry HC but feels it is better that he knows. Love from DC.

B95 A.L.s., St. Mark's College, Chelsea, Dec. 24th, [1843]. To: [Nab Cottage, Rydal]. 5 pp. Page 5 is crosswritten on page 1.

Thanks HC for the lines on Christabel ["To Christabel Rose Coleridge," DC, ed., HC, *Poems*, London, 1851] and his letters. Describes Christabel. Sees SC and Mrs. STC only seldom, since they are five or six miles away. Dervy [Derwent Moultrie Coleridge] is sixteen and they are very anxious about his principles. Sends DC's "Report" of St. Marks [?]. The copy is one of a few printed for private circulation and differs from the version to be printed in the National Society's Report. Asks HC's opinion of the pamphlet. Asks HC to tell Mrs. Wordsworth that John Hutchinson is improved and will, hopefully, turn out well.

B96 A.L.s., 10 Chester Place, Regent's Park, [London], Sepr 24th, [1845]. To: [Nab Cottage, Rydal]. 4 pp.

Alludes to the death of their son [see B86] and now has to announce an even more grievous loss [Mrs. STC died 24 September 1845]. Describes Mrs. STC's last days. She was much improved, and died suddenly. The doctor believes her heart failed. She was not in pain, and her faculties remained clear. Today is her [Mary Pridham Coleridge's] birthday. DC has gone to fetch SC.

B97 A.L.s., St. Mark's College, [Chelsea], Feb^ry 16th, [1847]. To: [Nab Cottage, Rydal]. 4 pp.

Writes of the new baby, Ernest Hartley [Coleridge]. Describes Christabel [Rose Coleridge]'s reception of her new brother. Dervy [Derwent Moultrie Coleridge], who is said to be much like HC, has just matriculated at Exeter College, Oxford. Sends news of Sara [SC], who badly misses Mrs. STC. Describes Herbert and Edith [Coleridge]. Sends a charade. Asks about the [Dr. Thomas] Arnolds, who often speak of HC.

EDITH COLERIDGE

B98 A.N., [No. 10 Chester Place, Regent's Park, London], [n.d.]. To: [Nab Cottage, Rydal]. Note on the verso of a drawing of cat with kittens.

Presentation note of this "trifle" to "Uncle Hartley."

B99   A.L.s., Highgate, Friday, 25 July, 1834. To: Mrs Fleming's, Grasmere, Ambleside, Westmorland. 3 pp.

Writes to announce the death of STC at 6:30 that morning. Although STC's mind was clear, he suffered great pain, and to the end had difficulty breathing. James Gillman was with him the night before. STC had difficulty speaking and could hardly bear the presence of anyone other than Harriet, the servant. Will miss STC deeply. SC is much shaken. She and Mrs. STC send their love. Begs HC to comfort his mother.

B100   A.L., Live. Inn., 16 August, 1834. To: [Grasmere]. 4 pp. With a note from SC. Accompanied by an envelope with contents summarized and the note, "upon the whole this letter would be of more use for the memoirs of Henry than for that of Hartley."

Says Mr. [Joseph Henry] Green is STC's sole executor. Will forward to HC a copy of STC's will. Mrs. Rickman talks of going to Keswick. Mr. Green proposes to send a copy of the will to Mr. Wordsworth and Mr. [Robert] Southey. All STC's property is willed to Mrs. STC for her use during her life and then in equal shares to HC, DC, and SC. HC's share is, by codicil, invested in Mr. Green, HNC, and Mr. [James] Gillman. All books and manuscripts go to Green with permission to purchase the former at his own price and publish the latter, any profits from publication to go to the estate. The will leaves a ring of hair to Miss [Sara] Hutchinson. Knows nothing of debts, especially at Highgate. Mentions [Thomas] Wedgewood's annuity, Herbert and Edith [Coleridge], DC, and SC. Gives long extracts from the will. Green wishes HNC to gather the literary and critical remains. Julius Hare and Sterling are to be in charge of the divinity, and Green will handle the philosophy himself. Mr. Gillman is to collect the letters. Discusses publication plans.
    SC says she has influenza. Speaks of STC's life. She is staying at the [Basil] Montague Place, Bedford Square. Love to friends at Rydal Mount.

B101   A.L.i., endorsed on letter face by HNC "London, Eighteenth Aug^t, 1834." To: [Grasmere]. 1 p. With a scrap note on "moles." Although on different paper, probably a continuation of B100.

Has a collection of STC's table talk and is thinking of publishing it [HNC, ed., STC, *Specimens of the Table-Talk of the Late Samuel Taylor Coleridge*, 2 vols., London, 1835]. Feels it would sell very well. Reports on the health of the family members, including SC, Herbert, Mrs. STC, and his father and mother [James and Frances Taylor Coleridge]. Love to Mr. and Mrs. Wordsworth and the others at Rydal Mount. [John Gibson] Lockhart has asked for a sheet of

Worthies [HC, *Biographia Borealis; or, Lives of the Distinguished Northerns*, Leeds, 1833]. Tells HC not to bargain with [Francis Edward] Bingley [his Leeds publisher]. Will try to sell the magazine article manuscript [unknown] HC sent but is dubious of his success.

B102   A.L.s., Live. Inn. 14. Jan., 1836. To: Mrs Fleming's, Grasmere, Ambleside. 3 pp. Accompanied by a blue paper wrapper endorsed by SC with a note on the contents. Address face is bordered in black.

Writes of the death of his father [James Coleridge] on 10 January 1836. He was restless and uncomfortable but not in severe pain. His mind failed for periods at the end. Mentions the death of old Sir John Kennaway. Says Mrs. STC was much relieved to hear HC does not intend to recommence any work for [Francis Edward] Bingley. Urges HC to print only in London. Urges HC to write articles on Retsch and Macbeth for the Q[uarterly] R[eview] [see A46]. Mentions Owen Lloyd, SC, and Herbert and Edith [Coleridge]. People have begun to distinguish HNC from HC by printing his name as *Nelson* Coleridge, which he abominates.

B103   A.L., Hampstead, 14 August, 1836. To: Mrs. Fleming's, Grasmere, Westmorland. 4 pp. Part of page 3–4 has been cut away. The letter contains a brief note from Mrs. STC. A letter from Nurse [Mrs. Ann Parrott] to SC is enclosed.

Thanks HC for his letter. Has a cold, which is inconvenient as they are leaving for Ottery on the 18th to stay with Frank [Francis George Coleridge]. Mentions his mother [Frances Taylor Coleridge] and Mrs. STC. Speaks of the publication of STC's *Remains* [HNC, ed., *The Literary Remains of Samuel Taylor Coleridge*, 4 vols., London, 1836-1839]. Will forward the volumes to HC, Robert Southey, and William Wordsworth by John and Mrs. Woollam. There is enough material for two more volumes. Mr. [James] Gillman is collecting material for a memoir [*The Life of S. T. Coleridge*, London, 1838]. Mentions Frank, John [Taylor Coleridge], the [Dr. Thomas] Arnolds' house [Fox How]. HC's packet of essays has not arrived. Supposes it contained an article for the Qu[arterly] R[eview] [unknown]. Mentions Mr. Kew, an admirer of STC's.

B104   A.L.s., 10 Chester Place, Reg[ent's] Park, [London], 5 July, 1840. To: [Nab Cottage, Rydal]. 4 pp.

SC is expecting a baby before the end of July [Bertha Fanny Coleridge, b. 13 July d. 24 July 1840] and asks if HC is willing to serve as godfather. Mentions Mrs. STC and Derwent [DC] and Mary [Pridham Coleridge] who are now with Miss [Emily] Trevenen in Belgium or on the Rhine. HNC hopes to visit Holland soon. The new volume of STC [HNC, ed., *The Literary Remains of Samuel Taylor Coleridge*, 4 vols., London, 1836–1839] is selling well. Holds an increasingly higher opinion of *Church and State* [HNC, ed., STC, *On the Constitution of Church and State*, London, 1839]. Thinks the American schools of Coleridge, [James?] Marsh and McVickers, very amusing. Herbert and Edith [Coleridge] are now at Ramsgate.

B105 A.L.i., [10 Chester Place, Regent's Park, London], 16 July, 1840. To: The Nab [Cottage], Rydal, Ambleside. 1 p.

Announces the birth of a daughter [Bertha Fanny Coleridge, b. 13 July d. 24 July 1840]. Mother and child are well. SC has been very ill. Thanks HC for his letter.

B106 A.L.i., [10] Chester Place [Regent's Park, London], 24 August, 1840. To: The Nab [Cottage], Rydal, near Ambleside. 3 pp.

Is going abroad for three weeks with a young Oxonian, Cowley Powles. Outlines his itinerary. Sara [SC] and Edith [Coleridge] will stay at Lady [Elizabeth Turner] Palgrave's. SC is improving. Reports on the sale of STC's works. The *Poems* have sold best, then *Aids* [*to Reflection*]. *Church and State* has done well, and the fourth volume of *Remains* sells better than the third. People always ask about HC's *Worthies* [HC, *Biographia Borealis; or, Lives of the Distinguished Northerns*, Leeds, 1833]. HNC thinks the title foolish. No news of R[obert] S[outhey] yet.

MRS. HENRY NELSON
[SARA] COLERIDGE

B107 Thirty-four letters from SC to HC are calendared and indexed by Carl D. Grantz in his doctoral dissertation, *Letters of Sara Coleridge: A Calendar and Index to Her Manuscript Correspondence in the University of Texas Library*, 2 vols., The University of Texas at Austin, June 1967. Grantz gives the following numbers and dates for SC's letters to HC:

508 A.L.s., [1834?]
509 A.L.s., [July?] 23, [1834?]
510 A.L.i., [winter 1834/1835?]
511 A.L.s., [April 1835?]
512 A.L.s., January 21, 1836.
513 A.L.(inc.), Saturday, January 14, [1840?]
514 A.L.s., postmarked March 16, 1840.

515 A.L., October 3, postmarked 1841.
516 A.L.s.(inc.), postmarked June 13, 1842.
517 A.L.s., March 9, 1843.
518 A.L. (inc.), [March 1843?]
519 A.L., Tuesday, May 30, [1843?]
520 A.L. (inc.), [mid–1844?]
521 A.L.s. (inc.), January 20–21, 1845.
522 A.L.s., [early October 1845?]
523 A.L.(inc.), October 13, 1845.
524 A.L.s., October 21, 1845.
525 A.L.s. (inc.), [October 1845?]
526 A.L.s. (inc.), [October 1845?]
527 A.L.s., February 16, [1846?]
528 A.L.(inc.), [April 1846?]
529 A.L.s., July 7, 1846.
530 A.L. (inc.?), Friday, August 7, [1846?]
531 A.L.(inc.), [March 1847?]
532 A.L.s., Tuesday, March 30, [1847?]
533 A.L., Saturday, April 17, [1847?]
534 A.L.s., April 28, 1847.
535 A.L.s. (inc.), [spring 1847?]
536 A.L., [June 1847?]
537 A.L.s., October 7, 1847.
538 A.L., Thursday, October 28, [1847?]
539 A.L.s., [autumn 1847?]
540 A.L.(inc.?), November 23, [1847?]
541 A.L.(inc.), Tuesday, August 15, [1848]?

HENRY NELSON, SARA
AND MRS. S. T. COLERIDGE

B108 A.L., [10] Chester Place, [Regent's Park, London], 22 Oct., 1839. To: Grasmere, near Ambleside, Westmoreland. 4 pp. A combined letter from HNC, SC, and Mrs. STC.

HNC heard HC intends to come to London and writes to say he is welcome. Reports on his trip abroad and Herby [Herbert Coleridge]'s schooling. Is working on a new edition of the *Biographia* [HNC and SC, eds., STC, *Biographia Literaria*, 2 vols., London, 1847].

SC repeats the offer of a hearty welcome. Asks for news of Robert Southey and refers to his marriage [to Caroline Bowles on 4 June 1839]. Feels it is a great blessing that he has found a companion and is sure that in time Kate [Southey] will come to appreciate having someone to share her responsibilities [the marriage was the cause of a bitter family quarrel]. Mentions Cuthbert

[Southey], Bertha [Southey Hill], DC, Mary [Pridham Coleridge], Mr. [John Wood] Warter, and Edith [Southey] Warter.

Mrs. STC hopes HC will come. Mentions Mr. [Edward] Moxon and the [William] Richardsons. Has seen the Massinger and Ford advertised [HC, *The Dramatic Works of Massinger and Ford*, London, 1840].

JOHN TAYLOR COLERIDGE

B109   A.L.s., Bedford Square, [London], Jan.ʸ 6, 1846. To: The Nab, Rydal, Ambleside. 3 pp.

Writes on behalf of SC and DC regarding the disposal of STC's estate. STC's will directs that upon the death of Mrs. STC the principal of his property be divided among the children. Matters are, at the moment, very inconvenient. Derwent [DC] cannot pay off his debts; Sara [SC] cannot advance money for her children; Mr. [Joseph Henry] Green is kept busy dividing the dividends; HC is dependent on Sara. Sara and Derwent are anxious to divide the principal, and he hopes HC will agree. HC's share can be invested or he can receive an annuity for life. Has just returned from Devonshire. SC is well but her eyes suffer from her work on the Biographia [HNC and SC, eds., STC, *Biographia Literaria*, 2 vols., London, 1847].

SAMUEL TAYLOR COLERIDGE

B110   A.N.i., [n.p.], [n.d., early 1808?]. To: [Greta Hall, Keswick]. 1 p. Note is in a wrapper of folded paper with endorsement of date and contents by EHC. The note is written on the back of a fragment of a letter from STC to Mrs. STC.

Is very busy for HC's sake and that of DC, SC, and Mrs. STC. Will write, and plans to join them in two months. Prays HC to think of God and the fallibility of man.

B111 A.L.s., [Greta Hall, Keswick], [ca. 20 June 1815]. To: with Mr.
Morgan, Calne, Wiltshire. 4 pp., including a half–page note from SC.
Letter was franked in London, 23 June 1815, by John Rickman.

> Has heard good reports of the Ottery St. Mary Coleridges from Miss Spedding.
> Mentions a list of books HC wants, then mentions Mr. [William] Jackson, and
> STC. Asks for details of HC's college life. Repeatedly mentions HC's cousin at
> Oxford [William Hart Coleridge]. Sends news of Aunt [Mary Fricker] Lovell,
> Wilsy [Mrs. Wilson, Greta Hall housekeeper], SC, Mrs. [William] Calvert, Miss
> [Mary] Barker, the Maudes [Mrs. Maude and Mrs. Calvert are sisters]. Thinks
> HC's desire to have silk stockings an affectation and an unreasonable expense.
> Lectures HC on cutting expenses and repeatedly stresses the family's poverty.
> Mentions Mr. [John] Morgan and Mr. Wordsworth. STC has kept his promises
> to write and send money. Mentions SC, DC, and William Hart Coleridge.
> Writes half a page of minute instructions on how HC should pack his trunk.
> Asks if HC has delivered the letter of introduction to Mr. [Isaac, of Berkshire]
> Knipe. Mentions Mr. Bedford and Uncle [Robert Southey]. Lectures HC on
> how to address a letter properly. Sends news of Sir G[eorge] and Lady [Mar-
> garet Willes] Beaumont, Sir J[ames] Mackintosh, the [William] Sothebys, Uncle
> [Robert Southey], Mr. [William?] Gifford, and Mr. Davison and Mr. Hamp-
> den of Oxford. Asks if HC's fellow students know of his family connections to
> Robert Southey. Lectures HC on cutting his expenses, mentioning Mr. W[ords-
> worth], Mr. J[ames?] Coleridge, and STC.
>
> SC writes news of a family excursion including Miss [Mary] Barker, Mrs.
> Cotes, Mary Cotes, and Betty [?]. Mentions Mr. Leathe's house and Charles
> and Henry Barker [Mary's brothers?].

B112 A.L.s., 10 Chester Place, Regent's Park, London, Thursday,
[July] 6th, 1837. To: Grammar School, Sedbergh, Yorkshire. 3 pp.

> Had expected a packet of essays for HNC and a letter on Mrs. [Dinah] Flem-
> ing's death. Has heard from Mrs. Wordsworth by way of Dora [Wordsworth
> Quillinan] that Miss J[oanna] Hutchinson settled HC's affairs with Mrs. Flem-
> ing's granddaughter. Asks what HC intends to do and certainly hopes he will
> not lodge in a public house again. SC and HNC like this new house, but she
> does not. There is far too much noise here. Mentions Derwent [DC], Mary
> [Pridham Coleridge], and Mr. [John Diston] Powles's house. Discusses SC's
> and HNC's health and Robert Lovell's visit. Hopes the [Isaac] Greens are well.
> Mentions the Parrys and Dora [Wordsworth Quillinan]. If HC has left Sed-
> burgh and Mr. Green opens this letter, she hopes he will write her about HC.
> Chides HC for not writing. Is ill and anxious about him.

B113 A.L.s., 10 C[hester] P[lace], Re[gen]t's Park, [London], Sunday, Nov[r] 20, [1842]. To: [Nab Cottage, Rydal]. 6 pp. With note on inside flap of accompanying envelope.

A few minutes after SC had complained that their friends in the north ignore them, DC entered with HC's letter. Writes at length of HNC's health. She is not optimistic. Frances Duke Coleridge Patteson's doctor has written from Feniton Court, Devon, to summon John Patteson. Feels Fanny's serious illness is due to her entertaining too much. Complains of the heaviness of afflictions, mentioning SC, HNC, DC, and Mary Pridham Coleridge, who has invited Edith [Coleridge] to stay with her. Discusses HC's clothes. Mr. [Edward] Q[uillinan] will bring a parcel. Would be thankful to hear HC *really* had sent the essays to [Edward] Moxon. Couldn't HC write for Blackwood[*'s Magazine*] for immediate payment? Continues the letter on Monday evening. The latest accounts of Fanny are not good, but the immediate danger is over. Mentions Mr. Joseph Henry Green, Sir B[enjamin] B[rodie], Dr. James [Duke] C[oleridge], HC's "Worthies" [*Biographia Borealis; or, Lives of the Distinguished Northerns*, Leeds, 1833], Bertha [Southey Hill], and HC's good health. STC's friend Mr. [Josiah] Wade has left the portrait of STC to his grandson. She is upset, because Wade had told Mr. Wordsworth he would leave the picture to SC, and at her death to Jesus College, Cambridge. Mr. [Joseph Henry] Green is trying to get permission from Mr. Bernard to have an engraving of the portrait made. Mentions Uncle [Robert Southey]. Note mentions Bertha [Southey Hill]'s letter, HNC's health, Mrs. W[ordsworth]'s health, and the great expense of a barber daily [for HNC].

B114 A.L.s., 10 Chester Place, Regent's Park, [London], Tues, [November] 29, 1842. To: Rydal, near Ambleside, Westmoreland. 3 pp.

Informs HC of the death of Frances Coleridge Patteson [27 November 1842]. As James [Coleridge] was not sure HC and DC would hear from Devonshire, he asked Mrs. STC to notify them. Says she will tell Kate [Southey] herself; will HC notify Bertha [Southey Hill] and their friends at Rydal Mount [the Wordsworths]. The result of a consultation between Mr. [Joseph Henry] Green, Sir B[enjamin] B[rodie], and Mr. [Edward] Newton [on HNC's health] was favorable. Mentions HNC, SC, HC's clothes, Mr. [Edward] Quillinan, and Kate [Southey].

B115 A.L., [10] Chester Place, Regent's Park, [London], May [n.d., 1843]. To: [Nab Cottage, Rydal]. 4 pp.

Cannot understand why HC will not write, especially after having witnessed the interesting scene at K[eswick]. Regrets that HC missed the funeral [of Robert Southey, who died 21 March 1843] and that HC stayed at the Q[ueen]'s Head. It was a needless expense, since he had an invitation to Mr. Denton's. Lectures HC on finishing the essays promised to Mr. [Edward] Moxon, mentioning the

Wordsworths. Complains at length of her own ill health. SC and Edith [Coleridge] are at Broadstairs with friends [the Thomas Farrers]. Mentions Herbert Hill, who is in London, Herbert [Coleridge], Herbert Hill's mother in Basingstoke, St. Mark's College, the Bishop of Salisbury [1837–1854, Edward Denison], the Archbishop of Canterbury [1828–1848, William Howley], DC, Mary [Pridham Coleridge] and her sister [Sara Pridham Dusautoy], and C[hauncey Hare] Townshend. Mary [Pridham Coleridge] is to be confined in June, but Mrs. STC dares not go to her for fear of falling ill.

B116   A.L.s., 10 Chester Place, Reg^ts Park, London [late October 1843]. To: [Nab Cottage, Rydal]. 8 pp.

Sent the money in the parcel, not the letter [see A114]. Mentions Mrs. [Eleanor] Richardson and DC. Hopes to see her family from Eton. Fay [?] was at Broadstairs with the [Thomas] Farrers, then at Margate, Tunbridge Wells, and Eton, where her brother and sister wish her to stay. Fay has been nervous and ill and has to take morphine to sleep. Says it was Fay's two and one half years of nervous derangement that broke her own [Mrs. STC's] health. Complains of her sufferings, and says HC does not know or care how she suffers. Mentions SC, Mr. [Edward] Q[uillinan], DC's ill health, Mary [Pridham Coleridge], and Christabel Rose and Derwent Moultrie [Coleridge]. Lectures HC on his clothes. Lady [Elizabeth Turner] Palgrave says Dr. Jennings admires HC greatly. Mentions Mrs. Charles [Sarah Hustler] Fox, the Hardens' move [from Ambleside], the Herbert Hills, Dora [Wordsworth Quillinan], Miss [Isabella] Fenwick, and Mr. C[hauncey] H[are] Townshend. Berates HC for not sending [Edward] Moxon more essays. Many writers, including Aubrey de Vere, cannot get published. Aunt [Mary Fricker] L[ovell] has gone to Cockermouth and Kate [Southey] is to follow. Letter continues "Monday, 30th" [October]. Refers to a letter from SC [Grantz 972]. Mentions Edward [Coleridge] and a portrait to be painted of SC by Mr. [George] Richmond. Letter continues "Wed., Novr 1st." Has not received notice of the arrival of the bundle she sent HC, so he should begin to make inquiries.

B117   A.L. (inc.), [10] Chester Place, Regent's Park, [London], Mon. 29th, 1844, Jany. To: [Nab Cottage, Rydal]. 4 pp.

Though HC apparently cares little about them, they think of him. The essays HC promised Mr. [Edward] Moxon months ago were not in the package Mr. H[enry] C[rabb] Robinson brought. Chides HC about the essays. Mr. R[obinson] reported that HC was well. Describes at great length SC's suffering from psoriasis. SC is still correcting proofs of the "Poetical Selections" [STC, Poems, London, 1844?]. Mentions the Judge [John Taylor Coleridge] and his lady [Mary Buchanan Coleridge], who is ill. Grieves for Kate [Southey] and Aunt [Mary Fricker Lovell], mentioning the death of Betty [Kate Southey's old servant]. A letter from Mrs. Wordsworth mentions Dora [Wordsworth Quillinan]'s health and Kate [Southey]. Gives an account of Herbert [Coleridge]'s progress at Eton.

B118   A.L.i., 10 Chester P[lace], Reg^ts Park, [London], July 1, 1844. To: [Nab Cottage, Rydal]. 6 pp.

Speaks of packages to HC by Mr. H[enry] C[rabb] Robinson and from HC by Miss [Isabella] F[enwick]. Was disappointed in HC's output toward a volume of essays. Repeats Mr. [Edward] Moxon's compliments, made to Mary [Pridham Coleridge] on HC. Mary told Moxon she thought HC's copyist was ill. Wasn't Miss [Juliet] Fox also transcribing for HC? SC is ill, but correcting STC's *The Friend* [HNC, ed., 3 vols., London, 1837, 1844] for the press. Is sending HC STC's *Poems* [London, 1844]. DC is now at Rugby with his friend [John] Moultrie. Speaks of DC's travels, mentioning Mr. John Pridham at Chelten-ham, [John] Moultrie and a son of Mr. Lynn's [son of James Lynn, Keswick rector?]. DC got the committee to increase the size of the college [St. Mark's] but failed to get it to increase his income. Discusses the shirts Mary [Pridham Coleridge] is making HC. Mentions Miss [Emily] Trevenen, Mrs. [Winthrop Mackworth (Helen)] Praed, SC's picture, Judge and Mrs. [Thomas] Erskine, and Edith [Coleridge]'s twelfth birthday. Edith is going to the [John] Pattesons and Herby [Herbert Coleridge] to the Bishop's [William Hart Coleridge's]. Tell Mrs. [Eleanor] Richardson to present his [HC's bills to R[ydal] Mount.

B119   A.L.i., [10] Chester Place, [Regent's Park, London] Monday 12 August, [18]44. To: [Nab Cottage, Rydal]. 4 pp.

Writes from her sickbed to ask about the fit of the shirts she has sent him. Trusts the shirts now being made at Chelsea [by Mary Pridham Coleridge] will fit better. Was informed of HC's visit by Mrs. W[ordsworth] and HC's hosts [William and Eleanor Richardson]. William Richardson wrote her that his brother [John Richardson] and HC have been good friends for sixteen years. Chides HC for not writing. Mentions Mr. [Edward] Moxon and Miss Briggs. She and SC are very ill, and the doctor says SC must go to the sea at once. HC should tell this to the W[ordsworth]s, who will pity them. SC leaves for Broadstairs on Friday. H[erbert] and Edy [Coleridge] are in Devon. Kate [Southey] is in Somerset. Mentions D & M [DC and Mary Pridham Coleridge] and young D[erwent Moultrie Coleridge].

B120   A.L., [10 Chester Place, Regent's Park, London], Sun. Evening, postmarked Sp. 16, 1844. To: Nab Cottage, Rydal, Westm^r–land. 1 p. Written on the back of a fragment of a discussion of Jacob Bryant by HNC.

Discusses the clothes she has sent HC. Asks him to call at Rydal Mount before he writes so that he can give the Wordsworths her regards and can write her news of the Wordsworths. Wants to know if Kate [Southey] is to go to Cum-berland or to stay at Warwick. Asks about young John Wordsworth and Mr. [John] Dawes. Thinks HC's poem on Owen Lloyd ["A Schoolfellow's Tribute to the Memory of the Rev. Owen Lloyd," DC, ed., HC, *Poems*, London, 1851] is very affecting. Mentions *Janus*. Has had letters from Kate [Southey] and Aunt L[ovell (Mary Fricker)]. Longs to see her northern relations.

B121 A.L., 10 Chester Place, [Regent's Park, London], Tu. Octr 8, 1844. To: Rydal near Ambleside, Westm^r–land. 8 pp. Written on two forms for recommendation for medical relief from St. Pancras General Dispensary.

Is sending HC a parcel. SC is still correcting STC's *The Friend* [HNC, ed., London, 1837, 1844]. Mr. [William] Pickering will not settle their account. Supposes the profit is small, since Pickering had only the volume of *Poems* [STC, *Poems*, London, 1844] and one other work. Mentions Mr. [Joseph Henry] Green and the contents of the parcel she has sent. She and SC think HC's poems are beautiful and should be reprinted. Has two copies of the "Worthies" [HC, *Biographia Borealis; or, Lives of the Distinguished Northerns*, Leeds, 1833] and two of the poems [HC, *Poems*, Leeds, 1833]. Mentions D [DC], SC, a couple who have just returned from France, the W[ordsworth]s, SC's maid, Nurse [Mrs. Ann Parrott], Cook, SC's picture, *Punch*, Kate [Southey] at Warwick, and Sir Jasper Nicholl. D [DC] and M[ary Pridham Coleridge] dined at Fulham with the Bp. [of London, Charles James Blomfield], who was much taken with SC's essay ["On Rationalism," HNC, ed., STC, *Aids to Reflection*, 2 vols., London, 1843, Vol. II, Appendix C, pp. 335–556]. The bishop pronounced passages of the essay to be worthy of the pen of Bp. Jeremy Taylor. M[ary Pridham Coleridge] wants to know if the shirts she made HC fit. Mentions the [William] R[ichardson]s, the W[ordsworth]s, HC's clothes, M. [John] Dawes, Mrs. [Louise] Claude, Mrs. [Sarah Hustler] Fox, and the [Joseph] Traceys. Scarlet fever has broken out at Eton, and SC has canceled her proposed visit there.

B122 A.L., [10 Chester Place, Regent's Park, London], Mon^y, Novem. 4, 1844. To: [Nab Cottage, Rydal]. 4 pp.

Is worried about a parcel HC promised them. Is anxious to get HC's papers in Mr. [Edward] Moxon's hands, to know if the shirts fit, and to know if the "Magnum Bonum Pens" suit him. Mentions Kate and Cuthbert [Southey]. Wants to know what book Mr. J[ohn] W[ood] Warter sent HC, and whether or not HC has responded. Mr. J[oseph] H[enry] Green has not yet been able to get [William] Pickering to settle their accounts. SC has just sent off the last proof of STC's *The Friend* [HNC, ed., 3 vols., London, 1837, 1844]. Mr. [Charles B.] Stutfield is very attentive to SC and the children. Mentions Derwent [DC], Edy [Coleridge], and Mr. [Sir Thomas] Acland. Bewails the loss of Judge [Thomas] Erskine as a neighbor. SC visited the Erskines often, and they often rode in the Erskines' carriage.

B123 A.L.i., [10] Chester Place, [Regent's Park, London], April 28,

1845. To: Rydal n^r Ambleside, Westm^r land. 4 pp.

Has just had a surprise visit from Mr. Wordsworth and Mr. [Samuel?] Rogers. The whole party is to dine at Mrs. [Samuel] Hoare's this evening. Mr. Matheson is lending SC and Edith [Coleridge] his carriage to go to St. Mark's. The name "Hartley" was given up at HC's request, and the baby is to be called Henry Nelson Praed Coleridge [b./d. 1845]. Mrs. Winthrop Mackworth (Helen)] Praed, Mrs. [Sara Pridham, Mary Pridham Coleridge's sister] Dusautoy, and the Judge [John Taylor Coleridge] are to stand at the font. Discusses DC's and SC's health. Mentions Dora [Wordsworth Quillinan] and Mr. [Edward] Q[uillinan]. Continues the letter on 5 May. Mentions Mr. Wordsworth, Dora, and Mr. [Edward] Moxon. John [Taylor Coleridge] and his daughters [Mary Frances Keble and Alethea Buchanan Coleridge] were here. The other godfather is to be Mr. Cowley Powles, a former pupil of DC's. The Bishop [William Hart Coleridge] will baptize the baby. Discusses HC's bills and clothes, mentioning Mrs. Wordsworth, Miss [Isabella] Fenwick, Herby [Herbert Coleridge], and Mary [Pridham Coleridge]. Says Kate [Southey] proposes to visit Rydal. Bemoans her own ill health. Is taking *The News of the World* [October 1843–]. Mentions HC's lines on Dr. [Thomas] Arnold ["On the Late Dr. Arnold," DC, ed., HC, *Poems*, London, 1851], Dr. Jenner, Miss [Emily] Trevenen, and DC.

B124   A.L. (inc.), [10 Chester Place, Regent's Park, London], Saturday 17 [May 1845]. To: [Nab Cottage, Rydal]. 2 pp.

Mentions Mrs. R[ichardson (Eleanor)] and Mrs. W[ordsworth]. Mrs. [Sarah Hustler] Fox told Miss [Emily] Trevenen that her daughter [Juliet Fox] had a nice pencil sketch of HC. She would like a copy of it. Wants to know which of the essays in *Janus* are HC's [HC, "Antiquity," "Pins," "Love Poetry," "A Preface–which may serve," *Janus*, 1826]. Mr. Aubrey de Vere, who often calls on SC, would like to read anything of HC's. The [Henry] Taylors' baby is named Aubrey after him. The christening [of Henry Nelson Praed Coleridge, b./d. 1845] at St. Mark's was interesting, although Uncle Wm [Hart Coleridge, Bishop of Barbados] could not stay for it. Their two judges [John Taylor Coleridge and ?] were there. Mentions Mrs. [Winthrop Mackworth] Praed. Discusses Herbert [Coleridge]'s handling of money. Sara [SC] has been better but was tired last night.

B125   A.L.s. (inc.), [n.p.], [n.d.]. To: [n.p.]. 2 pp. A fragment of a longer letter.

Kindest love to Rydal Mount and Dora [Wordsworth Quillinan]. They hear little from Dora. Hopes she and her husband [Edward Quillinan] and daughters are well. Says to tell Mrs. W[ordsworth] that SC's state of health is very trying. Brother John [Taylor Coleridge?] is a comfort to them. Mentions Edith [Coleridge].

SARAH COOKSON

B126 A.N.s., Pavement End, Tuesday, Decr 29, [n.d.]. To: [n.p.]. 1 p.

Invites HC to dinner at 2 o'clock on New Year's Day to meet Mrs. and the Misses Cookson.

JOHN CROSS

B127 A.L.s., Leeds, Aug. 23, 1841. To: Ambleside. 3 pp.

Encloses a post office order for six copies of "Poems" [HC, *Poems*, Leeds, 1833]. Is surprised that HC's London friends have been unable to find the "Lives of the Worthies" [HC, *Biographia Borealis; or, Lives of the Distinguished Northerns*, Leeds, 1833]. When [Rufus?] Whittaker's supply is exhausted, he will have another supply in a few days. Cross is awkwardly placed in regard to advertising, which is very expensive. Proposes to advertise it again in a few days. Has forwarded six copies of *Poems* to Mrs. Nichols[on] and Mr. [Thomas] Troughton [Ambleside booksellers] and four copies of Worthies to Troughton. Sends by this post a copy of the Publisher's Circular, May 18, [1841,] containing the previous advertisement.

THOMAS DEANS

B128 A.N.s., Maryport, [Cumberland], Novr. 15th, 1838. To: [Grasmere]. 1 p.

Sends HC a copy of John Younger's *Thoughts As They Rise* [Glasgow, 1834].

SIR AUBREY DE VERE

B129 A.L.s., Ambleside, Octr. 26, 1845. To: [Nab Cottage, Rydal]. 3 pp.

Sends copies of his latest [*A Song of Faith, Devout Exercises, and Sonnets,* London, 1842] and his son's first [Aubrey Thomas de Vere, *The Waldenses, or the Fall of Rora: A Lyrical Tale,* Oxford, 1842]. Enjoyed hearing HC recite his own poems and hopes he will publish them.

CLARA ECKERSALL

B130   A.L.s., Ambleside, September 12, [n.d.]. To: [n.p.]. 3 pp.

Has received a letter from her niece, Miss Wood, thanking HC for the sonnet he wrote to her.

MARIANNE EDMUNDS

B131   A.L.s., Moss Head, Grasmere, Tuesday morning, [n.d.]. To: [n.p.]. 3 pp.

Is going to drink tea with Mr. Harrison after the fair. Would like to read to Mr. Harrison HC's poem about Katy [Jones] ["To K. H. J., the infant grandchild of a blind grandfather," DC, ed., HC, *Poems,* London, 1851]. Will call for an answer Thursday on the way to Mr. Harrison's. Respects from Mrs. Jefferies and Edward.

B132   A.L.s., Moss Head, Grasmere, Monday morning, [n.d.]. To: [n.p.]. 2 pp.

Sends a copy of "To K. H. J., the infant grandchild of a blind grandfather" [DC, ed., HC, *Poems,* London, 1851]. Has sent the original to Katie's mother [Margaret Harrison Jones] in Liverpool. Told Mrs. Jones of HC's wish to publish the poems in the collection [*Childhood,* 1841] which Mrs. Claude's friend, [Hannah Mary Reynolds Rathbone] is compiling. Regards from Mrs. Jefferies.

JOHN EMMET

B133   A.L.s., Birkenshaw, near Leeds, [n.d.]. To: [n.p.]. 3 pp. Accompanied by one page of unrelated notes in unidentified hand, apparently a list of unpublished poems by HC in the possession of Miss [Anna Maria] Briggs.

Was one of two young people who called on HC two weeks ago to secure his autograph. Reminds HC of his offer to read and review a poem and encloses for HC's consideration four poems: "Lines suggested by seeing the Druidical Circle near Keswick, August, 1845," "Written while walking along the banks of Winandermere," "Written after walking over the mountains from the Swan Inn, Grasmere to Patterdale," and "To a Dew Drop."

MARGARET WILKINSON EVANS

B134   A.L.s., Edge Lane, W. Oldham, [n.d.]. To: [n.p.]. 4 pp. All pages are bordered in black.

Takes the liberty of addressing him though it is some years since she was in his company at her father's house. Her youngest sister has just died of consumption at age 21. Asks HC to write a few lines on the dead girl, whose name was Agnes ["Agnes," DC, ed., HC, *Poems*, London, 1851].

WILLIAM FENTON

B135   A.L.s., Stafford, March 29th, 1834. To: Ambleside, Westmorland. 3 pp.

Has been collecting material for a "Worthies of Staffordshire" [never published?]. Mentions Staffordshire men, the Dukes of Buckingham, the Ansons, the first Lord Aston, Earl St. Vincent, the Talbots, the Earls of Essex, Dr. Johnson, Elias Ashmole, Bishops Newton and Hurd, Congreve, Fenton, Cotton, Isaac Walton, Erdeswick, etc. Wants to know if HC will help him by revising and amending the manuscript and by writing a prospectus. The skeleton of Congreve's and Fenton's lives, which HC could begin immediately, would be [Samuel] Johnson's *Lives*. Whether HC helps or not, perhaps he will send the prospectus soon. HC will be glad to hear that he [Fenton] expects his position to be worth £500 a year. Hartley Green is in Paris.

ISABELLA FENWICK

B136   A.N.s., The Gale, Monday, 29ᵗʰ June [1846?]. To: [Nab Cottage, Rydal]. 1 p.

Is having some of his friends at dinner at 5 o'clock on next Wednesday. Would be glad if he would join the party.

J. FENWICK

B137   A.N.s., The Gale, Saturday, May 9 [1846?]. To: The Nabb [Cottage, Rydal]. 2 pp.

Will be glad if HC will have dinner with him before helping with the Ambleside Rushbearing.

MRS. ARCHIBALD [ELIZA DAWSON] FLETCHER

B138   A.N.s., Lencrigg, Monday Mornᵍ, [n.d.]. To: [n.p.]. 2 pp.

Asks HC to breakfast Tuesday at nine or to luncheon at one to meet Dr. and Mrs. Olesen from Edinburgh.

B139   A.N.s., Lencrigg, Saturday Mornᵍ, [n.d.]. To: [n.p.]. 1 p.

Asks HC to meet Miss Fencouk [?] and her friends for dinner at two.

B140   A.N.s., Lencrigg, Monday Mornᵍ, [n.d.]. To: Nabbs Cott.[age, Rydal]. 1 p.

Asks HC to tea at six to meet Dr. Roger, nephew of Sir Samuel Romilly's.

B141 A.L.s., Perran, [near Truro, Cornwall], 1st September, 1833. To:
[Grasmere]. 5 pp. Page 5 is crosswritten on page 1.

Is he not being ungracious to publish a volume of poems [HC, *Poems*, Leeds,
1833] without telling an old friend? But since she belongs to those people who
profess to return good for evil, she will congratulate him anyway. Has seen
Derwent [DC], who is much admired and was joined by his father [STC] at
Cambridge. Mentions little Derwent [Moultrie Coleridge] and SC. Speaks of the
death of her mother [Mrs. William Hustler] and describes in touching detail
the death of her five-year-old daughter, "Guinea Kitty" [Jane Katherine Fox].
Mentions [Professor John] Wilson's "The City of the Plague" [*The City of the
Plague, and Other Poems*, Edinburgh, 1816]. Dale End [the Fox Ambleside
home] is likely to be occupied by her brother [John Hustler] and his family. Is
glad HC is home from Leeds. Urges HC to write.

B142 A.L.s., Perran, near Truro, [Cornwall], [n.d., 1836–1838]. To:
Grasmere, Kendal. 5 pp.

Because of the long silence between them, playfully introduces herself. Heard of
HC's taking I[saac] Green's place for a time [a few months, early in 1837]. Introduces to HC her nephew, Barclay Fox, who is a great favorite of hers. Mentions Derwent [DC], Mary [Pridham Coleridge], and the dead child [Emily
Frances Gillman Coleridge, b. 1835, d. 1836]. Barclay is touring with his father
[Robert Were Fox] and two sisters [Caroline and Anna Maria Fox]. Will write
soon of Derwent [DC] and Sara [SC]. Regards from Charles [Fox], who still
reads HC's "Worthies" [HC, *Biographia Borealis; or, Lives of the Distinguished
Northerns*, Leeds, 1833].

B143 A.L.s., Bolton House, 18/12/38. To: Grasmere, Kendal. 4 pp.

Asks for news of HC to tell Derwent [DC] when she returns home. Hated to
part with Dale End [the Fox Ambleside home] and does not wish to be forgotten by her Grasmere friends. Derwent [DC] is much occupied with his sermons
and the state of the church. His inclinations are toward Pusey, Newman, and
Keble. Mentions Mary [Pridham Coleridge], Dervie [Derwent Moultrie Cole-
ridge], and the dead infant [Emily Frances Gillman Coleridge, b. 1835, d.
1836]. Her brother [John] Hustler has been very ill. Mentions the [James]
Greenwoods.

B144 A.L.s., Perran, [near Truro, Cornwall] 9th Inst, [September],
[1843]. To: [Nab Cottage, Rydal]. 4 pp.

Apologizes for not returning the manuscript of HC's poems sooner. Reminds him of his faithlessness to an engagement at the Commercial Inn. She sent the manuscript so often in thought that she forgot to send it in fact. Juliet [Fox] has copied many of the worn poems and she encloses the copies. Juliet has not yet finished copying "To Dear Little Katy Hill" [DC, ed., HC, *Poems*, London, 1851]. Thanks him for the pleasure his poems have given them. Speaks of a trip to Wales and local legends of the fairies. An old Welchman sadly said of the fairies that they no longer come to us, for the spirit of man is grown too strong for them.

B144b A.L.s., Perran, [near Truro, Cornwall] 17th Ins^t [September], [1843]. To: The Nab, Rydal, Ambleside, Westmoreland. 1 p.

Has detained the manuscript of HC's poems in order to send with them a copy of [John] Sterling's poem on STC ["Coleridge" in *Poems*, London, 1839]. Speaks of Sterling's admiration for STC. Juliet [Fox] has now finished copying the sonnets. Urges HC to publish another volume of poetry.

B145 A.L.s., Perran, Near Truro, [Cornwall], 20th Nov^r, 1844. To: [Nab Cottage, Rydal]. 4 pp.

If she does not explain why she did not answer his last letter, he may not write again. The letter came just before the family left for Germany; foreign letters are expensive and upon their return it was easier to go to visit HC than to write. Encloses Juliet [Fox]'s copies of three of HC's sonnets. Asks HC to send his poem on Dr. [Thomas] Arnold ["On the Late Dr. Arnold," DC, ed., HC, *Poems*, London, 1851]. Speaks of past days at Dale End [the Fox Ambleside home]. Wants to know if the railroad excitement is subsiding at Windermere and if Wordsworth still opposes the railroads. Mentions Miss Barrett's attempt to write poetry about a locomotive [ll. 11–12, "Lady Geraldine's Courtship," Harriet Waters Preston, ed., *The Complete Poetical Works of Elizabeth Barrett Browning*, Boston, 1900]. Has great sympathy with Wordsworth's sonnet ["On the projected Kendal and Windermere Railway," A. J. George, ed., *The Complete Poetical Works of Wordsworth*, Cambridge, Mass., 1932], which seems the most passionate thing Wordsworth has written for years. Thanks HC for the sonnet in his last letter ["To Mrs. Charles Fox," DC, ed., HC, *Poems*, London, 1851?]. Hopes HC will publish another volume soon. Lent HC's last volume to [John] Sterling just before he died [on 18 September 1844]. He returned it with words of high praise. Feels Tennyson's fantasies have not spoiled people for the thoughts and truths of HC's poems. Regards from Charles [Fox].

B146 A.L.s., Perran, near Truro, [Cornwall], 12/4/45. To: [Nab Cottage, Rydal]. 4 pp.

Has heard that J[ames] Greenwood has been long ill and that his case is hopeless. Asks HC for news. Sends news of Derwent [DC]; of his lady wife [Mary

Pridham Coleridge], who expects a brother [Henry Nelson Praed Coleridge, b./d. 1845] to Christabel [Rose Coleridge]; and of Derwent [Moultrie Coleridge]. Juliet [Fox] sends her love and reminds HC to send the promised verses ["On the late Dr. Arnold," DC, ed., HC, *Poems*, London, 1851]. Asks again for news of James Greenwood.

B147 A.L.s., [Perran, near Truro, Cornwall], [n.d., 1845?]. To: [Nab Cottage, Rydal]. 4 pp.

Thanks HC for the news of J[ames] Greenwood. Has been bewildered by "Vestiges of Creation" [(Robert Chambers) *Vestiges of the Natural History of Creation*, London, 1844] which has been answered by Prof. [William] Whewell [*Indications of the Creator*, London, 1845]. Gives an admirable summary of the major points of *Vestiges* and says that it will be remembered when Whewell's book is forgotten.

B148 A.L.s., Perran, [near Truro, Cornwall], 28th Nov^r, [n.d.]. To: Grasmere, Kendal. 5 pp. Pages 4 and 5 are crosswritten on pages 1 and 2.

Has heard Derwent [DC] is well and Mary [Pridham Coleridge] looking better than ever since she has grown stouter. Tries to tease HC into writing. Thanks HC for the autograph [apparently STC's]. She will put it up for safekeeping and consider it only lent. Would appreciate the autograph of Professor [John] Wilson. Would like to see more of HC's compositions. Regards from Charles [Fox].

JULIET FOX

B149 A.L.s., [Perran, near Truro, Cornwall], [n.d.]. To: [Nab Cottage, Rydal]. 4 pp.

Thanks HC for the lines he has sent and for his letter. Only wishes she could return the lines better copied. Speaks of past times in Ambleside. Was sorry to hear of the death of J[ames] Greenwood and sends love to Lily [Greenwood]. Apologizes for the length of her letter.

CHARLOTTE FRASER

B150   A.L.s., The Sands, Liscard, Liverpool, [n.d.]. To: [n.p.]. 3 pp.

Has been requested by a friend who is a great admirer of HC's to procure HC's autograph for her. Hopes he has been well since she saw him at Fieldhead last October.

B151   A.L.s., The Sands, Liscard, [Liverpool], March 21, [n.d.]. To: [n.p.]. 2 pp.

Thanks HC for his letter and the lines ["A Schoolfellow's Tribute to the Memory of the Rev. Owen Lloyd" and "Epitaph on Owen Lloyd," DC, ed., HC, *Poems*, London, 1851] she wished, but would not ask for. Intends to send them on to another lady. Knew Owen Lloyd through the Hardens and appreciates HC's remarks on him. Looks for the poem HC promised her.

B152   A.L.s., Wellfield Wigan, Feb. 22nd, [n.d.]. To: [n.p.]. 3 pp. Page one is bordered in black.

Requests a few lines in the hand of STC, for a friend.

JENNETTA GALE

B153   A.L.s., Oak Bank, Ambleside, February 18th, 1843. To: [Nab Cottage, Rydal]. 1 p.

Asks HC to compose a poem on the subject of second sight. Is leaving Ambleside in a month.

JOHN GIBSON

B154   A.L.s., Post office, Whitehaven, 16 Decr 1848. To: Grasmere, Kendal. 1 p. Letter is in a wrapper of folded paper with endorsement of date and contents by EHC.

Has as a good friend a Cumberland man, Mr. Thomas Dixon, who is now living in New York. Dixon sent him a case of New Town Pippins [apples]. Sends a box of them to HC along with thanks for HC's kindness to him and his wife, Maggie.

MRS. JOHN [MARGARET] GIBSON

B155 A.L.s., Whitehaven, December 3ᵈ, 1847. To: [Nab Cottage, Rydal]. 3 pp.

Thanks HC for his and his young friend's contributions to her album. Will thank HC personally if she visits Ambleside for the Rush Bearing and will introduce to him a young Scotch lady. Speaks of her album. Is good friends with [Thomas] Carrick, who painted Wordsworth's portrait a few weeks ago. Says it is a good likeness. Wishes HC a Merry Christmas.

MRS. JAMES [ANN] GILLMAN

B156 A.L. (inc.), [The Grove, Highgate, London], [n.d., 1834?] To: [n.p.]. 2 pp. With a four–page copy in Mrs. Ann Gillman's hand. The copy is endorsed "Copy of Fragment *H.C.*" and begins " 'Tis a clear sighted man that dare look to the bottom of his own heart.' "

HC has always been in the heart and prayers of STC, who has constantly prayed that HC might be removed from temptation and reformed. For the last six or eight months STC has been very ill and especially concerned about HC's welfare and about putting his own philosophic system into such shape that it can be finished by his friend [Joseph Henry Green].

B157 A.L.s., The Grove, Highgate, December 12, [1840]. To: [Nab Cottage, Rydal]. 7 pp. Pages 1 and 5 have black borders.

A reply to A131. The sight of his handwriting and his affectionate letter made her cry. Has never ceased to love him and to have faith in him. Has experienced many sorrows since she last saw him [James Gillman died 1 June 1839]. Speaks of STC's death [25 July 1834]. She and her husband were almost constantly with STC or discussing his virtues, and now her thoughts are constantly with the two dead men. Would love to see HC again. Says Mr. Gillman *did* like what HC printed, though it was not much. Assures HC that Mr. Gillman loved him dearly. Wishes to write him again but feels her life is very uncertain and hangs by a slender thread.

CATHERINE G. GODWIN

B158   A.N.s., Spring Cottage, Monday Morn, [n.d.]. To: Grasmere. 1 p.

Invites HC to tea at seven on Wednesday evening to meet Lady Farquhar and Mr. Hamilton.

ROBERT P. GRAVES

B159   A.L.s., Themey How, July 29, 1834. To: [Grasmere]. 3 pp.

A letter of condolence on the death of STC [25 July 1834]. Was glad to hear of the happy nature of STC's end, which will surely be a consolation to HC.

MISS CAROLINE GREEN

B160   A.L.s., [Grasmere], Jan^ry 15th, 1845. To: The Nab [Cottage, Rydal]. 2 pp.

Is knitting HC a pair of muffetees. Mentions Susanna [Green?] and her music teachers Miss Cookson and Mr. Harrison. Describes her games.

B161   A.L.s., [Sedbergh or Grasmere, 1845]. To: [Nab Cottage, Rydal]. 2 pp.

Has finished the muffetees and hopes he likes them. Will he lend her Phantasmion [SC, *Phantasmion*, London, 1837]?

B162   A.L.s., Sedbergh, Nov. 7, 1837. To: Grasmere, Ambleside. 3 pp.

Still finds scraps of HC's writings around the house, and the children make Mr. "Tolleridge" a character in their plays. Speaks of his health and school matters, mentioning two difficult boys, Hervey and Rudd. Sends local news of Mr. and Miss [Mary?] Upton, Stephen Sedgwick, Mrs. Wilkinson and her daughters, Caroline [Green], and Mrs. [Isaac] Green. Asks HC to come for a visit. Mentions Dr. [William] Fell.

B163   A.L.s., Sedbergh, The Queen's Birth-Day and a *Holiday*, postmarked Fe 11, 1840. To: Grasmere, Ambleside. 3 pp. The paper has narrow black borders.

Sends HC something he had left behind. Asks when the second volume [of HC's *Poems*, Leeds, 1833] will come out. Mr. Evans [a master in Green's school] gave "She is not fair to outward view" [*Poems*, Leeds, 1833] to the students to be translated. Buried the first person, a child, at Howgill, and expects to bury Mr. Wilkinson soon. Sends local news, mentioning Mr. William Wilson, Mr. [Andrew?] Matthews, Mr. Upton, and Mr. Maude.

B164   A.L.s., Sedbergh, Septr. 5th, 1842. To: [Nab Cottage, Rydal]. 4 pp.

Thanks HC for his note. Has enjoyed the beautiful season. Is concerned with too many things at home to be able to elevate his vision. Sends domestic news, mentioning his health and a balky cook. Speaks of the marriage and emigration of a young woman, a local curate, and the Mormons and Joe Smith. Regards from his children.

B165   A.L.s., Sedbergh, Decr 4th, 1842. To: [Nab Cottage, Rydal]. 4 pp.

Thanks HC for his letter, which helped the invalid [Mrs. Isaac Green]. She wants to answer, and if her letter should be strange, HC will know how to deal with it. Hopes her mind will slowly improve. She seems to enjoy her piano and her children. Would be grateful for another letter. Doubts that he will see HC this Christmas.

MRS. ISAAC [CAROLINE IBBETSON] GREEN

B166 A.L.s., [Sedbergh], [n.d., summer 1837–March 1838]. To: Mrs. Richardsons', Grasmere. 6 pp. Pages 4 through 6 are crosswritten on pages 1 through 3.

Intends to send some things HC forgot [when he taught at Sedbergh in early 1837]. Sends Sedbergh news, mentioning Mrs. Boucher and her sons Tom, George, and Charley; Mr. Davies; the five Misses Upton; Mrs. Wilkinson; Professor [Adam] Sedgewick; Stephen Sedgewick; Cowgill and Howgill; her daughter Caroline; Edward Green; and the school. Mr. W[ilkinson] & I[saac Green] have been singing HC's praises. Thanks HC for his kindness. Invites him for a visit. Has Miss Elizabeth Wilkinson of Howgill staying with her, as she is lonely and ill. Hopes her sister-in-law and grandpapa are well.

B167 A.L.s., [Sedbergh], [n.d., 1839]. To: Grasmere. 4 pp.

Is sorry his books were packed along with theirs and will return them. Mentions Miss [Mary?] Upton, Mother, the children, her daughter Caroline, and Mr. Evans [a master in Green's school]. Hopes HC will like his new aunt, her namesake [Caroline Bowles and Robert Southey married on 4 June 1839].

B168 A.L.i., [Sedbergh], [n.d.]. To: Grasmere. 4 pp.

Thanks HC for the Bible he sent her daughter Caroline, and for the verses inscribed in it ["Lines written in a Bible presented by the author to his godchild," DC, ed., HC, *Poems*, London, 1851]. Describes Mrs. Evans [wife of a master in Isaac Green's school]. Sends local news, mentioning the Rev. G. Simpson, Miss [Elizabeth] Wilkinson of Howgill and her sister Margaret, the five Misses Upton, James Greenwood, Mr. Atkinson of Lonsdale, and Mr. Palmer.

B169 A.L.s., Sedbergh, Feb. 18th, 1840. To: Grasmere. 2 pp.

Has made a drawing for Mary Upton's album. The sketch shows two donkeys with gypsies and cart. [See "On A Picture Representing Gypsies and Asses," Earl Leslie Griggs, ed., HC, *New Poems*, London, 1942.] The monument erected to Mr. Wilkinson [former headmaster in Isaac Green's school] is very beautiful. Is pleased with the reception her daughter Caroline has met at the Briggs'. Regards from Isaac.

B170 A.L.s., postmarked Ripon, March 19, 1841. To: The Nab. Rydal, nr Ambleside, Westmoreland. 6 pp.

Has gone to the Rev. James Charnock's to recover from her recent illness, during which Isaac [Green] was so very kind and patient with her. Sends local news of Mr. Frank Faber, Miss Curts, Frederick Faber, Mrs. Longley, and Mrs. Evans [wife of a master in Isaac Green's school]. Says the hallucinations of her recent illness equalled Mr. De Quincey's opium dreams. Describes in great detail her hallucinations in which appeared friends, relations, and the devil. Asks to be remembered to her friends at Pavement End [the Cooksons]. Describes Mr. Charnock's home.

B171   A.L.s., [Sedbergh], [n.d., 1843]. To: [Nab Cottage, Rydal]. 4 pp.

Forwarded to HC newspapers containing pictures of the little Count of Paris. Thanks him for his letter of December third. Mentions Mr. and Mrs. [Miss Simmons] James Brancker, Mrs. [Dora Wordsworth] Quillinan, her daughter Caroline Green, and Isaac [Green]. Is very thin now. Speaks of Isaac's new term and of her new cook.

B172   A.N.s., [Sedbergh], [n.d., 1845]. To: [Nab Cottage, Rydal]. 1 p.

She let Miss [Mary?] Upton read Phantasmion [SC, *Phantasmion*, London, 1837]. Invites him to visit.

JOSEPH HENRY GREEN

B173   A.L.s., 46 Lincolns Inn Fields, August 21st, 1834. To: [Grasmere]. 2 pp.

A letter on the death of STC [25 July 1834]. A post-mortem examination attributes STC's illness to a chronic disease of heart and lungs. Writes at length of STC's last days. Says STC's last words to him were an injunction to promulgate *truth*. Sends HC a copy of STC's will.

B174   A.L.s., [The Mount], Hadley, Novr 27th, [1848]. To: [Nab Cottage, Rydal]. 8 pp. Accompanied by a blue envelope addressed to "The Reverend the Principal" and endorsed by DC "Mr Green to HC | on the Theory of Life. S. T. C."

A critical discussion of STC's *Hints Toward the Formation of a More Comprehensive Theory of Life* [Seth B. Watson, ed., London, 1848]. Reviews the discovery of the manuscript and its publication. Feels James Gillman and Dr. Seth Watson had no right to put the book out [see B100]. Does not doubt that the work is STC's but thinks some passages have been changed. Feels Watson has given proof that he does not understand STC's philosophy or reasoning. Gives his understanding of STC's theories of physics, Will, and the nature of reality. Continues to discuss STC's philosophy at length. Feels that STC has removed much of the difficulty standing in the way of the union between physics and morals. Discusses STC's theory of polarity.

G. R. GREENHOW

B175 A.N.s., Kirkland, Wednesday, 30th Dec^r, [1835?]. To: Grasmere. 1 p. The back of the letter is covered with notes on "Massinger, Decker, &C" in HC's hand.

Sends the copy of [Sir Henry Taylor's] *Philip Van Artevelde* [*a Dramatic Romance*, 2 vols., London, 1834] which his sister had promised HC when she was in Grasmere.

M. E. GREENWOOD

B176 A.L.s., Lythan, April 22nd, [n.d.]. To: Rydal. 3 pp.

Has been expecting a letter and begs HC to write. Says Mr. Lord, father of Mr. John and Mr. Edward [Lord], whom HC knows, has been teaching dancing in Lytham. Mr. Lord gave a ball for his pupils, and she and Miss Catherine [Wilson?] went to watch. Enjoyed HC's valentine very much and thinks she knows who wrote it, as she remembers the handwriting. Enjoyed the Easter holidays very much. Asks him to send the poetry he had promised her. Miss C[atherine?] Wilson sends her respects.

FANNY GURSTON

B177 A.L.s., Southshore, near Blackpool, Lancashire, Saturday 15th, [n.d.]. To: [n.p.]. 4 pp.

Should have thanked HC for the sonnet he sent her earlier. Has had a narrow escape. Has been kept at the seaside with her friend Miss Sutton. Values his lines very highly. Has been reading "Coleridge's Remains" [HNC, ed., STC, *The Literary Remains of Samuel Taylor Coleridge*, London, 1836–1839], which she finds interesting. Encloses her "Question and Reply." Has borrowed a copy of HC's *Poems* [Leeds, 1833].

MR. AND MRS.
BENSON HARRISON

B178   A.N., Scale How, Tuesday morning, [n.d.]. To: The Nab [Cottage, Rydal]. 1 p.

Invitation for tomorrow evening at half past six.

B179   A.N., Scale How, Monday Mor^{ng}, [n.d.]. To: The Nab [Cottage, Rydal]. 1 p.

Invitation for Thursday evening at half past six.

EDWARD HAWKINS
[FELLOW OF ORIEL]

B180   A.L.s., Oriel College, [Oxford], June 11th, 1820. To: [n.p.]. 2 pp. Letter is in a wrapper of folded paper with endorsement of contents and date by EHC. See Introduction for an account of the Oriel affair.

Has read HC's letter to the Dean. Hopes to see HC reform as he promises, but thinks it unlikely that Oriel College will grant him a further probationary term. The Fellows of Oriel will continue to be interested in his future.

Quoted in full in *LHC*, pp. 305–306.

ANN HEPPLE

B181   A.L.s., Kendal, Jan 5th, 1844. To: [Nab Cottage, Rydal]. 6 pp.

Pages 5 and 6 are crosswritten on pages 4 and 3.

Thanks HC for his favor from Mrs. [Eleanor] Richardson. Reminisces about "Knabbe" Cottage. Speaks of the weather and her pastor's stand. Wishes HC a happy new year. Mentions her father and sisters. Hopes Mr. and Mrs. [William and Eleanor] R[ichardson] are well.

REBECCA AISLEY HEPPLE

B182　A.L.s., Lowther Street, August 7th, 1843. To: [Nab Cottage, Rydal]. 4 pp.

Sends by Mr. [William?] Richardson "Verses by a Poor Man," by the Rev. Tom Garnett of Kirkby Lonsdale, who resided some years in Durham [?]. Regards from her father and sister.

B183　A.L.s., [Ambleside, summer, 1846]. To: [Nab Cottage, Rydal]. 6 pp.

If HC will have the tailor cut a pattern, she and Ann [Hepple] will embroider him a waistcoat. HC has promised her the "Christmas Mother" and the lines on the Hutchinson family. Miss [Anne] Addison would like him to write in her scrapbook. Regards from her father and sister.

B184　A.L.s., Ambleside, Saturday 12th Sepr, [1846]. To: Nab [Cottage, Rydal]. 3 pp.

Received his note. Is on an excursion to Rydal Mount. Mrs. [Cornelius] Nicholson is bringing to him this note and Miss [Anne] Addison's book in which she wishes him to copy a poem or two. Intends to begin his waistcoat soon. Mentions Ann [Hepple], the Misses Richardson, and Miss [Anne] Addison.

B185　A.L.s., Lowther Street, October 27th, 1846. To: [Nab Cottage, Rydal]. 3 pp.

Will send the parcel privately or by coach. Mentions a waistcoat which she had wanted him to have on his arrival from Kendal. Regards from her father and Ann [Hepple].

B186   A.L.s., Greta Hall, [Keswick], Feb^{ry} 18th, [n.d.]. To: [n.p.]. 4 pp.

> Asks if he will visit next week. As a letter from Hampstead is now at Rydal [Wordsworth's], HC has probably heard its contents. Edith [May Southey Warter] is to be in London and will meet Sara [SC] if the latter is well enough. Sends local news, mentioning Mr. Townshend, who was bitten by his favorite dog.

B187   A.N.s., [n.p.], Friday afternoon, [n.d., 1842?]. To: The Knabbe [Cottage, Rydal]. 2 pp.

> The letter from Mrs. Wordsworth to Miss [Isabella] Fenwick gives a very satisfactory account of Henry [HNC], who is now out of danger. Hopes HC's cold is better. Herbert [Hill] improves daily.

B188   A.L.s., Greta Hall, [Keswick], Monday Morn^g, Jan. 2nd, [n.d.]. To: [n.p.]. 3 pp.

> Invites HC to visit. There has been much illness at Greta Hall, but all are now well. Mentions Kate [Southey], Papa [Robert Southey], and Aunt [Mary Fricker] Lovell. Cuthbert [Southey] went to the dentist, Cartwright, and then on to Oxford. Had a good account of Edith [May Southey Warter] and the baby [Ellen Caroline Warter]. Sara [SC] will be godmother to Ellen-Caroline [Warter]. Wrote Mrs. STC. Asks HC to come soon.

JAMES JOHNSON

B189   A.L.s., Kendal, April 24, 1840. To: The Knab, Rydal, Ambleside. 2 pp.

> Has been reading STC's *On the Constitution of Church and State* [London, 1830] and wishes to borrow HC's copy of STC's *Aids to Reflection* [London, 1825]. Sends the two sonnets he showed HC. Has had a letter from his cousin heavily criticizing his poetry. Would like to see HC publish a volume of collected essays. Has been reading again HC's "On the Character of Hamlet" [*Blackwood's Magazine*, November, 1928]. Feels that in Hamlet Shakespeare

may, for once, have failed to create a believable character. Realizes the weakness of his reasoning. Has just read that there are 5,023 poets in the United States. Of these 94 are are in prison, 511 in lunatic asylums, and 200 in debtor's prisons. The day has been glorious. Will come to Rydal some Sunday.

THOMAS JOHNSON

B190 A.L.s., Lancaster, 20 February, 1840. To: [Grasmere?]. 4 pp, including enclosed poem.

Thanks HC for his letter, though it came too late to do any good. Wrote an article for *Blackwood's Magazine*, "On the Characters of Hircius and Spungius, in Massinger's Virgin Martyr" [Philip Massinger and Thomas Decker, *The Virgin Martyr*, London, 1622]. The object of it was to defend Decker against Mr. [William] Gifford's charges [in William Gifford, ed., Philip Massinger, *The Plays*, 4 vols., London, 1805, 1813, 1840, etc.] that Decker prostituted his genius and his judgment. Has contrasted Hircius and Spungius with Congreve's dangerously entertaining libertines. Signed the article "Ignotus." Mr. [Christopher] North [John Wilson] rejected the article at once. Encloses his "Sonnet, On resuming a hard task" [unpublished?].

MRS. MARGARET HARRISON JONES

B191 A.L.s., Rodney St., [Liverpool], Novr 4th, [n.d.]. To: [n.p.]. 4 pp.

Thanks HC for the poem he has sent her ["To K.H.J., the infant grandchild of a blind grandfather," DC, ed., HC, *Poems*, London, 1851]. Mrs. Jones and little Katie's grandmother also admire the tribute. The allusion to her father [Mr. Harrison] brought tears to her eyes. Her friend Marianne Edmunds told her that HC's reading of the poem much pleased Mr. Harrison [see B131]. Does not object to the publication of the poem if only initials appear. Has said for Mrs. [Louise] Claude to tell Mrs. Richard [Hannah Mary Reynolds] Rathbone so [see A13]. Regards from Mr. Jones.

EDWARD LLOYD

B192   A.L.s., Kendal [?], 5 May, 1842. To: [Nab Cottage, Rydal].
4 pp.

Thanks HC for his long letter and his verses on Owen Lloyd ["A Schoolfellow's Tribute to the Memory of the Rev. Owen Lloyd" and "Epitaph on Owen Lloyd," DC, ed., HC, *Poems*, London, 1851]. Has been prevented from answering sooner by the illness of his wife's sister, who lives with them. Feels exceedingly obliged for an offer [?] HC has made. Thinks the penny post has something to do with the dwindling of the traditional long letter. Is glad to have news of Ambleside and the neighborhood.

JOHN LORD

B193   A.L.s., 14 Berners St., Oxford St., [London], Augt 14/[18]43.
To: [Nab Cottage, Rydal]. 1 p.

A comic letter. Is working hard. Has met Turner [Charles Tennyson Turner], whom he likes. Is going to make a man of himself. Will HC please write?

B194   A.L.s., 14 Berners St., Oxford St., [London], [n.d.]. To: [n.p.].
2 pp.

Alludes to the loneliness of HC's position in the north. Is utterly alone here, and heartily wishes for HC's presence. Feels HC badly underrates himself. Since HC wishes it, he will begin drawing the Preston cast of the infant Hercules [see "Lines, suggested by a cast from an ancient statue of the infant Hercules strangling the serpents," DC, ed., HC, *Poems*, London, 1851]. Discusses the proposed drawing. Is reading Spenser's *The Faerie Queen* for the first time. The book is in fashion with artists, who find it stimulating.

B195   A.L.s., Manor Villa, Upper Holloway, London, Sept. 13/[18]47.
To: [Nab Cottage, Rydal]. 4 pp.

Alludes to his distresses and depression. Speaks at length on the loneliness of life in London. A brother artist has just returned from Windermere and speaks ill of Lord's reputation there. Begs HC to tell him truly how he is spoken of, for he tried to make no enemies. Wordsworth's parting words to him were kind. Repeatedly refers to his feeling of closeness to HC at Randy Pikes and speaks of their first meeting and of their subsequent misfortunes. Thinks that HC is misused, though he does not complain. Has painted a miniature of Mrs. [Francis] Mountjoy Martyn. Many painters had tried, but his is the first she has accepted. The spiral propeller he invented has been submitted to the Admiralty. Plans to publish a "Treatise on the Science of Skaiting" [no record of publication]. Asks HC if he would like to contribute to the work. Mr. Wordsworth is so fond of skating that Lord thinks he will send the treatise to him in the hope that he might sanction it or even allow Lord to dedicate the treatise to him. Profits from the treatise are to be devoted to his new invention, the water-wings. Hopes HC won't laugh at his project [the treatise]. Mentions Anne [at Randy Pikes], Jackson Thompson, and Capt. [Herbert] White, who is in Wales.

MARGARET LOUGH

B196   A.L.s., Chro[?]ile office, Novr 6, 1833. To: Grasmere. 3 pp.

A letter of introduction for Mr. Sinclair. Assures HC her family will be happy to see HC when he can visit for a few days. Asks HC to send her the promised lines on the name Margaret.

ROBERT LOVELL

B197   A.L.s., Keswick, Nov. 28, [n.d., 1837?]. To: [n.p.]. 3 pp.

Plans to stop in Grasmere on his way southward and asks if HC will be at home Saturday at one o'clock. Offers a series of excuses for not having visited HC sooner. The [Mary Fricker] Lovells have had letters from Mrs. STC and SC. Hears that HC is going to Sedbergh, but hopes he has not left yet.

J. MacKEIETH TO
[ISAAC?] GREEN TO HC

B198   A.L.s., Altringham, Feby. 15th. [18]42. To: [Isaac?] Green, [n.p.]. 2 pp. Page 1 is a letter, MacKeieth to Green, annotated by Green for HC's benefit and sent on to HC. Page 2 is an extract, McKeieth to HC via Green.

Describes an elaborate practical joke involving the disguising of Johnny Walton. Has been promised the curacy of Halsham.

Sends HC an extract from *The Regular Book of Winestead*. Extract concerns the birth and baptism of Andrew Marvell. [See HC, *Life of Andrew Marvell*, Hull, 1853.]

MARY MILNER

B199   A.L.s., The Vicarage, Appleby, Nov. 29, 1844. To: Grasmere. 5 pp.

Begs pardon for addressing him. Her *Christian Mother's Magazine* carries a series called *Original Letters*. The only published letters she has used are those from her life of Dean Milner [her uncle], [Mary Milner, *Life of Isaac Milner, D.D.*, London, 1842]. Has seen in the *"Saturday Magazine* for 1834" [STC, "Address to a Godchild," *Saturday Magazine*, No. 138, 30 August 1834, p. 79] a letter from STC to Adam Steinmetz K–[ennard]. Asks HC if he would and could give her permission to publish this letter and if he would assist her in any other way. Would like to have *anything*, prose or verse, of HC's or STC's. HC must not be repelled by the title of the magazine. It is intended to be for family reading. Begs pardon for thus troubling him.

B200   A.L.s., The Vicarage, Appleby, Dec. 3, 1844. To: [Nab Cottage, Rydal]. 3 pp.

Thanks HC for his verses ["To an Infant," *Christian Mother's Magazine*, January, 1844]. Asks again for permission to publish STC's "Address to a Godchild," [*Saturday Magazine*, No. 138, 30 August 1834, p. 79]. Thanks HC for his contribution.

B201   A.L.s., The Vicarage, Appleby, Dec.ʳ 4, 1844. To: [Nab Cottage, Rydal]. 4 pp.

Thanks HC for his letter. His verses have gone to the press ["To an Infant," *Christian Mother's Magazine*, January, 1845]. Hopes for more contributions from him. Thanks HC for his permission to use his published works. Does not usually use published works, but if she does, will make no alterations. The letter to Adam Steinmetz K[ennard] will appear in the January issue.

B202   A.L.s., The Vicarage, Appleby, Dec.ʳ 13, 1844. To: [Nab Cottage, Rydal]. 4 pp.

Miss Barrett's Poems [Elizabeth Barrett Browning, *Poems*, 2 vols., London, 1844] have just been sent to her for review in the January *Christian Mother's Magazine*. Feels that Miss Barrett's poetry, though mystifying and a little pedantic, shows genius. Asks HC to review the *Poems* for the February issue [HC's only known contribution to the *Christian Mother's Magazine* is "To an Infant," January, 1845]. Feels that if these poems are as good as she thinks they are, they can only be reviewed by a poet.

M. C. MINTO

B203 A.L.s., 26 Devonshire St., [Portland Place, London], 31st June, [1847]. To: [Nab Cottage, Rydal]. 16 pp.

Thanks HC for his letter and the sonnet on Lady Grizzle ["XXIV, On Reading the Memoir of Miss Grizzle Baillie," DC, ed., HC, *Poems*, London, 1851]. Has had great difficulty in reading HC's hand. Says most women criticize as Mrs. STC did, by the relation of the poetry to sentiment and to life. Discusses HC's poetry and urges him to finish "Prometheus" and to publish another volume. Has been reading Shelley's life by Medwin [Thomas Medwin, *The Life of Shelley*, 2 vols., 1847]. The book makes one love Shelley, but it is bad biography. Asks if HC has read Jane Eyre [Charlotte Brontë, *Jane Eyre*, 3 vols., London, 1847]. Feels that it has an amount of analysis of motivation unusual in the English novel. Recommended it to Mr. [John] Crossfield. Mentions Miss Claude's poems for children [Mary S. Claude, *Little Poems for Little People*, London, 1847]. Asks HC to send him some charades for a party. Discusses his visit to Rydal. Mr. Kenyon is a great admirer of HC's. Asked Mrs. Fletcher to get Wordsworth's autograph for him. Mentions the red herrings ["To a Red Herring," DC, ed., HC, *Poems*, London, 1851]. Has been reading Robert Browning and is impressed by his grand mind. Asks if there is anything he can do for HC in London. Would give much to see beautiful Rydal.

EDWARD MOXON

B204 A.L.s., London, April 20th, 1848. To: [Nab Cottage, Rydal]. 1 p. The back of the letter bears notes in pencil in the hand of HC.

Asks HC to return some proof sheets and trusts HC will excuse the trouble he has given him.

B205   A.N., Water-head, Thursday, [n.d.]. To: Grasmere: 1 p.

An invitation to dinner on Wednesday evening.

CORNELIUS NICHOLSON

B206   A.L.s., Cowan Head, Kendal, Feby 23, 1842. To: [Nab Cottage, Rydal]. 1 p.

Thanks HC for the poem on his daughter ["To Mary Agnes Nicholson – Born March 4, 1834," unpublished] and is gratified HC is so interested in her. Hopes HC will forgive the injury Nicholson did him by setting one of his poems to music. Is relieved to confess his sin. Respects from Mrs. Nicholson.

B207   A.L.s., Cowan Head, Kendal, March 12, 1842. To: [Nab Cottage, Rydal]. 2 pp.

Acknowledges receipt of HC's verses on Owen Lloyd ["A Schoolfellow's Tribute to the Memory of the Rev. Owen Lloyd," DC, ed., HC, *Poems*, London, 1851], which he will try to print nicely. It is to be printed on cardboard or vellum board. Any sum earned beyond the cost will be given to HC. [The poem was printed as a broadside by "Hudson & Nicholson, Printers, Kendal." A copy of this broadside is in the Humanities Research Center, The University of Texas at Austin.] Regards from Mrs. Nicholson.

B208   A.L.s., Cowan Head, Kendal, Jany 30, 1843. To: [Nab Cottage, Rydal]. 2 pp.

Thanks HC for his poem on the birth of Nicholson's second daughter, Cornelia ["On the Birth of Cornelia," broadside dated January 28, 1843]. Regrets to hear of the death of HC's brother-in-law. [HNC died 26 January 1843.] Nine years part Mary Agnes [Nicholson] and her sister [Cornelia Nicholson]. Mrs. Nicholson and his sister Hannah send regards.

B209   A.L.s., [Cowan Head, Kendal?], [n.d., 1842?]. To: [Nab Cottage, Rydal?]. 2 pp.

Thanks HC for his poem ["To Mary Agnes Nicholson – Born March 4, 1834," unpublished] and the cake. Hopes her relations in Ambleside are well; has not heard from them for a long time. Hopes her parents will like their new house and that HC is well.

JOHN WALKER ORD

B210   A.L.s., Guisborough, Yorks, June [n.d.], 1833. To: The [*Leeds*] *Intelligencer*, [Leeds]. 1 p.

Sends HC a copy of "The Wandering Bard" [written circa 1830, John Walker Ord, *The Bard, and Minor Poems*, London, 1841]. Wants HC to review the poem in the [*Leeds*] *Intelligencer*. Does not have HC's address.

B211   A.L.s., Guisborough, [Yorks.], May 29th 1834. To: Grasmere, Westmoreland. 3 pp.

Sends HC his work "England" [John Walker Ord, *England: a Historical Poem*, 2 vols., London, 1834–1835]. HC will find in it a great deal of abuse of Scotland and the Whigs. Has sent copies for HC to deliver to Wordsworth and [Robert] Southey. Mr. M. L. Milton encloses a copy of his poem "The Ocean Bride." Notes that the "Concluding Address" [to *England*, see above] is addressed to Miss [Margaret] Wilson, despite the fact that he and Mr. Wilson are not on good terms. Mentions [John Abraham] Heraud's *The Judgment of the Flood* [London, 1834], which he feels is overpriced. Vastly dislikes magazine reviews of Ebenezer Elliott [*The Splendid Village; Corn-Law Rhymes; and Other Poems*, 3 vols., London, 1833–1835?] and Pilligren's *The Moral of Flowers* [(Mrs. Rebecca Hey) London, 1833]. Speaks of the loveliness of the Lake District. Feels the world is against him. Has sent two challenges in the last two days to Scotsmen who were offended by his book. Feels poets are persecuted by the world. Comments on religion.

B212   A.L.s., Guisborough, Cleve[d], Yorks., July (?), 1834. To: [Grasmere]. 1 p.

He is well. Wants HC to write one hundred to three hundred lines, Spencerian stanza, on any period of English history after Richard III, for the second volume of his work [John Walker Ord, *England: a Historical Poem*, 2 vols., London, 1834–1835]. Forwarded the first volume to HC by Mr. [M. L.] Milton. Wishes HC success. The [Professor John] Wilsons will be coming north soon. "Marg^t. W**" in the poem is Miss Wilson ["Concluding Address: To Margaret W*****," 260 ll, *England*, see above].

B213 A.L.s., Conservative Journal Office, London, September 30, 1838. To: Grasmere, Westmoreland. 1 p. Written on the back of a prospectus for *The Gift* [William Anderson, ed., *The Gift. Dedicated to Her Most Gracious Majesty, Victoria*, no record of publication]. See A57.

Asks HC to send a contribution for *The Gift*. Plans to publish the book in December. Has been establishing the [*Metropolitan*] *Conservative Journal* [October 1836 to December 1838. Continued as *The Conservative Journal and Church of England Gazette*, January 1839–December 1842]. Feels he is prostituting his poetic gifts, but one must eat. Hopes HC is happy and busy.

MARY LOUISA ORRELL

B214 A.N., The Cottage, Tuesday [May], 17th, 1842. To: [Nab Cottage, Rydal]. 1 p. Signed only "the ladies of the Cottage."

Invitation to dinner on Thursday at five o'clock.

B215 A.N.s., The Cottage, July 20th, [18]42. To: [Nab Cottage, Rydal]. 1 p.

Invitation to breakfast at 10 a.m., July 27th.

B216 A.L.s., The Grove, Cheadle, N^r Manchester, July 24th, [n.d., 1843]. To: [Nab Cottage, Rydal]. 2 pp.

Reminds HC he promised to get her Mr. Wordsworth's autograph for a friend. Is sorry not to have seen him before their departure. Will he please send her a few lines of poetry on any subject?

B217 A.L.s., The Grove, Cheadle, Monday, August 14th, [n.d., 1843]. To: [Nab Cottage, Rydal]. 3 pp.

Thanks HC for the song and Mr. Wordsworth's autograph [see B216]. Wishes she could come over for a few days, for the weather was so unfavorable during their visit. Mr. Orrell hopes to see HC soon. Drove to Castleton, where she was delighted with the castle ruins. Regards from Mr. Orrell and her sister.

W[ILLIAM?] PEARSON

B218   A.L.s., Christhwaite, 7th June, 1836. To: Grasmere. 3 pp.

Returns the two volumes he had borrowed. Thinks highly of STC as a poet, but cannot agree with his later political and religious opinions. Would like to understand STC's philosophy but knows of none of his works in which it is completely developed. Can see STC's distinction between Reason and Understanding, but cannot understand how STC reconciles the Trinity with reason. Discusses this problem, mentioning Locke and Newton. Hopes when he sees HC again, HC can enlighten him on these subjects.

MARY PEDDER

B219   A.L.s., postmarked Ambleside, Fe. 3, 1845. To: The Nab [Cottage, Rydal]. 3 pp.

Copy of a sonnet by HC, June 2nd, 1841 ["To Margaret Mary Pedder," unpublished]. The second page consists of notes on the sonnet in Mary Pedder's hand, signed "Hartley Coleridge." "For H. Coleridge, Esqre with Mary Pedder's kind regards and love."

ELIZA M. POWELL

B220   A.L.s., Bredleigh Salterton, Novr. 20th, 1848. To: [Nab Cottage, Rydal]. 4 pp.

Informs HC that their friend George Hillard has arrived safely in the Far West. Hillard was seasick and is now afraid he has lost his friends because of the hot political debate on the presidential question. Speaks of their stay in Westmorland. Regards from her brother. Hopes to hear from HC.

BRYAN WALLER PROCTOR
[BARRY CORNWALL]

B221 A.L.s.[?], 4 Grays Inn Square, London, April 9, 1839. To: Grassmere, Cumberland. 4 pp. The signature has been cut off, but a corner of the address face bears the initials "BWP." Endorsed on the address face by Proctor "with a Book."

Is glad to hear [Edward] Moxon has engaged HC to preface a volume [HC, ed., *The Dramatic Works of Massinger and Ford*, London, 1840]. Despite STC's opinion, Proctor does not like Philip Massinger, who, he feels, is not a truly imaginative writer. Is sure that HC will do so good a job as to make Massinger as agreeable as possible. Found the little hill in Grasmere, let alone Helvellyn and Skiddaw, too much for him. Has been rereading HC's lives of the worthies [HC, *Biographia Borealis; or, Lives of the Distinguished Northerns*, Leeds, 1833], which he greatly admires. Why doesn't HC put out a volume of essays or a history of English poetry? Has requested Moxon to send HC a volume of songs [Bryan Waller Proctor, *English Songs and Other Small Poems*, London, 1832]. Thinks HC will like the dramatic extracts best, then the songs. [The remaining four lines were partly cut off with the signature.]

MRS. EDWARD [DORA WORDSWORTH] QUILLINAN

B222 A.N.s., Rydal Mount, [n.d.]. To: [n.p.]. 2 pp.

Will HC please come and write in Rotha Quillinan's album as he promised to do? Wishes to send the album to Rotha with Miss Graves, who leaves for London in two or three weeks. Has had good news of SC's health.

MRS. RICHARD [HANNAH MARY REYNOLDS] RATHBONE

B223 A.N.s., Woodcroft, January 15, [n.d., 1842?]. To: [Nab Cottage, Rydal]. 1 p.

Presents HC with a copy of the book [Hannah Mary Reynolds Rathbone, ed.,

Childhood, 1841] in which he kindly allowed her to publish some of his poems [HC's contributions are "The Sabbath Day's Child," "The First Birthday," "Primitiae," and "To K. H. J."].

JOHN EDMUND READE

B224   A.L.s., 45 St James Square, Bath, Feb. [n.d.], 1839. To: [Grasmere?]. 2 pp.

Has had Longmans forward a copy of "Italy" [John Edmund Reade, *Italy, A Poem with Historical and Classical Notes,* London, 1838] to HC but as he has not heard from him, fears HC did not receive the book. Has recently forwarded to HC "The Deluge" [John Edmund Reade, *The Deluge, A Drama,* London, 1839] through the same channel. Asks HC to apply to Longmans if he does not receive the books. Hopes HC will like "The Deluge."

HENRY HOPE REED

B225   A.L.s., Philadelphia, December 19, 1836. To: [n.p.]. 3 pp. Accompanied by a blue envelope with notes in the hand of EHC.

Has forwarded to HC via Messrs Baldwin and Cradock, London, a copy of a recent number of the *American Review* containing an article on HC's *Poems.* Feels HC will appreciate the candid expression of opinion and the sympathy in the article. Urges HC to publish the second volume promised in the Preface of *Poems* [no more published]. Wrote the article after procuring a copy of *Poems* to express his gratification with the book and sends it, as an afterthought, to assure HC that he has, in America, friends and supporters who are anxious to read more of HC's poetry. Was also prompted, in writing his review, by his intellectual and moral debt to the works of STC, who has formed his character. Is superintending the preparation of a complete edition of Mr. Wordsworth's poems. In some of the notes to this edition has used passages from HC's writings. The edition is to be published shortly by the Philadelphia press; will send HC a copy [William Wordsworth, *Poems,* H. Reed, ed., Boston, 1837]. Respects and affection.

CAPT. DAVID LESTER RICHARDSON

B226   A.N., Calcutta, [India], August 15th, 1837. To: [n.p.]. 1 p. Seal face bears signed note by Dora W[ordsworth Quillinan] "The book will follow. London | April 11th."

Sends his book *Literary Leaves*, published in Calcutta [1836], and would appreciate an acknowledgement of its receipt. Mr. John Richardson, 91 Royal Exchange, London, would forward any communications.

THE REV. JOHN RICHARDSON

B227   A.L.s., Appleby, Aug. 4th, [n.d.]. To: [n.p.]. 4 pp.

His sister-in-law, Mrs. Tom Wilson, sends HC a manuscript. Says her verses are pretty. She was at Miss Dowling's School, where she recalls HC's saying that chimneysweeps and Scotchmen wash their faces on a Sunday. Drops into Scottish dialect and mentions the Judge [John Taylor Coleridge?] Would be glad to have HC visit.

B228   A.L.s., Appleby, August 22nd, [n.d.]. To: [n.p.]. 4 pp.

Has at last deciphered HC's letter. He and his wife are packing. Describes his diocesan's letters. Has delivered HC's message to Capt. Bennet and Mrs. [Elizabeth Scambler] Bell. Mentions Mr. Airey, grocer of Kendal. Has paid a visit to Lord [Harry] Brougham to have him explain the act for release of debtors. Regards from Miss [Mary Hannah] Wilson and his wife [Eliza Richardson]. Mentions Edith [Richardson] and Thomas Atkinson.

B229   A.L.s., Appleby, Wednesday Evening, [n.d.]. To: Grassmere. 2 pp.

Urges HC to come to Appleby and make use of their library. Has been trying to read Bishop [John] Jewel [1522–1571]. Again urges HC to visit.

JOHN AND ELIZA RICHARDSON
AND MARY HANNAH WILSON

B230   A.L.s., Appleby, Aug. 6th, 1844. To: Nab Cottage nr Ambleside. 4 pp.

It is a gloomy evening which he will escape by writing HC a letter. Begins to write in thick Scottish dialect. Mentions Wadsworth, Geordy Dixon, and Jack Poolay, about whom he sends much news. Speaks of a church service he attended. Says Edith [Richardson] has searched everywhere for HC. Regards from Eliza and Mary Hannah.

MARTYN ROBERTS

B231   A.L.s., Leeds, 2nd October [1843?]. To: [n.p.]. 3 pp.

Has been delayed by the publisher's absence, but has now, as requested, sent HC copies of some of Swedenborg's works [Emanuel Swedenborg, *Wisdom of Angels concerning Divine Love, Wisdom, and Providence*, London, 1788–1790 and *Treatise concerning Heaven and Hell*, London, 1778]. Also, Mrs. Roberts sends a copy of her poem [see B232].

MRS. MARTYN [ANNIE] ROBERTS

B232   A.L.s., [Leeds], 2nd October, [1843?]. To: [n.p.]. 4 pp.

Reminds HC of his promise to send her a treatise on versification. Has he done anything about it yet? Is sorry HC did not return home before she and Mr. Roberts left. Sends HC her volume [Mrs. Martyn Roberts, *The Spiritual Creation, or Soul's New Birth. A Poem*, London, 1843]. Feels she should have had more experience in blank verse before she tried the subject. Regrets having published in haste. Seeks HC's opinion of her book.

JAMES CRAIGIE ROBERTSON

B233   A.L.s., Trinity College, Cambridge, Decr. 9th, 1836. To: [Ambleside]. 4 pp.

Although HC may have forgotten him, he hopes his petition will not go unheard. An anthology [*The Tribute*, 1837] has been proposed to relieve the distress of a literary man [Edward Smedley] and his family. The editor is Lord Northampton, and contributions have already been received from Wordsworth, [Walter Savage] Landor, and Henry Taylor. Will HC contribute? Hopes HC will soon publish a second volume of poems. Has interested a Senior Wrangler in HC. A new volume of poems has every prospect of success. Left Ambleside at the beginning of June with the intention of going abroad with his brother. His family objected, and after three weeks at home he went to the Isle of Skye and other places. Finding Aberdeen unsafe, he returned to Cambridge early. Has been asked to appear at Gloucester for examination in relation to a curacy at Bitton near Bath. His patron is the Bishop of Gloucester's examining chaplain. The income is less than £60. Mentions Mrs. Louisborough. Hopes to hear from HC.

MR. AND MRS. ROUGHSEDGE

B234   A.N.s., Flosghyll, Monday, [n.d.]. To: [n.p.]. 1 p.

An invitation to dinner tomorrow at six o'clock and to spend the night.

ELIZABETH S. RUTTER

B235   A.L.s., Ivy Cottage, Nov. 9th, [n.d.]. To: [n.p.]. 2 pp.

Asks HC for a few words of his writing.

THE REV. WILLIAM SANDFORD

B236   A.L.s., Long Burton Newcastle on Tyne, Sepr 4th, 1841. To: [Nab Cottage, Rydal]. 8 pp. Pages 5 through 8 are crosswritten on pages 1 through 4. Letter is in a wrapper of folded blue paper with endorsement of date and contents by EHC.

Thanks HC profusely for the two sonnets HC sent by Sandford's brother. Hears that Cumberland and Westmorland are filled with tourists. Dr. Besly speaks of visiting the north, and Sandford thinks Besly and HC will get along well. Asks to be remembered to Mr. [John] Dawes. Speaks of his curacy and the character of the people to whom he ministers.

B237   A.L.s., Johnstone H., Annan, [Dumfries], [n.d., late 1843?]. To: [Nab Cottage, Rydal]. 2 pp.

Many changes have taken place since Bessy [Elizabeth Scambler]'s marriage more than a year ago. She and Mr. Bell had twin girls [Mary and Elizabeth Bell] who died. Then they moved to Appleby. Dorothy [Scambler] is pregnant. Sends news of Tom and Henry [Scambler]. Hopes HC will write.

B238   A.L.s., Annan, [Dumfries], Feby. 20, [184]4. To: [Nab Cottage, Rydal]. 2 pp.

Is sorry she has been unable to answer HC's letter before now. Her sister Dorothy [Scambler] died 14 February. She had been preparing herself, and was ready to die. Eliza [Scambler Bell] and her husband came for the funeral. Hopes to hear from HC soon and begs him for a few lines on Dorothy's death.

B239   A.L.s., [Annan, Dumfries], postmarked Oc. 8, 1844. To: The Nab, near Rydal, Westmoreland. 3 pp.

Thanks HC for his letter and the lines he sent. Sends family news of Henry and Mrs. Scambler and Elizabeth [Scambler Bell] and family. Suggests the possible marriage of HC and Mrs. Luff. Mentions George Newton, Mr. [William] Fell and family, and Tom [Scambler]. Asks HC to write.

B240   A.L.s., [Annan, Dumfries?], [n.d., 1844?]. To: [Nab Cottage, Rydal]. 4 pp.

Has visited Appleby to assist in Eliza [Scambler Bell]'s confinement. She now has a fine baby boy. Jane [Scambler] has a girl. Writes news of Tom and Henry [Scambler]. A suspected murderer, Graham, and Mary Bickerley live in the same town. Mrs. Scambler has taken a pretty little house called Vine Cottage.

B241   A.L.s., Vine Cottage, March 3, [1845?]. To: [Nab Cottage, Rydal]. 9 pp. Page 9 is crosswritten on page 8.

Is sorry to hear of the death of Mrs. STC. Her own health is very bad, but she is thankful for the comforts around her. There has been a family reunion at Lancaster, but she was unable to attend. Tom [Scambler] is married. Asks HC to write her a few lines on Walton Cottage. Reminisces of the good old times at Ambleside. Thanks HC for writing and asks him to write again. Asks HC to forgive the blunders in her letters, as she could never go to school like her sisters and is self-taught. Asks to be remembered to Mr. [William] Fell.

ELIZABETH SCAMBLER

B242 A.L.s., George Town, [St. Vincent Island], Feby 23rd, 1837. To: Grasmere, readdressed to Mr. Green's, Sedbergh. 5 pp. Pages 4 and 5 are crosswritten on pages 1 and 2.

Is presently in the home of the Government Secretary, Mr. [William Bertie] Wolseley, nephew of Sir Charles Wolseley, [William] Cobbett's friend. She is introduced by the Wolseleys to everyone and is well treated. Wishes HC could see the black ladies in all their finery. HC's Uncle [William Hart Coleridge] is Bishop [of Barbados] here. Has been out picking up Cocoa Nuts. Has been to two pleasant balls. The Wolseleys have two sons [William Augustus and John Henry] at Exeter and seven daughters [Charlotte Elizabeth, Frances Anne, Celia Lewis, Eliza Jane, Catherine Norval, Louisa Tollemache, and Henrietta Augusta] at home. Says HC would love to walk in the garden and pick oranges, grapes, mangoes, limes, etc. Must conclude as the vessel sails tomorrow.

B243 A.L.s., Chalkside House, nr Wigton, May 18, [18]40. To: Grasmere, Ambleside, Westmoreland. 6 pp. Pages 4 through 6 are crosswritten on pages 1 through 3.

Asks HC to write. Says her family has been forgotten by HC. Writes family news of her mother, Alice, Jane, Doll, Tom, and Henry [Scambler]. John [Scambler?] has died suddenly. Begs HC to write. Saw Mrs. Warden's and Mr. [William] Fell's weddings in the paper, but has not seen HC's. Gave up her school and is now a governess. Met Dr. [Neil] Arnott, the Scottish physician who attended Bonaparte in his last illness. Asks about the Dowlings, Miss Eliza [Dowling], and Mr. Carr.

B244 A.L.s., Chalkside House, Jany 4th, [18]41. To: [Nab Cottage, Rydal]. 5 pp. Page 5 is crosswritten on page 1.

Likes, at this season, to think of old friends. Thanks HC for his letter. Describes her visit to a friend at Birmingham. Sends news of her family, mentioning Alice, Tom, and Henry [Scambler]. Is moving closer to Wigtown. Writes of Owen Lloyd, Jane [Scambler], Mrs. and Miss Jones, and Mrs. Barker. Asks if Miss [Dora] Wordsworth is really getting married [Dora Wordsworth married Edward Quillinan 11 May 1841].

B245   A.L.s., Tarnside House, n^r Wigton, May 8th, [18]41. To: Rydal, n^r Ambleside, Westmoreland. 4 pp. With accompanying envelope.

Chides HC for not writing. Was shocked at Owen [Lloyd]'s death. Thinks he may have died because Miss Harden married. Asks about Ambleside, mentioning Dora Wordsworth [Quillinan], Julia, M[ary] A[nn] Harrison, Mr. [John] Dawes, and William Fell. Sends local news of Alice, Tom, Jane, Doll, and Herbert [Scambler]. Asks HC to write. Treasures HC's presentation copy of *Biographia Borealis* [; or, *Lives of the Distinguished Northerns*, Leeds, 1833. This copy is inscribed with HC's poem "Dear Bessy, 'tis all that I can," unpublished].

B246   A.L.s., Tarnside House, nr Wigton, Decr 30th, [18]41. To: [Nab Cottage, Rydal]. 4 pp.

Chides HC for not answering her two previous letters. Says that if this goes unanswered, she will think he wishes to sever their friendship. Peter, the bearer of the note, will give HC the local news. Regards from her mother, Alice, and Henry [Scambler].

B247   A.L.s., High Street, Annan, Dumfrieshire, April 16th, 18[42]. To: [Nab Cottage, Rydal]. 4 pp.

Was delighted to receive HC's letter. Thought they had been forgotten. Has a new school position, a house and garden, two boarders, and seventeen day students. Sends family news of Doll, Jane, mother, Alice, Henry, and Tom [Scambler]. Asks for a copy of the verses on Owen Lloyd ["A Schoolfellow's Tribute to the Memory of the Rev. Owen Lloyd," DC, ed., HC, *Poems*, London, 1851]. Thanks him again for writing.

B248   A.L.s., Annan, Dumfrieshire, June 21st, 1842. To: [Nab Cottage, Rydal]. 3 pp.

Chides HC for not answering her first letter. Asks if the piece on Owen Lloyd ["A Schoolfellow's Tribute to the Memory of the Rev. Owen Lloyd," DC, ed., HC, *Poems*, London, 1851] has been published yet. Has had smallpox but is not marked. Sends family news of Jane, Henry, Tom, Doll, Alice, and mother [Scambler]. Mentions Mr. and Mrs. [William] Fell. Begs HC to write.

G . WALLWYN SHEPHEARD

B249   A.N. on verso of calling card of M^r. G. Wallwyn Shepheard, 11

Queen Square, Bloomsbury.

In Italian: "Remember your friend, the poor painter."

JOHN FRANCIS SMITH

B250   A.L.s., Salutation Inn, Ambleside, Oct. 27, [18]35. To: Grassmere. 2 pp.

Is a stranger to HC, but introduces himself and invites HC to dine with him
tonight. Has introductions to Wordsworth and Southey, neither of whom he has
seen yet.

MISS SOUTHERN

B251   A.L.s., Lawford, September sixteen, [n.d.]. To: [n.p.]. 2 pp.

Thanks HC for favoring her with the autograph. Hopes HC has recovered from
his cold and will have a happy birthday.

KATHERINE SOUTHEY

B252   A.L.s., [Greta Hall], Keswick, March 21, 1843. To: [Nab Cottage, Rydal]. 3 pp.

Informs HC of the death of her father [Robert Southey], who went quite calmly at the last. Though no longer what it once was, Greta Hall will remain dear
to them all for the happy times they shared there. The strongest ties she had on
earth are now gone, and she is lonely. Gently expresses her love and respect
for her father.

WILLIAM SUART

B253   A.L.s., Cockerham School, Augt 11th, 1838. To: Grasmere, Ambleside, or Elsewhere. 3 pp.

A letter to his godfather, HC, in doggerel verse and exquisite penmanship. Has now grown from a baby to the stature of HC in height though not in genius. Wishes he could be a poet and begs HC to send news of himself.

MISS SWAINSON

B254   A.N., Bridge Street, May 3rd, [n.d.]. To: [n.p.]. 1 p.

Presents kind regards to HC and begs him to accept the enclosed piece of music.

SIR THOMAS NOON TALFOURD

B255   A.N.s., Rolle Cottage [?], Friday morning, [n.d.]. To: [n.p.]. 1 p.

An invitation to dinner at five o'clock on Monday next.

ROBERT TEMPLE

B256   A.L.s., Stokesley, Cleveland, Yorkshire, Aug. 5th, 1835. To: Grassmere, Westmoreland. 4 pp. Page 4 is crosswritten on page 1.

Writes to say how much he enjoys HC's company and to express regret at the death of STC [25 July 1834]. Feels that he himself has lost a friend and guide. Believes STC and Wordsworth the two greatest poets of the age. Thanks HC for introducing him to Wordsworth, for pointing out Wordsworth's beauties, and for teaching him to prefer pure and natural beauties to the artificialities of an excited mind [Byron]. Criticizes Byron. Says HC's sonnets are beautiful. The only fault is not with the sonnets but with HC, who speaks too mournfully of himself. Says HC has no reason to be discontent with himself. Begs HC to write. Has written before and had no answer.

ROBERT TYSON

B257   A.L.s., Miss Delaney's, 79 Georges St., Whitehaven, Saturday, [n.d.]. To: [n.p.]. 4 pp.

HC was no doubt surprised by Tyson's sudden departure for Whitehaven. Whitehaven is dirty compared to Ambleside, and he has been lonely. Has a couple of pictures to paint which may lead to more. HC has promised him a poem; would he please send it soon?

MISS WALKER

B258   A.L.s., Grasmere, Saturday morning, [n.d.]. To: [n.p.]. 2 pp.

Thanks HC for the lines he wrote in her album.

JOHN WOOD WARTER

B259   A.L.s., Vicarage, West-Tarring, [n.d., 1848?]. To: [Nab Cottage, Rydal].

Asks if HC has ever received the copy of *The Doctor* in one volume [John Wood Warter, ed., Robert Southey, *The Doctor &c.*, London, 1848. See A72]. HC's copy was given to SC in London. Longmans was to send out copies to several members of the family. They are anxious as the edition sold out at once.

RICHARD WHATELY
[FELLOW OF ORIEL]

B260   A.L.s., [Oriel College, Oxford], [June 1820]. To: [n.p.]. 4 pp. Letter is in a wrapper of folded paper with endorsement of contents and date by EHC. See Introduction for an account of the Oriel affair.

Is still interested in HC's welfare. Says HC does not understand the nature of the case. No punishment is contemplated. The probationary period is to determine what a man already *is*, not what he will become. HC's plea for a further probationary period is, therefore, pointless, since the Fellows have already had time to see what he is. The Fellows will meet in October. At that meeting his vote will follow the dictates of his conscience. Has a duty to the college. HC should cherish no hopes, as his delinquencies are moral as well as academic. Reminds HC that life is also a probationary period at the end of which there is no hope of eluding the judgment of God.

Quoted in full in *LHC*, pp. 304–305.

GEORGANNA WILSON

B261 A.L.s., The Craig, Monday, [n.d.]. To: [n.p.]. 4 pp. The paper is bordered in black.

Apologizes for not having thanked HC sooner for "The Solace of Song" [DC, ed., HC, *Poems*, London, 1851] and the sonnet. Has sent the sonnet to her sister. Has not yet set "The Solace of Song" to music. Thanks HC for his compliance with her request.

F. M. WOOD

B262 A.N.s., Rollinshaws Lodgings, Ambleside, Wednesday Ev^g, [n.d.]. To: [n.p.]. 1 p.

Invites HC to a family dinner party Saturday at half past five. Mentions Mrs. F. Wood and his aunt Miss [Clara?] Eckersall.

ELLEN WOODSON

B263 A.L.s., Kendal, Nov. [n.d.], 1843. To: [Nab Cottage, Rydal]. 3 pp.

Thanks HC for his poem, which reminds her and her husband of their own infant daughter who died.

WILLIAM CHARLES
BONAPARTE WYSE

B264 A.L.s., Manor of St. John, N^r Waterford, Ireland, December 4th, 1846. To: [Nab Cottage, Rydal]. 8 pp.

Reminds HC of their agreement to correspond. While HC has been leading the life of a stoic philosopher, he has been the solitary wanderer, and thanks HC for the letters of introduction he furnished him. Visited many cities, including Manchester, which particularly pleased him. Spent an evening in Manchester with [Charles] Swain, who is a great admirer of HC's. At Sheffield presented

HC's sonnet ["To the Poet James Montgomery," unpublished] to James Montgomery, who considered HC's poems worthy of STC and most remarkable. Since his return to Waterford, has been bored and ill and has written a great number of bad sonnets and epigrams. Sends HC two epigrams on E[ugene] Sue [unpublished?], whom he dislikes. Mentions the two Aubrey de Veres, whose volumes he saw, uncut, in HC's library. Discusses his recent reading and sends HC a poem, "Sonnet while reading Festus: To H. Coleridge" [unpublished?]. Begs HC to read Festus [Philip James Bailey, *Festus*, London, 1839] and discuss it with him. Apologizes for sending HC his own work. Speaks of his love for the lake district and its inhabitants. Wants to know whether "Poet Wordy" [Wordsworth] is still fond of batter-pudding. Mentions Miss Wordy [Dorothy Wordsworth] and "The Rime of the Ancient Mariner." Mentions Nelson and Galand, who enclosed in a letter the elegy he had repeated to HC and Wyse in the Swan. Asks about Miss [Anne] Addison [see B2]. Will send his "Farewell Poem," addressed to HC, and a copy of the poem HC wrote for Miss Dickenson at the Salutation [Inn] Ball ["Sounds I have heard," DC, ed., HC, *Poems*, London, 1851].

B265 A.L.s., Manor of St. John, N^r Waterford, Ireland, [n.d., early 1847]. To: [Nab Cottage, Rydal]. 4 pp.

Is afraid HC did not receive or mislaid his letter of last November [4 December 1846, see above]. Asks if HC has forgotten him. May visit the lakes soon. Asks where he can get a copy of HC's *Poems* [Leeds, 1833]. Asks if Nelson is still at Ambleside. Invites HC to Ireland.

CORRESPONDENT UNKNOWN

B266 A.L. (inc.), postmarked Ex., Ja. 16, 1836. To: Grasmere, N^r Ambleside. 1 p.

Has read HC's B[*iographia*] B[*orealis; or, Lives of the Northern Worthies*, Leeds, 1833] but disapproves of the way HC speaks of politics and religion. Quotes several passages which he wishes to contradict on doctrinal grounds.

STRAY ENVELOPES

B267 A.E., postmarked Liverpool, Mr 23, 1842. To: [?], Ambleside, Westmoreland.

B268 A.E., postmarked Liverpool, Dec [?], 18[?]. To: The Nab, Rydal, Ambleside.

Appendix

THE LEEDS AFFAIR

In 1832 the Leeds publisher Francis Edward Bingley invited Hartley Coleridge to undertake a series of lives of "worthies" of Yorkshire and Lancashire. According to the original agreement (in the Humanities Research Center, The University of Texas at Austin), dated December 22, 1832, the series was to be delivered in twelve parts of forty pages each, octavo, at weekly intervals. Parts one and two had been delivered before the agreement. For the twelve parts and the copyright Bingley was to pay Hartley £250 in payments made throughout the series. For each part not delivered, Hartley was to pay Bingley £10.

The agreement for the subsequent volume (of poems) and a pamphlet is not in the Texas collection, but seems to have been that Bingley would pay Hartley £50 for a volume of poems to be followed by a second volume. Hartley gives his account of these arrangements with Bingley in letter A95. Not being a good businessman, Bingley went into bankruptcy in 1833. Hartley employed the aid of his good friend James Brancker to free him of his obligations to Bingley, and the record of this effort is given below in chronological order.

FRANCIS EDWARD BINGLEY
TO JAMES BRANCKER

1   A.L.s., Leeds, Jany 5, 1836. To: James Brancker, Liverpool. Sent on to HC, Grasmere. 3 pp.

> Says HC is bound by agreement to complete the Worthies [HC, *Biographia Borealis; or, Lives of the Distinguished Northerns*, Leeds, 1833] or forfeit a penalty. Cannot understand why HC will not deal directly with him. Is willing to negotiate for the copyrights of Worthies and Poems [HC, *Poems*, Leeds, 1833]. If HC's friends will remit to him £20, he will resign his claims on HC for the second volume of Poems and the Pamphlet. Has lost £1000 by HC's books.

FRANCIS EDWARD BINGLEY
TO HC

2   A.L.s., Leeds, Jany 9, 1836. To: Grasmere. 1 p.

Releases HC from all claims for a pamphlet, a second volume of *Poems*, and more of the *Worthies*, and from all other engagements.

FRANCIS EDWARD BINGLEY
TO JAMES BRANCKER

3   A.L.s., Leeds, Jany 9, 1836. To: James Brancker, Liverpool. 1 p. James Brancker notes on the letter face that he answered on the 11th and remitted £20.

Notifies Brancker that he has released HC from all claims [see 2]. Asks for £20 and says he is ready to deal for the copyrights.

FRANCIS EDWARD BINGLEY
TO HC

4   A.L.s., Leeds, Jan^y, 1836. To: Grasmere. 1 p.

Releases HC from all claims for a second volume of *Poems*, a pamphlet, and more of the *Worthies*. Would be glad to publish anything HC might send to him.

Quoted in full in *Memoir*, pp. civ–cv.

FRANCIS EDWARD BINGLEY
TO JAMES BRANCKER

5   A.Ls., Leeds, Jany 14, [18]36. To: James Brancker, Liverpool. 2

pp., including extract. James Brancker notes at the top of the letter that he answered. Letter is accompanied by an extract in Brancker's hand.

> Says his [Bingley's] letter to HC is not in the terms he wishes. Will Brancker please return it and substitute the annexed letter [probably 4 for 2]. The copyrights for *Poems* and *Worthies* do not belong to him, but he is empowered to negotiate a sale. There is no fixed price. The same answer has been made to a London bank which is interested in the copyrights.
>
> Extract of a letter to F. E. Bingley, January 16th [1836]. Is not prepared to make an offer for the two copyrights, nor does he think one will be made. Trusts the copyrights will be offered to HC before they are disposed of to strangers. Bingley forgot to acknowledge the £20 Brancker sent him.

6   A.L.s., Leeds, Jany 20, 1836. To: James Brancker, Liverpool. 2 pp.

> Regrets Brancker's having sent his letter [3] to HC. Says that because of his bankruptcy he had not the power to release HC from every agreement. Has the power to release HC from completion of the *Worthies*, a second volume of *Poems*, and a pamphlet. Considered Brancker's £20 as compensation for any profit he might have had from the publication of the manuscript mentioned above. Does not consider the £20 as a payment of HC's £25 debt to him. Intends to sell HC's debt along with others to the assignees.

JAMES BRANCKER
TO FRANCIS EDWARD BINGLEY

7   A.L., Liverpool, Jany, 22nd, [18]36. To: F. E. Bingley, Leeds. 1 p. Copy in Bingley's hand.

> Is sorry Bingley is having second thoughts. When he saw Bingley in Leeds, it was clearly understood that when HC supplied Bingley with a second volume of poems and a pamphlet, all Bingley's claims upon HC would be satisfied. Bingley had valued his property in the volume and pamphlet at £20; the sum is paid and the account closed. The only debatable ground left is the purchase of the copyrights.

The subsequent history of the copyrights may be traced through legal documents in the Humanities Research Center. On 3 May 1834, Bingley put up copyrights for *Poems* and *Worthies* (along with rights to a newspaper and patents on "Abernethy's Pills") as security for £630 and interest owed to Mr. John Chiesham, a schoolmaster. On 21 March 1835 John Chiesham agreed to sell the two copyrights plus two hundred and fifty copies of parts one and two of the *Worthies* to James Young Knight, a bookseller and publisher, for £40, £30 to be paid in three installments and "£10 in stationary." On 7 October 1835 the assignment of copyrights was made. On 29 November 1850 the copyrights returned to the Coleridge family when Derwent Coleridge bought them from James Young Knight for £50.

All arabic numerals refer to letter numbers. In each entry, letters from HC are listed first, letters to HC second, citations in letters from HC third, and citations in letters to HC fourth. For the convenience of the reader, immediate families are listed as groups, with the exception of HC's most frequent correspondents, the Coleridges, the Wordsworths, and the Claudes. Each member of these three families is listed separately.

Brancker, Mrs. James (1st, Jane Moss) A5, 8, 13, 19, 30, 51, 103, 107, 108, 125; B14, 15, 41, 42, 46, 47, 49, 50, 51, 52, 53, 56, 70

Brancker, Mrs. James (2nd, Miss Simmons) A111; B16, 17, 57, 60, 171

Brancker family A8; B54, 55, 64, 72

Brancker, John (James B's brother?) B54

Brancker, Mr. (James B's father) A5; B15, 41, 42, 60

Brancker, Mrs. A30

Brancker, William (James B's brother?) A159

Brancker, the Rev. Thomas (James B's nephew) A8

Brent, Miss A116

Brians, Mr. A108

Brice, Penelope (of Asholt) A116

Briggs, Dr. W. Letter to, A6; Letter from, B27; A11, 69, 121, 155; B25, 26, 30

Briggs, Mrs. W. (Anna Maria) Letters from, B28, 29, 30; A6, 19, 69, 121, 155; B17, 19, 20, 23, 25, 26

Briggs, (son) B28, 29

Briggs, Anna Maria (daughter) Letters from, B18, 19, 20, 21, 22, 23, 24; A5, 69; B29, 133

Briggs, Margaret (daughter) A6; B27, 29

Briggs, Herbert (Margaret's son) B27, 29

Briggs, Mary Jane (daughter) Letter from, B25; A6, 20, 121

Briggs, Robert (Mary Jane's husband) A20

Briggs, Miss (daughter) B55, 119

Briggs, Sara (daughter) Letter from, B26; A6, 11, 114, 117, 119

Briggs family A108; B28, 46, 169

Bristowe, Anne A57

British Critic, The A7

Broadlands (Claudes' Ambleside home) B70

Brodie, Sir Benjamin A102; B92, 113, 114

Brontë, Charlotte Letters from, B31, 32; *Jane Eyre*, B203; Percy-West romance, B31; *Poems*, B32

Brontë, Patrick Branwell Letter to, A7; tr. Horace's *Odes*, A7

Brooke, Lord A47

Brooks, William C. and Mrs. Cards of, B33

Brougham, Lord Henry Peter A22; B228

Brown, Thomas (1663–1704) A127, 128

Browning, Dr. A144

Browning, Robert B203

Browning, Mrs. Robert (Elizabeth Barrett) A71; B145, 202; *Poems* (1844), B202

Bryant, Fanny Letter from, B34

Bryant, Jacob B120

Bryant, Mr. (Fanny B's brother, of Belfield) B34

Buckingham, Dukes of B135

Bullock, Mr. A71

Bulwer-Lytton, Edward George Earle Lytton, 1st Baron Lytton of Knebworth B31

Burleigh, Lord B31

Burton, Mary Letter from, B35

Burton, Robert (1577–1640) *Anatomy of Melancholy*, A109

Burton, Robert A42

Bussey, George Moir Letter from, B36

Bussey, (son) B36

Butler, Charles A88; *Book of the Roman Catholic Church*, A88

Butler, Jane A117

Byron, George Gordon Noel, Lord B256

Caesar, Julius A16

Calvert, Thomas (fellow of St. Johns, Cambridge) A23

Calvert, Mrs. William B111

Calvert, Mary (daughter) (see Stanger)

Calvert, Dr. William (son) A113

Cameron, Mr. (of Wakefield) B39

Appendix; children, A30, 36, 74, 126; criticism of, A9, 14, 19, 26, 29, 30, 34, 45, 50, 56, 58, 59, 60, 61, 62, 66, 71, 72, 75, 76, 79, 83, 84, 89, 99, 100, 101, 103, 104, 105, 107, 113, 114, 117, 123, 125, 126; difficulties of translation, A7, 45, 66; education, A47, 56, 69, 74, 83, 90, 105, 131; handwriting of, A16; B24, 80, 203, 228; humor, A8, 25, 30, 101; Nab Cottage, A14, 147, 148; B181; Oriel affair, A2, 21, 24, 80, 81, 82, 83, 143, 151, 155; B180, 260; politics, A21, 35, 46, 92, 93, 95, 125, 126, 133, 140, 154; portraits of, A64, 122; religious controversy, A8, 17, 64, 76, 114; self-criticism, A9, 28, 30, 33, 34, 35, 37, 51, 60, 69, 85, 86, 87, 110, 131; STC's death, A31, 48, 98, 131; Mrs. STC's death, A62, 63
—Works: "Address to Certain Gold Fishes," A153; "Agnes," B134; *Andrew Marvell*, B198; "Angel of the Rose," A160; "Antiquity," A121, B124; *Biographia Borealis ("Worthies")*, A43, 44, 49, 51, 94, 95, 105, 123, 124, 126, B36, 39, 80, 101, 106, 113, 121, 127, 142, 221, 245, 266, Appendix 1, 2, 4, 5, 6; "Can man rejoice," A30; "Character of Hamlet," B189; "Come listen," A23; contributions to *Childhood*, A12, B48, 50, 52, 70, 223; "De Omnibus Rebus," A29; "Dear Bessy," B245; "Dedicatory Sonnet." A124; *Dramatic Works of Massinger and Ford*, A9, 10, 34, 49, 50, 107, 141, B47, 108, 221; "The Fourth Birthday," A112; "From Michelangelo," A57; "God Save the Queen," A57; "The God-child," A50; "Gypsies and Asses," B169; "I fear you think," A147; "Ignoramus," A89, 90, 91, 92; "In Holy Books," A138; "Into the heart," A14; "It comes, it goes," A13; "Keswick," A61: "Laugh No More," A66; "Like a winter wind," A136; "Lines on the infant Hercules," B194; "Lines written in a Bible," B168; "Lollypops," A19; "Long has thou laboured," A6; "Miss Grizzle Baillie," B203; "Nephew, a term," A36; "The Nightingale," A18, 19; "No Revelation," A65; "Now is the time," A33; "Not such a Marriage," A148; "Now the old trees," A130; "Oh, why my Brother," A32; "On the Birth of Cornelia," A61, B208; "On the Late Dr. Arnold," A116, 121, B83, 123, 145, 146; "Pins," A121, B124; *Poems*, A44, 49, 51, 54, 94, 96, 99, 108, B73, 121, 127, 141, 145, 177, 225, 265, Appendix 1, 2, 4, 5, 6, 7; "poetical description," A97; "Poetry," A88; "Poetry on an Ass," A149; "The prattling tongue," A111; "Preface – which may serve," A121, B124; "Prometheus," A22, 23, 26, 31, 51, 83, 96, 124, B47, 203; proposed *Essays*, A9, 10, 37, 59, 109, 110, 111, 120, B40, 56, 113, 115, 116, 117, 118, 122; proposed pamphlet, Appendix 1, 2, 4, 6, 7; proposed *Poems*, A9, 10, 96, 109, 128, 135, 146, B38, 52, 56, 144, 144b, 147, 163; "Sabbath-Day Child," A90, B48; "Schiller's Translations of Macbeth," A46, 101, 125; "Schoolfellow's Tribute," A16, B12, 120, 151, 192, 207, 247, 248; "Second Nuptials," B16; "She is not fair," B163; "The silent melody," A98; "Solace of Song," B261; "Sounds I have heard," B264; "Stay where thou art," A69; "Sweetest Lord that wert so blest," A137; "Tea Table," A90; "They lived awhile," A147; "To a Red Herring," B203; "To a Snowdrop," A1; "To an Infant," B200, 201, 202; "To Christabel Rose Coleridge," A37, B95; "To Dear Little Katy Hill," A12, B144; "To

Dr. Briggs," A11; "To H. N. Coleridge," A48; "To James Montgomery," B264, "To Joanna Baillie," B5; "To K. H. J.," A12, B48, 50, 52, 70, 131, 132, 191; "To Margaret Mary Pedder," B219; "To Mary Agnes Nicholson," B206; "To Mrs. Charles Fox," B145; "To My Unknown Sister-in-Law," A30; "To S. T. Coleridge," A102; "To the Rev. Frederick Faber," A8, 17, B69; "Twins," A54, 98, B52; unfinished essay on STC, A10, 47, 56, 60, 75, 78, 104, 107; "A wanton bard," A12; "What sound awakened," A34; "When thoughts too mighty," A20; "Why Damon, why in sable suit," A136; "Write when you can," A23

Coleridge, Henry James (John Taylor C's son)   A121

Coleridge, Henry Nelson (James C's son, HC's brother-in-law) Letters to, A43, 44, 45, 46, 47, 48, 49, 50, 51; Letters from, B99, 100, 101, 102, 103, 104, 105, 106, 108; A22, 26, 29, 30, 31, 32, 36, 53, 54, 57, 58, 59, 60, 68, 70, 73, 74, 90, 91, 92, 94, 95, 96, 98, 100, 101, 102, 103, 104, 105, 106, 110, 111, 112, 114, 124, 125, 129, 135; B80, 83, 87, 89, 90, 91, 92, 93, 94, 112, 113, 114, 120, 187, 208; ed. *Aids to Reflection*, A63, 114, B106, 121; ed. *Church and State*, A58, B104, 106; ed. *The Friend*, B118, 121, 122; *Introduction to the Study of the Greek Classic Poets*, A30, 43, 92; ed. *Remains*, A46, 104, B103, 104, 106, 177; review of *Biographia Borealis*, A45, 100, 128, B80; *Six Months in the West Indies*, A29; ed. *Table Talk*, A45, 99, B80, 101

Coleridge, Mrs. Henry Nelson (Sara Coleridge, HC's sister)   Letters to, A52, 53, 54, 55, 56, 57, 58, 59, 60, 61, 62, 63, 64, 65, 66, 67, 68, 69, 70, 71, 72, 124, 125; Letters from, B107 (33 letters), 108; A11, 22, 23, 26, 27, 28, 29, 30, 32, 35, 38, 40, 43, 44, 45, 46, 48, 49, 50, 51, 73, 74, 78, 88, 89, 91, 92, 93, 94, 95, 96, 97, 98, 99, 100, 101, 103, 104, 106, 108, 109, 110, 111, 112, 113, 114, 115, 116, 117, 118, 119, 120, 121, 122, 124, 125, 129, 135, 155; B48, 57, 83, 89, 92, 93, 94, 95, 96, 97, 99, 100, 101, 102, 104, 105, 106, 109, 110, 111, 112, 113, 114, 115, 116, 117, 118, 119, 121, 122, 123, 124, 125, 141, 142, 186, 197, 222, 259; ed. *Biographia Literaria*, A69, 78, 102, B108, 109; "Dyce's Beaumont and Fletcher," A71; essay on beauty, A70, 111; "On Rationalism," A63, 114, B121; *Phantasmion*, A56, 108, 109, 113, B161, 172; ed. *Poems* (1844), A117, B117; *Pretty Lessons*, A99, 129; "Tennyson's *Princess*," A71

Coleridge, Henry Nelson Praed (DC's son)   A121, 122; B85, 86, 87, 123, 124, 146

Coleridge, Herbert (HNC's son) A19, 44, 51, 55, 56, 57, 58, 59, 61, 63, 69, 70, 90, 92, 97, 101, 106, 108, 112, 114, 117, 118, 119, 120, 121, 124, 127, 131; B91, 92, 93, 97, 100, 101, 102, 104, 108, 115, 117, 118, 119, 122, 123, 124

Coleridge, James (HC's uncle) A22, 39, 40, 41, 125, 129; B89, 101, 102, 111, 114

Coleridge, Mrs. James (Frances Taylor)   A22, 104; B101, 103

Coleridge, James Duke (James C's son)   A41, 58; B91, 113

Coleridge, Sir John Taylor (James C's son)   Letters to, A73, 74, 75, 76, 77, 78; Letter from, B109; A22, 30, 35, 40, 58, 60, 62, 65, 68, 70, 80, 82, 95, 101, 102, 103, 113, 139; B87, 91, 103, 117, 123, 124, 125, 227

Coleridge, Mrs. John Taylor (Mary Buchanan)   A40, 73, 78, 82; B117

Coleridge, Mrs. John (Anne Bowden, HC's paternal grandmother)   A62

B140

Rogers, Samuel   A16; B123

Romilly, Sir Samuel   B140

Roscoe, William   A45

Rose, George (1744–1818)   A23

Rothay Bank (Crossfields' Ambleside
home)   B74

Roughsedge, Mr.   A135
  Roughsedge, Miss (daughter)
    A108, 135
  Roughsedge, Mr. and Mrs.   Letter
    from, B234

Rousseau, Jean-Jacques   B31

Rubens, Peter Paul   A59

Rudd (boy in Isaac Green's school)
B162

Russell, John (1st Earl Russell)
A57, 126

Rutter, Elizabeth S.   Letter from,
B235

Ryan, Mr. (Louis Claude's tutor)
B49, 54

Rydal Mount (Wordsworths' home)
A62, 92, 103, 108; B120, 123,
184, 186

Sadler, Michael Thomas   A126

St. Aubyn, Sir John   A22, 90
  St. Aubyn, Edward (son at
    Cambridge)   A22
  St. Aubyn, (son, HC's pupil)   A22,
    30, 151
  St. Aubyn, W. J. (Grasmere
    tradesman?)   A91

St. Vincent, Earl   B135

Sandby, George (Merton College
friend)   A151

Sanford, Mrs. John (Miss Poole)
A117

Sanford, Mr.   A135

Sanford, the Rev. William   Letter
from, B236; A76

Saturday Magazine   B199;
  "Address to a Godchild," B199,
  200

Savage, Richard   A3

Scambler, Mrs.   A146, 147; B239,
240, 243, 246, 247, 248
  Scambler, Alice (daughter)
    Letters from, B237, 238, 239,

240, 241; A146, 147; B243, 244,
245, 246, 247, 248

Scambler, Dorothy (daughter)
A146, 147; B237, 238, 243, 245,
247, 248

Scambler, Elizabeth (daughter)
(see Bell, Mrs. Elizabeth
Scambler)

Scambler, Henry (son)   A147;
B237, 239, 240, 243, 244, 245,
246, 247, 248

Scambler, Jane (daughter)   A146,
147; B240, 243, 244, 245, 247,
248
  Scambler, (Jane's daughter)
    B240

Scambler (?), John (son?)   A147;
B243

Scambler, Thomas (son)   A147;
B237, 239, 240, 241, 243, 244,
245, 247, 248

Scambler, William (son)   A29

Schiller, Johann Christoph Friedrich
von   B44; Turandot, B70

Scot, John   A21

Scott, Sir Walter   A34, 72

Scratchey (Merton College friend)
A42

Sedgewick, Professor Adam   A57;
B166; Discourse on Studies, A56

Sedgewick, Stephen   A155; B162,
166

Senhouse, Miss   A125

Shakespeare, William   A9, 34, 103,
141; B189; Hamlet, B189; Lear,
A34; Macbeth, A46; Titus
Andronicus, A34

Shelley, Percy Bysshe   Medwin's
Life, B203; Poetical Works, A50

Shelton, Miss   A117

Shepheard, G. Wallwyn   Letter
from, B249

Shepherd, Mr.   A5, 10

Sheppard, Mr.   B73

Sidmouth, 1st Viscount   (see
Addington)

Sidney, Sir Philip   A26

Simpson, the Rev. G. (of Sedbergh)
A146; B168

Sinclair, Sir John   A46

Sinclair, Mr. (Margaret Lough's
friend) B196
Sloane, Mr. B24
Sloane, Mrs. B24
Smedley, Edward A57, 74, 104;
B233
Smedley family A74, 104; B233
Smith, Janetta A44, 97
Smith, John Francis Letter from,
B250
Smith, Joseph (Mormon leader)
B164
Smith, Miss A42
Smith, Mr. (writer for *Ency. Brit.*)
A45
Smollett, Tobias George A72
Sotheby, William *Polyglott
Georgics*, A92
Sotheby family B111
Southern, Miss Letter from, B251
Southey, Edward (Robert S's
brother) A116
Southey, Robert Letter to, A150;
A10, 16, 23, 25, 30, 34, 38, 43, 46,
52, 53, 55, 56, 57, 58, 60, 74, 76,
88, 93, 94, 99, 101, 103, 105, 106,
113, 116, 117, 118, 125, 126, 141,
152, 155; B26, 34, 100, 103, 106,
108, 111, 113, 115, 188, 211, 250,
252
—Works: *Book of the Church*,
A88; "Cataract of Lodore," B26;
The Doctor, A53, 57, 72, 76, 101,
B259; *History of Brazil*, A39; *Life
of Wesley*, A39; *Peninsular War*,
A39; "Pilgrim to Compostella,"
A89; *Progress and Prospects of
Society*, A89; *Vindiciae Ecclesiae
Anglicanae*, A88; "Vision of
Judgement," A26; *Voyage to
Moscow*, A105
Southey, Mrs. Robert (1st, Edith
Fricker) A10, 43, 45, 54, 56,
88, 95, 105, 155
Southey, Mrs. Robert (2nd,
Caroline Bowles) A58, 113;
B108, 167
Southey, Charles Cuthbert (son)
A30, 55, 65, 89, 102, 112, 113,
118, 119; B108, 122, 188

Southey, Mrs. Charles Cuthbert
A112, 113
Southey, Edith May (daughter)
(see Warter)
Southey, Herbert (son) A149
Southey, Kate (daughter) Letter
from, B252; A10, 30, 33, 54, 55,
58, 63, 65, 92, 105, 106, 109,
113, 117, 118, 149; B108, 114,
116, 117, 119, 120, 121, 122,
123, 188
Southey family A27, 52
Spectator, The A118
Spedding, James A10, 57, 71, 104
Spedding, Miss B111
Spedding, Thomas A113
Spenser, Edmund *Faerie Queene*,
B194
Spinoza, Baruch A29
Spring Rice, Thomas (Lord
Monteagle) A5
Spring Rice, Mary Alicia Pery
(daughter) (see Marshall,
Mrs. James Garth)
Staël, Madame de A120
Stanger, Joshua A113
Stanger, Mrs. Joshua (Mary
Calvert) A113
Stanley, Arthur Penrhyn *Life of Dr.
Arnold*, A116, 121
Stephens, Mr. A142
Sterling, John A71; B100, 144b, 145
Sterne, Laurence A72, 76;
Tristram Shandy, A69, 71, 72;
B84
Stevenson, William *Gammar
Gurton's Needle*, A58
Stockford, Captain (of Cowley) B8
Stockford, Miss (see Radford)
Stolterforth, Dr. A71
Stolterforth, Miss (daughter) A71
Stuart, Mr. A88
Stutfield, Charles B. B122
Suart, William (HC's godson)
Letter from, B253
Sue, Eugene B264
Sutton, Miss (Fanny Gurston's
friend) B177
Swainson, Miss Letter from, B254
Swann, Charles (of Oxford) B8

May Southey)   A30, 38, 43, 53, 55, 64, 92, 116, 125, 149, 155; B108, 186, 188

Warter, Edith Frances (daughter) A125

Warter, Ellen Caroline (daughter) B188

Watson, Dr. Seth   B174; ed. *Theory of Life*, B174

Watts, Alaric Alexander   Letters to, A152, 153; A88, 89

Watts, Isaac   A12

Wedgewood, Thomas   B100

Wetherall, Sir Charles   A4

Whately, Richard (Archbishop of Dublin)   Letter from, B260; A21, 66, 80, 107, 140, 151

Whately, (son)   A10

Whately, (daughters)   A66

Whewell, William   *Indications of the Creator*, B147

White, Fanny (Herbert W's sister?) A28, 29, 34, 125

White, Herbert   A11, 12, 16, 29, 34, 114, 126; B16, 57, 74, 75, 77, 83, 195

White, Mrs. Herbert   A34, 126; B57, 75, 77

White, Emily (daughter)   B57 natural son   A34

White family   A34; B59, 65, 66, 70, 72

White, Howard (Herbert W's brother?)   A34

White, Sophy (Herbert W's sister?) A29, 34, 125, 147

Whittaker, Rufus (bookseller)   B127

Wilberforce, Robert Isaac   A6

Wilberforce, Samuel   A6

Wilberforce, William   A6, 21

Wilkes, (John? Thomas?)   A26

Wilkins, Miss   A64

Wilkinson, Agnes (Margaret W. Jones's sister)   B134

Wilkinson, Mr. H. (headmaster of Isaac Green's school)   A106, 135; B166, 169

Wilkinson, Mrs.   A106, 134; B162, 166

Wilkinson children   A106, 134,

135; B162

Wilkinson, Mr. (of Howgill)   A134; B163

Wilkinson, Elizabeth (daughter?) B166, 168

Wilkinson, Margaret (daughter?) B168

William IV, King   A21

Williams, John   A84

Wilson, Catherine   B176

Wilson, Edward (Merton College friend)   A151

Wilson, Georgianna   Letter from, B261

Wilson, John (1800–1849)   B78

Wilson, Professor John (Christopher North)   A30, 50, 53, 54, 89, 90, 92, 152; B31, 148, 190, 211; *City of the Plague*, B141

Wilson, Mrs. John   A30, 56

Wilson, James (son)   A30

Wilson, Jane (daughter)   A30

Wilson, John Jr. (son)   A54

Wilson, Margaret (daughter) A30; B211, 212

Wilson, Mary (daughter)   A30

Wilson, Kate   A144

Wilson, Mary Hannah (Eliza W. Richardson's sister)   Letter from, B230; B228, 230

Wilson, Miss   A138

Wilson, Mrs. ("Wilsy," Greta Hall housekeeper)   A22, 23, 40, 52, 53, 58; B111

Wilson, Mrs. Thomas (Eliza W. Richardson's sister-in-law)   A119; B227

Wilson, William (of Sedbergh) B163

Winter's Wreath, The   A92, 127; B38

Witheburn   A4

Withington, Mr.   A8, 92, 160; B50, 51, 54

Withington, Mrs.   A92; B47, 53, 61

Withington, Agnes (daughter) A11

Withington, Alice (daughter) B47, 51, 52, 59, 73

Design and typography by J. E. Bagg, Jr.